ISBN 978-1-331-35145-0
PIBN 10178011

This book is a reproduction of an important historical work. Forgotten Books uses
state-of-the-art technology to digitally reconstruct the work, preserving the original format
whilst repairing imperfections present in the aged copy. In rare cases, an imperfection in
the original, such as a blemish or missing page, may be replicated in our edition. We do,
however, repair the vast majority of imperfections successfully; any imperfections that
remain are intentionally left to preserve the state of such historical works.

BY HIS SON

The Rev. M. C. F. MORRIS, B.C.L., M.A.

RECTOR OF NUNBURNHOLME, YORKSHIRE

WITH PORTRAIT AND ILLUSTRATIONS

LONDON

14 KING WILLIAM STREET, STRAND

MDCCCXCVII

Printed by BALLANTYNE, HANSON & Co
At the Ballantyne Press

TO

MY SISTER LAURA

THE FOLLOWING PAGES

ARE AFFECTIONATELY INSCRIBED.

PREFACE

AN author's memoir may sometimes be said to be in a great measure written in his lifetime. This was, perhaps, especially true in the case of my father.

To so many, however, he was known only as a popular writer on natural history, and birds in particular, that I have been induced to write this sketch of his life, which may give those to whom his name is thus familiar, as well as others, a fuller account of his many-sided activities than they might else have gained.

While it is clear that a son, as such, is from one point of view the best-qualified person to write a memoir of his father, so from another is he the least so. Still, if the close ties of kinship have at times led me to say less or more than I might otherwise have done, I cannot but cherish the hope that any shortcomings and oversteppings may on this ground be indulgently regarded.

Holding the pronounced views my father did with regard to Darwinism and vivisection, it might by some have been thought advisable to have omitted in these pages special mention of questions which for many years formed with him the arena of so much contention. Knowing, however, that such omission would have been strongly resented by him, there seemed no other choice than make such allusions to them as will be found in the memoir under that head. It is hoped that in the brief space allotted to these subjects no more has been said than was necessary to make his attitude towards them plain to those who may perhaps to some extent have misjudged him in the past.

My thanks are cordially given to those friends and relatives who kindly furnished me with information on many points while the memoir was in course of preparation.

The engraving of the portrait in the frontispiece has been made from a photograph taken by Messrs. Gowland of York less than a year before my father's death.

M. C. F. M.

NUNBURNHOLME,
    June 6th, 1896.

CONTENTS

FRANCIS ORPEN MORRIS

I

PARENTAGE AND EARLY LIFE

FRANCIS ORPEN MORRIS, the eldest son of Admiral
Henry Gage Morris, was born on 25th March 1810,
at Cove, near Cork, at a time when his father was
serving his country in command of one of his
Majesty's ships on the Irish station. Half a century or more before this his grandfather, Captain
Roger Morris, was engaged on active duty in the
other branch of the service in America, and took
part in some of the most stirring events preceding
the War of Independence. He was aide-de-camp
to General Braddock during the luckless campaign
against the French and Indians at Fort du Quesne
in 1755, and was severely wounded in the memorable battle of the Monongahela River, when Braddock paid dearly for his wrong-headedness and lack
of caution. The General himself was among the
fallen on that disastrous day, while, out of eighty-
six officers in the engagement, twenty-six were
killed and thirty-seven wounded; of the privates,

A

the killed and wounded amounted to seven hundred and fourteen. Had Braddock listened to the counsels of others, the result must have been far otherwise than the event proved; but he was new to the Indians' mode of warfare, and they took him unawares. Of the other two aides-de-camp who served under Braddock at this time, one was George Washington, then a young officer in the Virginian Militia. The only one of the three who escaped untouched was the young Virginian colonel, though, seeing that he had two horses shot under him and four bullets through his coat, it was little short of a miracle that the first President of the United States was not some other than he. Unhurt as he was, Washington was able to attend to the wants of his brother aides-de-camp when they withdrew from the battle-ground. He and Captain Morris were then on terms of intimacy.

It was not long, however, before these two were rivals in a campaign of another kind.

In the February following the battle of the Monongahela, Washington left his residence at Mount Vernon on a journey to Boston to confer with General Shirley on military affairs. On reaching New York he stayed at the house of his old friend, Beverley Robinson, with whom he had served under Braddock. While there he met for the first time Mary Philipse, the sister-in-law of his friend, then a young lady of many charms. She was the daughter of Frederick Philipse of Philipsburg, and with her sister, Mrs. Beverley Robinson, had inherited large estates from an uncle. Washington paid much attention to the fair sister of Mrs. Beverley Robinson, and each day of his sojourn with his former comrade-in-arms made him less inclined to bring the visit to an end. It was no secret to his friends that this young lady's attractions had made a deep impression on his heart.

Irving, in his "Life of George Washington," alludes to this episode, but he evidently could not bring himself to believe that his hero had proposed to Mary Philipse, and that his offer had been refused. Such, nevertheless, is the tradition in her family, and that it was a generally accepted belief is proved by the frequent allusions to it in American literature. There is, at least, no doubt as to his affection for her, as, when he was at last compelled to leave Colonel Beverley Robinson's hospitable roof in consequence of pressing military affairs, he confided the state of his feelings to his friend, who shortly afterwards wrote urging his immediate return, as another admirer of Mary Philipse was in the field, and was pressing his suit. This rival was Washington's former companion-in-arms, the young English officer, Captain Roger Morris, who succeeded in securing the lady's hand.

. In January 1758 Mary Philipse was married to Captain Roger Morris, in the presence of a brilliant gathering. Members of the leading families of the province and representatives of the British forces in America were present on the occasion. A strange episode happened during a great feast that followed the wedding ceremony. Without any warning a tall Indian, closely wrapped in a scarlet blanket, appeared at the door of the banqueting-hall, and in measured tones gave utterance to these words: " Your possessions shall pass from you when the Eagle shall despoil the Lion of his mane." The Indian vanished as suddenly as he came, but his penetrating accents were never forgotten by those whom they mainly concerned. Later events proved the truth of the Indian's forecast.[1]

Before his marriage, Roger Morris had built for himself a handsome mansion upon his estate on Manhattan Island, near New York. There he brought his young bride, and there his children (two sons and two daughters) were born. His military career, however, did not yet come to a close. In 1759 he served in the campaign of that year under General Wolfe at Louisburg, and was present at the taking of Quebec in command of grenadiers. He remained on active service till the conquest of Canada was completed and the Indians around the western lakes were subdued. For meritorious services he received the rank of lieutenant-colonel, and in 1764 he left the army and retired to his seat, Mount Morris, on Manhattan Island. For some time he served as a member of the Executive Council of the province of New York. Mrs. Morris was the original from whom Fenimore

---

[1] This account of the wedding is the same as that told by Angevine (son of the favourite coloured valet of Philipse), who was sexton of St. John's Church at Yonkers for forty-five years.

Cooper drew the character of the heroine of his novel, "The Spy."

From the time of their first acquaintance more than twenty years elapsed before Washington and Mary Philipse (then Mrs. Morris) again met ; this meeting took place when Washington was on his way to take command of the American army before Boston. On this occasion he stopped at the house of Colonel Roger Morris, who, with his wife, extended every courtesy and hospitality to their distinguished guest. This proved their last meeting, for Colonel Morris and his wife had remained faithful to the Royal cause throughout the struggle, and the result of the war was most disastrous to them. After experiencing great reverses of fortune they ultimately settled in England, and thus the Atlantic finally separated Washington from these friends of his younger days.

Colonel Morris and his wife occupied their Manhattan residence at intervals till the close of the War of Independence. For a short period in 1776 the Americans held the upper portion of the island, during which time Washington made Roger Morris's house his headquarters. The adherence of Colonel Morris to the side of the mother country compelled him to fly to England in April 1775, remaining here till the autumn of 1777 ; and again at the general emigration of loyalists from New York in 1783, when the city was evacuated by the British troops. Mrs. Morris with her husband were attainted of treason, and their American estates were confiscated. The amount assigned them as compensation was comparatively small, the property having been valued to the Commissioners in 1784 at over £53,000; the value of this, being so close to New York, would at the present day be almost incalculable. It is believed that Mrs. Morris and her sister were the only two women attainted at the conclusion of the war.

Colonel Roger Morris died in 1794, and both he and his wife were buried at St. Saviour's Church, York. Mrs. Morris survived her husband thirty years, and lived to reach her ninety-sixth year.

Roger Morris's sons entered the royal navy. Amherst, the elder of the two, so named after his godfather, Lord Amherst, to whom his father was for a time aide-de-camp, gallantly distinguished himself in the celebrated engagement on June 18, 1793, between the English frigate *Nymphe* and the French frigate *Cleopatre*. He was the first officer to board the enemy's ship, and to him the French lieutenant surrendered his sword, which is still preserved as a family relic.

The second son, Henry Gage, joined the service at the tender age of six, though he did not go to sea till he was twelve, and served in many ships. The last that he commanded was the *Jalouse*, being employed in her from 1809 to 1812 on the Irish station. Shortly before this time, while acting as flag-lieutenant to Admiral Lord Gardner, the young naval officer met his future wife, Rebecca Newenham Millerd Orpen, the youngest daughter of the

Rev. Francis Orpen, Vicar of Kilgarvan, in the county of Kerry. To them were born a large family of sons and daughters. Of the former, the eldest is the subject of this memoir. He was born in the house purchased by his father near the Cove of Cork, opposite the harbour-mouth. This situation was a very beautiful one. The charm of the scene, the constant coming and going of men-of-war and other ships, the brilliant verdure of the trees and meadows that seemed to touch the very waters of the lovely estuary that reached its limits at the city of Cork, the song of the birds on land, the graceful sailing of the sea-gulls through the air, or their light buoyancy as they rested on the top of the waves—sights and sounds such as these made a deep and a lifelong impression upon his active mind and retentive memory, and perhaps first kindled, or at least fanned, the flame of that strong passion and admiration for the wonders and beauties of nature which from those early days up to the very end of his long life never left him. As an infant, he seemed so delicate that it was thought there was but little chance of his living; but in reality his constitution was a remarkably good one. When reading with a tutor for Oxford as a young man, he had successively scarlet fever, ague, jaundice, and inflammation of the lungs, and when about eight-and-twenty he nearly lost his life with an attack of small-pox. But these ailments in no way injured his constitution; indeed, after the last dangerous illness was over, he was, as he used to say, if possible, in better health than ever. From that time till old age stole upon him he may be said never to have had an ache or pain.

His earliest associations were connected with the sea, for which he always had a strong liking. For eight years his father continued to be employed on the Irish station, and when not actually afloat or otherwise hindered by duty, he enjoyed the pleasures of home life at his house near Cove. To one who had any taste for the sea and appreciation of the beauties of such coast scenery as that which may be viewed in the West of Ireland, a life such as this must have had in it much that was enjoyable. Not always, however, was his ship confined within the limits of the Irish station. When occasion required he had to convoy a greater or lesser fleet of vessels to some distant port, and when his eldest son was but a few days old he was thus called away for a time on foreign service, and April 1810 found him convoying twenty-nine sail to Madeira. A voyage of that kind was, in those days, a matter of months; but, though lengthy, the log of the *Jalouse* shows that the cruise was anything but monotonous. Frequently on their return from Madeira they gave chase to, and came to close quarters with, "strangers;" sometimes it was found necessary to clear for action and fire several shot before the unknown craft was brought to submission; now and again an English brig would be sighted, chased, and boarded, and some of her crew impressed. It was not till July 7 that this voyage was ended and the good ship dropped her anchor once more in Cork harbour in five fathoms of water.

Thus the months rolled by till September 1812, when my grandfather was made post-captain, and his period of service on board the *Jalouse* came to an end. Captain Morris was a strict disciplinarian, and had a very stern sense of duty. He continued to live in his delightful home near Cove for some years after this, and did not take up his abode in England until Francis Orpen was fourteen years of age. Meanwhile his son's education was not neglected, and it was in these early years that the religious principles which were the guide and rule of his whole life were deep sown in his mind and heart. After the way of those days, but especially so, it would seem, in the case of my grandfather, a strict obedience to parental authority was demanded of all his children. Such obedience was willingly given, and was never for a moment questioned. My father used frequently to allude to this, and contrasted the respect and obedience shown to parents at the time when he was a boy with the laxer and more indulgent discipline in this matter at later times. It certainly resulted well in his case, for he ever looked back to those days of his boyhood and home life with feelings of the greatest happiness.

The sterner and determined nature of the father and the exceeding gentleness and tenderness of the mother were united in the son to a remarkable degree. It was this extraordinary co-existence of determination and tender-heartedness in him that gave force to his character and actions.

His love for natural history showed itself in his earliest years; indeed, it may be said that as soon as he could think and speak, his powers of observation in this direction were brought into action. These, gathering strength as time went on, afforded him endless channels of delight. If there was one branch of his favourite pursuits that gave him greater pleasure than another, it was what he used to call the "gay science" of entomology. It is hard to say how soon this was first noticed in him; certainly when but four or five years of age he was wont to observe and remark upon the different kinds of moths and butterflies that flitted about his home. One of them, the buff-tip moth (*Pygæra bucephala*), he always called, even at that tender age, "the piece-of-stick-moth," from its likeness to a bit of a small branch of the silver birch.

He was naturally quick at learning, and was gifted with a remarkably good memory. When he was nine years old he gained his first prize, consisting of a prayer-book; this was awarded to him, after a public examination in Cove Church, for proficiency in religious knowledge; and again, at eleven years, he obtained the second of two prizes after another examination held under similar circumstances. These books he carefully kept and treasured.

Captain H. G. Morris returned to England in 1824, when his son's education received a fresh

impetus. Originally it was intended that he should
be sent to Winchester School, but his father seeing
something there of which he greatly disapproved
when he went to inspect the school, it was determined
that he should be sent elsewhere. Accordingly, this
same year he was entered as a pupil at Bromsgrove
School in Worcestershire, which at that time was
under the head-mastership of the Rev. John Topham,
a most estimable clergyman of the old school.
Bromsgrove was one of the so-called grammar
schools of King Edward the Sixth. A boy educated there, and gifted with good abilities, had a
pretty certain prospect of gaining one of the scholar-
ships attached to the foundation, which led afterwards to a fellowship at Worcester College, Oxford.
It was with this object in view that he entered the
school. Under ordinary circumstances he would
in all probability have obtained a scholarship
without difficulty, for he rose rapidly in the school,
winning several prizes, and ultimately gaining the
silver medal as being second in the school. His
ambition, however, was doomed to disappointment;
for, as it happened, there was no vacancy in the
year that he left the school, nor in the two years
that intervened before he went to Oxford—a most
unusual occurrence—while on the very next occasion, when it was just too late for him to compete,
there were no fewer than four scholars elected.
This was naturally a trial to him, though, being of
a sanguine and hopeful temperament, and always
looking on the bright side of things, he in nowise

took it to heart, but regarded it as in every way for
the best.   For two years after my grandfather's
return to England he settled at Worcester, but
removed thence in 1826 to Charmouth, in Dorsetshire, a pleasantly situated village on the coast.

His school-days at Bromsgrove my father always
looked back upon with the greatest pleasure.   He
many times in later years had thought of jotting
down what he called "A Brief Biograph of a
By-gone Bromsgrovian."   Had he done so, "Tom
Brown's School-Days" would, as he playfully
expressed it, "be found to be as nothing to it, nor
those of any other boy of any other school in England."   The head-master was a kindly hearted man,
and his rule reflected his character ; learning was
not made burdensome to the boys, and the discipline
was, to say the least of it, easy.   The country around
Bromsgrove was picturesque, and in those days well
wooded ; it was a happy hunting-ground for the
young naturalist.   While there he made the most
of his opportunities as a student in nature's wide
field ; frequently in summer he would be off on long
expeditions to catch butterflies and other insects, or
to look for some uncommon bird, accompanied by
a congenial companion or two, of whom he found
several among his schoolfellows.   Sometimes he
would go out shooting or fishing ; for, strange to
say, the enforcement of the game laws, as well as
the discipline of the school, were such in those days
that the boys could go out shooting or hunting
exactly as they liked without let or hindrance, not

even going through the form of asking permission
of masters, landowners, gamekeepers, or anybody.

An amusing illustration of the prevalence of these
sporting propensities, not only among my father's
school friends, but also among those living in the
town and neighbourhood of Bromsgrove, was given
on a certain occasion during school hours, which
was often called to mind afterwards, and told with
a lively sense of the ridiculous. An unfortunate
"day boy," who was continually getting into trouble
with the masters for his extraordinary faculty for
making "false quantities," was one day "up" with
a Greek lesson before an under-master, one of
whose *prænomina* was the appropriate one of Rod-
well. The unhappy youth was asked by the said
master, "Where did you find the *first aorist?*"
Thinking he said, "Where did you find the *first hare,
sir?*" the boy, under the influence, seemingly, of the
ruling passion, *naïvely*, as the record hath it, replied
(it was soon after the 1st of September, and the
lad's father a gentleman farmer in the neighbourhood), "If you please, sir, my father found him
in the wheat stubble, and he fired both barrels at
him and missed him, and then he 'whanged' the
gun-barrel after him." I will not dwell on the
sudden consequences of this slight misunderstand-
ing on the part of the luckless boy more than to
say that the master on this occasion at least proved
himself worthy of his name !

The Bromsgrovian schoolboys were enthusiastic
entomologists. A simple device was theirs for catch-

ing moths after they had retired to bed. A candle was placed near an open window, and a long string tied to the handle of the frame—they were old-fashioned lattice ones—the boys then got comfortably into bed, and when a moth made its *entrée* the window was pulled to by the string, and the insect secured and captured within.

While at school he made, as most boys do, some lifelong friends. Of these none were more highly valued by him than Richard Alington and Henry Hilton, both true lovers of nature, and the former a very accurate observer of bird life ; indeed, my father used to say of him that he was the best outdoor naturalist he ever knew. Many were the letters which passed between the old schoolfellows in latter years, when Richard Alington occupied the sequestered rectory of Swinhope in Lincoln-shire, and Henry Hilton that of Milstead in Kent. Richard Alington was an excellent authority on the ornithology of his own county ; and not only so, but he had a rare power, left-handed though he was, of reproducing with his pencil the attitudes of the birds he had for many years watched so closely.

It was at school that the future author of the " History of British Birds " began in earnest his collections of birds and insects, the latter of which ultimately grew to large dimensions. Of birds he never had any great number, probably for lack of the requisite space in arranging them ; but as time went on there were other reasons that militated against it, for, though an excellent shot, he never could bring himself in his latter .years to take the life of any bird. The first stuffed bird he ever possessed was a jay which his father brought him just after he had gone to school. This bird he kept carefully all his life, and from it the engraving in his " History of British Birds " was made. Many were the stories which he used to relate of his school-days ; and his journeys to Bromsgrove on the top of the coach, when he was about fifteen years of age, were graphically described by him. These were to him good old days, and he frequently alluded to them as such. After leaving school, which he did in 1828, he went for about two years to a private tutor, the Rev. J. M. Butt, then Vicar of East Garston, near Lambourne, in Berkshire. It was while reading here that he was struck down, as stated above, no less than four times with serious illnesses. With the exception of these times of sickness, the two years passed pleasantly enough. Needless to say, while a pupil of Mr. Butt's, he eagerly followed up his outdoor studies, and his observations of bird life were in constant exercise. He records in one of his volumes the fact of his obtaining here two specimens of the Cirl Bunting, a bird of some rarity, having been attracted to them by their note, which differed from that of the common yellow Bunting.

From East Garston he proceeded directly to Worcester College, Oxford, staying on the way for a few days with Rev. R. L. Cotton, then a tutor, and afterwards Provost, of the College. Of Dr. Cotton he always spoke in terms of affectionate regard, and the acquaintance which was then formed was kept up for many years. He matriculated at the University on June 17, 1829, and took up his residence there in the Michaelmas term following. The beautiful gardens of Worcester College were peculiarly attractive to him, being then, as now, the haunt of many species of birds, and often did he linger in them in the bright hours of the summer term to watch the movements and listen to the notes of his favourite songsters.

While at Oxford his inborn taste for the study of natural history gathered fresh strength, although in those days the University did but little for an undergraduate whose studies took that turn. The School of Natural Science was not even thought of at that time. Still, he found scope for his energies as a naturalist while he was at Oxford. It was at this time that he made the acquaintance of the keeper of the Ashmolean Museum, Mr. J. L. Duncan, at whose request he arranged the collection of insects in the Museum—a labour of love which met with grateful acknowledgment.

During his residence in Oxford he received frequent communications from his friend, J. C. Dale, Esq., of Glanvilles Wootton, Dorsetshire, an ardent and noted entomologist. These letters were always full of entomological notes and news, telling of this or that rare capture, the doings of various entomological societies, writings in magazines, &c. Thus, for instance, in a letter dated May 30, 1833, Mr. Dale is full of entomological talk, as may be gathered from the following brief quotation, which is only one of many such :—" I have done nothing extraordinary this season yet (though warm enough for *Podalirius*). But I found *Melitæa Lucina, Lycæna argiolus, Thecla rubi, Melitæa Artemis,* and *Lycæna cymon* at Glanvilles Wootton lately, which is rather unusual. *Lucina* I never saw there before, and not at Grange even for twelve years. *Cymon* is a fortnight earlier ; *rubi* I have not seen for several years ; *Argiolus* I have only seen there for the last two or three years, and *Artemis* (now in plenty) I only took two of before last year at Glanvilles Wootton, and those twelve or thirteen years ago." Few letters interested him more keenly than those which he had from Mr. Dale, some of which reached an unwonted length, and literally bristled with caterpillars, chrysalises, moths, and butterflies.

It is hard to realise the changes that have taken place at Oxford since 1829—changes in manners, customs, modes of thought, to say nothing of those of a material kind ; so that the Oxford of that date is very far removed from the Oxford of to-day. Not least among the many changes that have passed over her is that which has been brought about in the system of the University examinations. That many of these alterations are beneficial is beyond dispute, but whether the University turns out better-educated men on the whole is, perhaps, somewhat doubtful. There is more encouragement given to an undergraduate under the present system to follow up a particular line of study for which he has special aptitude, and these avenues of learning are far more varied than of yore, but in the opinion of many there is more probability of one who had taken, say, a first class in the Classical School half a century ago being an "all-round man," to use a common phrase, than one who has taken equally high honours at this day in any one of the various "schools" for which *Alma Mater* trains her children. This, however, is a point which cannot here be discussed.

My father used frequently to admit that he had no taste whatever for mathematics. The fifth proposition of the first book of Euclid always puzzled him ; indeed, it is doubtful if he ever fairly got over it ! The classics, to use his own words, he "drank in like water ;" he delighted in them, and even to his latest years it gave him pleasure to quote from them, as he frequently and aptly did in his sayings and writings.

When he entered the University, and for many years after, there were but two examinations for a degree, Responsions, or "Little Go," and the final examination, or "Great Go," as it was then called. Being naturally of a studious turn of mind, and having such a strong liking for classics, he determined at the outset of his career to read for honours, and to that end he applied himself diligently. Before taking his degree he read for a short time with Rev. G. A. Jacob, then head-master of Bromsgrove

School, and previously Fellow and tutor of Worcester College. He was wont to do a good deal of his work at night, and was accustomed on retiring to rest, after some hours' study of Aristotle's Ethics or a play of Æschylus, to place under his pillow a small musical-box, which he set going and allowed to run itself out, his mind and nerves being soothed the while by the familiar strains of some well-known air, to which he never wearied of listening.

He went in for his "Great Go" in Michaelmas term 1833, the examiners on that occasion being Augustus Short; Richard Michell, afterwards Public Orator at Oxford ; George Moberly, the late Bishop of Salisbury ; and William Sewell, afterwards Professor of Moral Philosophy. It may be worth while to note the subjects taken up by him at this examination, as being typical of the kind of mental training which the Oxford men of that day underwent who read for honours. The list is taken from a memorandum, made apparently at the time, in his own handwriting. It ran thus :—1. Divinity ; 2. Logic ; 3. Butler's Analogy ; 4. Paley's Natural Theology ; 5. Aristotle's Ethics ; 6. Aristotle's Politics ; 7. Aristotle's Poetics ; 8. Herodotus ; 9. Thucydides ; 10. Xenophon's Hellenics (first two books) ; 11. Livy (the second decade) ; 12. Tacitus (The Annals) ; 13. Æschylus ; 14. Sophocles ; 15. Aristophanes (Aves, Plutus, Vespæ, Nubes) ; 16. Euripides (Orestes, Medea, Rhesus, Iphigenia in Aulis) ; 17. Virgil ; 18. Horace ; 19. Pliny's Natural History (Books 8, 9, 10, 11). The selection of the last

named as one of the subjects caused no little
astonishment, not to say consternation, among the
examiners; for Pliny's "Natural History" had, it
was said, never before been taken up for examination at the University, and it is probable that it has
never been since. He acquitted himself creditably
in his *vivâ voce;* but he used to say, and, it must
be admitted, not without a touch of glee, that the
examiner who tested him in his knowledge of Pliny
was more than once caught tripping, and had to
make his apology. When the result of the examination was made known his name appeared in the
second class. There were six in the first class,
one of them being his brother collegian, Rowland
Muckleston, now Rector of Dinedor, in Hereford-
shire; and another, A. C. Tait, of Balliol College,
afterwards Archbishop of Canterbury.

His four years' residence in Oxford left its mark
upon him, and his study of Logic, as well as of such
works as Aristotle's Ethics and Butler's Analogy,
together with the active exercise and development
of his mind which his varied pursuits at the University afforded him, stood him in good stead in
after-years, when he took up his well-worn pen to do
battle for the sacred cause of religion or humanity;
to stand up for what he believed to be right, no
matter what powers might be arrayed against him;
to protect the weak against those who cruelly
oppressed them; to expose that which was false,
and, if possible, bring it to naught. It was certainly amazing to find, as we shall see presently,

what a multitude of varied channels he chose for himself in which to exercise his energies on the side of right and goodness. Though at times he might be thought lacking in discretion, his quickness of perception, his excellent memory, his dexterity in wielding his weapons whether of defence or attack, his perseverance, as well as his unconquerable determination, made him a tough adversary to encounter. Opposition, however strong, could never silence him ; and if driven into a corner, as he occasionally was, he had an extraordinary faculty of fighting his way out of it. He loved Oxford dearly, and the memories of it were ever fresh in his mind and often dwelt upon. He now and again revisited the place, but never to take a higher degree than that of Bachelor of Arts.

His favourite classical author was Horace, whom he seemed pretty well to know by heart, though he seldom looked into a Latin or Greek classic after he took his degree ; indeed, at no subsequent period of his life was his study of books so close as when he was at Oxford. For the remainder of his days, one, at least, of his chief books was that commonly called Nature, and of this he never grew weary for lack of novelty, for its last page could never be reached, and each one as he looked upon it filled him with fresh wonder and delight.

II

EARLY CLERICAL LIFE

ON leaving Oxford, or more probably before that time, Mr. Morris had determined to take Orders, and in the interval that elapsed between November 1833 and August 1834 he applied himself to a careful preparation for the step he was about to take. He obtained a title to the curacy of Hanging Heaton, near Dewsbury, and was ordained deacon on 3rd August by the Archbishop of York (Dr. Vernon Harcourt), the whole county of York being then comprised in that diocese. This examination he passed with credit, and in consequence, on the recommendation of his examining chaplain, Archdeacon Wrangham, a refined scholar as well as a man of deep learning, the Archbishop presented him the following year with a prize of books when he came up for priest's orders; he was, moreover, appointed to preach the ordination sermon in the event of the absence of another gentleman who had been invited to preach on the occasion. He did not remain long at Hanging Heaton, and after leaving that place he held the curacy of Taxal, in Cheshire, for three months.

On New Year's Day 1835 he married Anne, the

second daughter of Charles Sanders, Esq., of Broms-grove, a lady who was eminently fitted to be the wife of a clergyman, ever ready as she was to perform cheerfully and with unfailing good temper even the smallest duties and most trivial matters connected with her position, and to help forward every good work. She was beloved by all who knew her. To be in her presence was to live in sunshine; and every parishioner felt that they had in her a true, sympathetic, and warm-hearted friend, one who was ever ready to share their sorrows and do what lay in her power to lighten them, and to render the lives of those with whom she came in contact brighter and more joyous.

Their married life, which extended over a period of more than forty years, was in the highest and best sense of the word happy. To them were born three sons and six daughters.

Devoted though Mr. Morris was to the study of natural history even from his earliest days, it was not until he was past forty years of age that his name became at all widely known as a writer on those subjects for which he had such a strong inborn taste. Long before that time, however, his pen had been at work in various ways, and as early as the year 1834 his first publication was issued. This was a small matter, and was entitled "A Guide to an Arrangement of British Birds," being, as he expressed it on the title-page, "A Catalogue of all the Species hitherto discovered in Great Britain and Ireland, and intended to be used for labelling cabinets or collections of the same." The plan followed in the arrangement was that devised by Mr. J. Curtis, the well-known author of "British Entomology," the genus and species in each case being given in Latinised form, together with the English appellation. Being printed on one side of the paper only, the names could be cut out and affixed as required.

Shortly after his marriage he took up his abode at Doncaster, and became assistant curate of Armthorpe and Christ Church, which formed one parish, the vicar at that time being the Rev. Henry John Branson, from whom he received his title for priest's orders. He worked happily and harmoniously with Mr. Branson for two years, from October 1835 to October 1837, living in a house called Beechfield, then in the outskirts of the town, but now surrounded by streets. His clerical duties were faithfully performed, and his labours in the parish much appreciated. Still, he found time amid the work of his calling to pursue and cultivate his taste as a naturalist, the neighbourhood of Doncaster being by no means an unfavourable one for the purpose. Many a visit did he pay to Sandal Beat, a wellknown wood not far distant, as well as other favoured spots, such as Thorne Moor and Edlington Wood, where he took many rare specimens of butterflies and moths, which he added to his already extensive and well-ordered collections.

Towards the close of 1837 he left Doncaster, and undertook the sole charge of the parish of Ordsall,

near East Retford, Nottinghamshire, occupying the
Rectory house.   Here he spent four years and a half,
and, among other works, greatly interested himself
in the extension of the church accommodation of
his rapidly increasing parish.

With the exception of the time he was at Ordsall
and the few months at Taxal, the whole of his
clerical life was spent in the county and diocese
of York.   To that diocese he returned on leaving
Ordsall about May 1842, when he became curate in
charge of Crambe, a small and prettily situated parish
between York and Malton, where he remained,
living at the Vicarage, till nearly the end of 1844.

On 22nd November in this year my father was
presented by Archbishop Harcourt to the living of
Nafferton, a large and scattered parish in the East
Riding.   Although the parish was somewhat an
exacting one for a clergyman, it was here that his
literary work began in earnest, and his name as a
writer on natural history became by degrees more
widely known.

At no period of his life could his time have been
more fully occupied, one would suppose, than it
was during the nine years he was vicar of this
place.   The parish extended over six thousand
acres, being about six miles long and three wide;
it contained a population of fourteen hundred, of
whom something like a thousand were in the
village itself, and the remainder in two hamlets
and scattered houses.   Under the most favourable
circumstances. this would have given any parish

priest at all times more than enough to do, but the state of Church feeling in most of the Yorkshire wold villages during the first half of the present century was at a low ebb. Nafferton, it would seem, was no exception to the rule. The work that lay before him when he took up his abode here, which he did on the very first day he was able after presentation, would have daunted the courage of many less sanguine and hopeful men than the new vicar, but he always carried a good heart with him, and had the happy faculty of looking on the bright side of things; this, indeed, he had almost to a fault, but he used to say that he considered such a frame of mind and temperament a far greater blessing even than good health. Such a stimulus proved of special value to him during his residence at Nafferton, where he had from the outset many difficulties to fight against, and not a little opposition to confront.

The value of the living was very small—£170 a year gross at most—while the net yearly income was but £40. The Vicarage house was miserably poor and insufficient. The place itself was long considered as one of the strongholds of Dissent, and contained four meeting-houses for three different religious bodies. The church at Nafferton was a large one, and presented some interesting features, but the internal arrangements when first Mr. Morris went there were unsuitable, not to say deplorable. Huge box-like pews filled the nave and blocked up the entrance to the chancel. The old "three-

decker" was there in all its massiveness and un-
sightliness, with a sound-board to crown the whole.
Organ there was none, and the very name of choir
was then unknown ; the singers, as they were called,
occupied a gallery at the west end of the church,
being led by the village harmonious blacksmith,
and accompanied by fiddles, clarinets, and other
instruments. Whenever these struck up, the whole
congregation turned round and faced them. Tate
and Brady, or some similar psalmody, was in full
force, and the tunes to which the words were sung
can be better imagined than described. Innumerable coats of whitewash covered the walls, and the
whole appearance of the building was dreary in
the extreme. The new vicar was not long in
effecting changes, and reducing things to something like decent order. Two full services were
now, of course, held regularly every Sunday, and
Holy Communion was celebrated once a month
instead of three or four times a year. Within
little more than a year the number of communicants had doubled, and the morning congregation
had increased from a very small number to one
of a hundred and fifty people or so, and in the
afternoon the improvement in the attendance was
equally marked.

A good church school was established in the
village, a portion of the cost of the building having
been collected by the previous vicar. Nearly a
hundred and fifty names were soon on the books
of the school.

The internal arrangements of the church were completely changed. A new roof was given to the nave, the unsightly pews were altered, a new organ placed at the west end of the church, and the old singing-gallery swept away. The belfry arch was opened out, which had previously been bricked up, and a number of minor alterations were made in and about the church. Kneeling during the service seems to have been a practice unknown at Nafferton previously to this time, while other "uses" prevailed which it was found desirable to discontinue. For instance, some of the notices in church, as well as the psalms, were given out by the clerk, and at funerals it was customary to meet the procession at the church door instead of at the entrance to the churchyard.

Old customs of various kinds survived in the village; "riding the stang," as it was called, was the salutary corrective for such as ill-treated their wives, while a period of fixture in the stocks and incarceration in a dismal hovel near the churchyard, fittingly called the "black hole," were standing warnings to drunkards and other offenders against decent behaviour. The material well-being of the people was not lost sight of. Progress was made towards under-draining the village, while Mr. Morris was instrumental in having improvements effected in many of the dwellings of the poor. The glebe land, or a portion of it, was let out in a considerable number of allotments, and additional glebe land adjoining the Vicarage was purchased.

A village library and clothing club were established. These, with many other changes and improvements of various kinds, were accomplished in the space of a year and a quarter.

For nearly two years the vicar had the advantage of the valuable gratuitous assistance of a curate, the Rev. Alexander Joseph, an excellent clergyman, and deservedly respected. The two worked together most amicably, and wrought still further changes. A third service was now established in the village of Wansford; this was held in the new schoolroom there. These services were much appreciated by the inhabitants.

As may be supposed, changes so numerous and so rapidly effected gave alarm, not to say offence, to some of the parishioners, and a party arose in violent opposition to the vicar. At one time the indignation of·the malcontents rose to a high pitch, and found vent in various ways which did not redound to the credit of the prime instigators; but happily Mr. Morris remained long enough at Nafferton to live down much of this ill-feeling, and when he and his family left the place there were many, not to say general regrets.

While at Nafferton he saw a good deal of some of the neighbouring clergy. Almost the next parish was Burton Agnes, of which place Archdeacon Wilberforce was at that time rector. He was the friendliest of neighbours, and my father was a frequent visitor there. On the occasions of parochial meetings, school‑feasts, and social gatherings at either place some members of both families were generally to be seen. On many ecclesiastical questions the Archdeacon and he did not agree, but their friendship was never broken, and on many matters of difficulty my father found in the Archdeacon a valued counsellor and guide. Of all relaxations from work, there were none more congenial to his tastes at that time than entomology and fly-fishing. He rarely, however, took a holiday in the modern acceptation of the word ; that is to say, he seldom, if ever, left home for a few Sundays, as most clergy now do, although few worked harder than he. Still, he managed to find time for pursuing his favourite study. Sometimes he would visit a distant place to catch some rare entomological specimens, or spend, though very occasionally, a few days with an old friend at a distance ; but what he enjoyed perhaps more than anything else in the way of sport was a day's fishing in the Lowthorpe trout-stream. This noted water ran within a couple of miles of Nafferton Vicarage, and it afforded perhaps as good sport as any stream in England. It was strictly preserved, and, through the kindness of the owner, Colonel St. Quintin, my father had permission to fish there whenever he liked — a privilege which, though he availed himself of it but sparingly, was most thoroughly appreciated. He generally used a rod and flies of his own making, and he seldom failed to catch a good basket of fish. The following note from his fly-fishing book is worth recording :—" 1848, Lowthorpe, July 29th, nineteen brace ; put in one brace

and a half. September 9th, seventeen brace and a
half ; put in five brace ; the rest weighed twenty-two
pounds. 1849, June 18th, twenty-one brace ; put in
twelve brace : of the rest, two weighed two pounds
one ounce each ; two, two pounds all but one ounce
each ; and the next two, three pounds between them.
1851, June 16th, seventeen brace ; put in nine brace.
October 1st, eleven brace and a half ; put in eight
brace. 1853, August 2nd, thirteen brace and a half ;
one fish caught with an artificial minnow ; put in
two brace and a half. August 26th, eight brace ;
put in one brace and a half : the largest weighed
three pounds all but two ounces ; the next three
pounds all but three ounces and a half ; the next
one pound and three-quarters. September 30th,
thirteen brace and a half ; put in seven brace."

Nafferton and its neighbourhood was not a favourable district for the entomologist ; but frequently on
his walks when visiting parishioners in outlying
houses, as well as on other occasions, he would take
his net with him, in the hope of capturing some fresh
specimen for his cabinets.

It was at Nafferton where my father and mother
had their first great sorrow, in the death of their
eldest child—their dearly loved little daughter Emily,
who died at the age of twelve in 1847, and was buried
in Nafferton churchyard.

Although he had so many duties to attend to in a
parish like Nafferton, yet he contrived to find time
for a considerable amount of literary work, especially
in the last three or four years of his residence there.

"The History of British Birds," "The History of the Nests and Eggs of British Birds," and "The History of British Butterflies" were all partly before the public between 1850 and 1854, in which latter year he left Nafferton for Nunburnholme. The authorship of these works added considerably to his correspondence.

It must not be supposed that his literary activities were confined to one groove. They embraced widely divergent topics. In 1850 he published an essay on "The Eternal Duration of the Earth," in which he endeavoured to show by Scriptural arguments that the world we inhabit will not be annihilated by fire, although subjected to its action for the purpose of purification and renovation. He held that the work of fire might be a counter-effect of the action of water at the Flood on the whole surface of the globe. Many of the arguments brought forward were not new, but the whole was carefully worked out. The essay, or the substance of it, had, previously to publication, been read before the Malton Clerical Society. Another essay, also read before the same Society, and published in 1850, was that on "Baptismal Regeneration," extending to thirty-one pages. It would take too much space to give even a sketch of its subject-matter here, but that regeneration accompanies baptism according to the teaching of the Church of England he found it impossible to deny. In this year also he published another dissertation on "Scientific Nomenclature," which had been previously communicated to the British Association (of which he was a life-member) in 1844, when its meeting was held at York. This paper was written only at the particular request and wish of one of the most active of the leading members of the Association. It was a short and practical treatise, the main object of it being to create greater uniformity and distinctness in the nomenclature of animated nature.

Read at the same meeting of the British Association, and published also in 1850, was a short paper on a subject which for many years since must have exercised the minds of successive Postmasters-General, viz., "A Plan for the Detection of Thefts by Letter-Carriers." The plan suggested was one which might have worked satisfactorily in those days, when the number of letters passing through the Post Office was comparatively few, but the check recommended, which involved the stamping and directing of a slip attached to each letter, and afterwards torn off, filed, and preserved at the Post Office, would be impracticable in these days.

These writings are here alluded to in order to show the varied character of the subjects in which he was at that time interested. It is remarkable how this mental habit was kept up all through his life. His mind seemed ready to interest itself in almost any matter that came before it ; perhaps it would be best described by saying there was a wide-awakedness about him which let nothing escape notice that came within the range of his observation.

The last year that he was at Nafferton—1853— he attended the meeting of the British Association,

which was held in Hull. At this meeting a paper
of his was read on " National Adult Education," a
subject in which he felt great interest. In this
paper suggestions were made for the improvement
of Mechanics' Institutions, or rather for the substitution of something better in their place, for
they had then already failed to fulfil the purpose
for which they were designed. Something more
attractive was needed. He advocated the establishment of national colleges, with buildings of handsome appearance, as a continuation of the national
school system, in towns. "This building," he observed, "open throughout the day and evening,
should, if carried out to a complete extent, contain,
among other departments, a museum, a library, a
reading-room, a lecture-room, and a room for philo-
sophical experiments." He argued that a taste for
scientific pursuits might be fostered by the sight
of natural and artificial objects. "The first sight
of a butterfly or a bird may excite the dormant
spirit of a Le Vaillant or an Audubon, or the
model of an engine some otherwise 'inglorious'
Fulton or Watt." Strongly urging the importance of
encouragement being given also to outdoor amuse-
ments and recreations, he proposed that in every
village and town open spaces should be set apart
for this purpose, and suggested also the establishment of cricket-grounds, bowling-greens, gymna-
siums, quoit-grounds, bathing-places, and public
promenades. "Garden allotments," he added, "are
most advantageous, and might in a vast number of

places be easily procured by enclosing waste lands, by purchase, exchange, or long lease. No more beneficial means of improving the health and morals of townspeople can be thought of than this. All encouragement should likewise be given to the study of music, the establishment of the botanic garden, the museum of natural history, the procuring a gallery of arts, an agricultural museum, as also to the promotion of annual, half-yearly, or more frequent flower shows, cattle shows, horticultural *fêtes*, and exhibitions of farm produce, implements, and various other productions ; and prizes should be awarded to successful competitors. A savings-bank was part of the plan of the Manchester Mechanics' Institution ; but though it failed of success and was discontinued, I cannot but think that the idea is a good one, and might be most advantageously carried out throughout the country at large. For all these purposes land should be provided, and endowments invited by deed of gift or bequest."

He held firmly that the study of the arts and sciences should promote morality and religion, that the general tone of the mind would be improved by such studies and rendered more susceptible of higher impressions. "There is nothing," he said, "in being a better artist or a better mathematician to hinder the student from being a better member of society, a better man, and a better Christian. I would have every Government scheme so ordered that no handle be given to any mere party to gain an ascendency and degrade institutions that ought to be noble and truly handmaids to religion into vehicles of irreligion, impiety, scepticism, and sedition. The very contrary is their legitimate result. The discoveries of Herschel do not lead men to disbelieve in God, nor do the compositions of Handel act as hindrances to the singing of His praise in worship."

I should like to have quoted more from this paper on "National Adult Education," but perhaps enough has been said to show that the writer's views on that important subject were in advance of the time at which he wrote. Taken as a whole, his ideas seemed best to correspond with those which at the present time are being carried out under the High School movement in Denmark with such excellent results. The aim of that movement is not to prepare the young people for examinations, which in this country can hardly be dissociated from the idea of education, but rather to enlarge and humanise their minds, to create new and healthy tastes, to brighten their lives, and to put before them higher aims and altogether more invigorating objects than they would otherwise have in the midst of their daily occupations and callings in life.

Before leaving Nafferton he issued a farewell address to the inhabitants, as he had been accustomed to do in parishes that he had previously left. After taking affectionate leave of his parishioners, he thus ends what he has to say :—

"I am deeply thankful to leave the parish in a
very different state from that in which I found it.
When I first came among you there was no school;
now there are two excellent ones, each with a master
and mistress, and at the beginning of this year there
were no fewer than 253 children on the books.
Every house I have seen provided with a Bible and
prayer-book. The congregation is manifold more
than it was; the church has been restored in the
most creditable manner, so as to have more the
character of a house of prayer; and the whole tone
of the village is so changed as to be obvious to
those who pass through it. Glad shall I be to see
further improvements carried out in the parish and
in the church, and thankful always to hear of the
still greater prosperity of the cause of God's Holy
Church, to His glory, and the salvation of the souls
of the people. Never can I cease to retain the
deepest interest in this place. Here our first-born
child was removed from us and awaits the Resurrec-
tion; here we have spent nine long, and yet nine
short, years; here we have many friends who have
proved themselves sincere ones; and here, I trust,
the means of grace and the preaching of the Gospel
have been blessed to souls. We have, indeed, had
our trials, but our mercies have been far greater;
nor have we known one dull moment since we have
been here. I need not recall the recollection of any
'root of bitterness,' which I would rather forget
and forgive, as I hope to be forgiven, but am contented to have endeavoured to do my duty in that

state of life into which it hath pleased God to call me, and to have seen a better spirit prevail amongst others, and hostile feelings become ' beautifully less.' A more quiet village than this now is it would be difficult to find anywhere, and I trust that peace may ever prevail among you, and righteousness flourish and abound to the praise and glory of God."

Soon after he came to Nafferton his father removed from Charmouth, where he had passed twenty happy years, and took up his abode at Beverley, in the East Riding, where he died in 1852.

III

NUNBURNHOLME

THE nine years spent at Nafferton (1845–1854) were years of ceaseless work with Mr. Morris. Some of the obstacles that had stood in his way might have been removed with less friction than they were had he bided his time and exercised more tact ; but he preferred to go straight and speedily at anything that seemed to him to be wrong, and take the consequences in his endeavours to right it. It was, however, an agreeable announcement to him when Archbishop Musgrave, in the most kindly and considerate manner, offered him the Rectory of Nunburnholme, which had been vacated by the Hon. and Rev. John Baillie on his appointment to a living in Northumberland. Had all England been searched through it would have been hard to find a place that was more to his taste and liking. The parish was a small one, the whole population being not more than about 240 souls, while the value of the living, though not great, was considerably in excess of that which he then held. This offer was made to him about the beginning of 1854, and he thankfully accepted it, for he would now have more spare time at his disposal for carrying on his literary work, for which he then, and ever after, had so strong a leaning. The quiet seclusion of the spot and its pleasant surroundings made it the home of all others for an author, and especially a naturalist. Despite some stormy times at Nafferton, he had, nevertheless, met with a vast amount of real kindness and staunch support, and he and his family left the place with many regrets.

The move, or *flitting*, as it is called in Yorkshire, was made in the early spring of 1854, a season remarkable for its forwardness, for in that year the lilacs in the Rectory garden were fully out about the middle of April—a sight which we have never been permitted to see here since.

A *flitting* in those days was a very different thing from what it is now, when the removal of household goods is reduced almost to a science. At that time a man's bag and baggage had to be rumbled over the country in carts and waggons, at no little risk of breakages : in this case, however, the transit across the wolds was safely accomplished ; even the numerous and delicate entomological specimens, by which their owner laid so much store, were landed at Nunburnholme none the worse for their shaking.

Nunburnholme, or Burnholme, as it was named three hundred years ago, was a place scarcely heard of outside a radius of twenty miles at the time of which we are speaking. It lay far removed from the highways of the world, and had nothing of its own to make itself a name. If its Benedictine House possessed any lustre in bygone days, the glory thereof

had long since faded, the very name of its founder
being not beyond doubt. The active mind and dili-
gent pen of the late rector did, however, after a
course of well-nigh forty years, tell their tale, and the
name of this quiet little Yorkshire village became
more widely known than that of many a place of
much greater size.

The village itself lies snugly sheltered from
northerly blasts in a well-wooded valley at the
foot of one of the East Riding wolds. This valley
runs in a south-westerly direction, and as you stand
above it, on the top of the steep hill—fittingly
called Totterdown—the scene is a striking one
indeed, being one of the most extensive views in
the Riding. Right away to the north-west can
be seen the range of the Hambledon Hills, many
miles beyond the northern capital, while the whole
of the fertile vale of York lies open before you.
The eye takes in a wide field, including Selby
Abbey and Howden, together with Doncaster in
the extreme distance. The silvery line of the
Humber, with the Lincolnshire hills beyond, bounds
our vision towards the south; while the little village,
in its peaceful seclusion, nestles immediately below
you. Towards its easternmost boundary is the site
of the old nunnery just alluded to, with the remains
of its moat and fish-ponds, the plan of the whole
being clearly traceable; at the opposite end of the
village stands the ancient church of St. James, with
the Rectory house hard by. As you look at them
from afar, both church and parsonage appear to

be almost enveloped by trees. The whole district, indeed, is well timbered, and Nunburnholme Brant, or 'Brant,' as it is called, a wood of about a mile in length belting the opposite side of the valley, is at all times of the year a pleasant object on which to fix one's gaze. In autumn its ever-changing tints are attractive, while its choice carpet of variegated wild-flowers is fairly a feast for the eye to behold in the month of May. At that season of the year the place is alive with the voices of many kinds of birds, from the perky chatter of the magpie and the jay to the softest pipings of the bullfinch and the long-tailed tit. Beyond a flutter of excitement when a sparrow-hawk or kestrel makes an occasional descent into the wood, there is but little to disturb the freedom of its inmates. The members of an ancient rookery at one extremity of the Brant cling tenaciously to the trees within the confines of their own colony, and have nothing to say to the neighbouring songsters of other feathers. Their curious and inscrutable ways, however, always give food for reflection to those who are careful to observe their movements. But this is not all. Down the little vale runs the nameless beck which rises a mile or so higher up in the never-failing pool, known far and near in the district as Warter Bucksea. This bright stream is fed from the hills by tiny rills—sykes, as they are called in the country-speech; these, by the forces of nature, bubble forth from the chalk here and there in many parts of the wold country, and form one of its features. The sequestered valley of Nunburnholme, through which this little beck makes its ceaseless way, though by no means claiming to be called romantic, is certainly one of the most charming bits of country in the Riding.

The church, though small, is an interesting building, dating from the time of the Norman Conquest; its rich and perfect western Norman arch and small north window of unique pattern giving unmistakable proof of its high antiquity. Features such as these tell us that its walls, or portions of them, have withstood the storms of eight hundred winters. Inside the sacred fabric, where the "rude forefathers of the hamlet" have worshipped for so many generations, are to be seen other interesting relics of the past, among which may be named an Easter sepulchre, a curious low-side window on the south-west of the chancel, above which is a graceful Early English lancet one, the other windows of the chancel being of subsequent date, though probably not later than 1330; while on the north side of the nave are the tracings of an Early Norman doorway. The chancel is nearly as large as the nave, though the whole building will not accommodate much more than a hundred people. Such was the church to which my father was inducted in the spring of 1854, and beside whose wall his body was laid to rest in 1893. The churchyard—God's-acre, as he liked to call it—is an ideal one in its peaceful seclusion and pretty surroundings.

Fifty paces from the south door of the church,

along the gravel-walk, brings you to the Rectory garden, which forms a sheltered retreat, and has for years past been a veritable paradise of birds. Thanks to the good taste of a former occupant of the benefice, the ground, though not extensive, has been well laid out, and the touch of time has aided the hand of man in making the place what it is—a home of delight. Lying as it does at the end of a valley, the view from the low terrace in front of the house is not a wide one ; but this is made up for by many interesting peeps which the garden itself affords. Stand where you will, there is always something pleasant to look upon ; it may be a glimpse of the grassy slopes of the abutting wold as you peer through an opening beneath the boughs of a lime or a sycamore ; or if you turn your eye in another direction you will see, through the light and graceful foliage of the birch, a Gothic window of the little church hard by, with the steep and wooded ascent of the Brant in the background ; or you can sit in the summer-house and watch the swallows skimming over the beck which runs through the garden ; at the same time you may gain sight of the fly-catcher making sudden darts after its scarcely visible prey from ·the rustic bridge over the stream, returning ofttimes, as is its wont, to the point from which it started.

The main charm of the place seems to centre in the little stream of water, a never-failing source of pleasure. Along its banks the water-voles make their home, and they can constantly be seen nibbling the grass near the water's edge, looking up at you the while with their soft black eyes, till a slight motion on your part sends them like a flash headlong into the stream; and for an occasional treat you may hear the wild cry of the heron as it drops down by the water-side at no great distance off in search of a trout or some smaller fry. For many years after my father came to Nunburnholme you could seldom walk half-a-mile down the beck without seeing a kingfisher or two; now you may think yourself lucky if you meet with three or four in a year, so ruthlessly have they been destroyed in the lower reaches of the stream. In the winter-time, when other brooks were frozen, our little beck was the haunt of many a snipe and wild duck, though these, alas! are not so frequent as of yore; and the dipper, though rarely seen even forty years ago, is now quite a thing of the past, so far as the Nunburnholme beck is concerned.

Happily there is no lack of trees and shrubs in the Rectory garden. These are the haunts of countless birds of the commoner sorts, such as sparrows, blackbirds, thrushes, chaffinches, robins, dunnocks, wrens, starlings, and others; while in years past the boughs of the yew-trees have given a building-place for our smallest bird, the golden-crested wren, as well as for the pleasant-voiced wood-pigeon. Hundreds of families of martins have been reared from year to year under the eaves of the Rectory, and many generations of swallows have found nesting-places for themselves within the boundaries of the

garden fences, and brought off their broods unmolested in happiness and peace.

What home could have been more congenial to
one who regarded all birds with feelings of the
keenest interest, not to say affection, and whose
movements and voices were to him a never-ending
source of delight ? He thoroughly appreciated his
new abode, and in later years was often heard to
confess that if, by some compelling power, he were
forced to confine himself for the remainder of his
days within the limits of his own garden, such a
decree would not in any way distress him.

From whichever side you approach Nunburnholme, the view is a pleasant one ; and to one who,
like its late rector, had a keen appreciation for the
beauties of nature, whether animate or inanimate,
the many and varied walks in the parish and
neighbourhood gave endless supplies of interest,
to which his published writings so frequently bore
witness.

To strangers the wold country, pure and simple,
is apt to appear lonesome and monotonous. True,
the district is sparsely populated and somewhat
uniform in its character, but the trim, well-cultivated,
and extensive farms which cover its surface give it
an appearance of prosperity and richness which
compares favourably with many other parts of
England. The freshness and dryness of the air
makes it peculiarly healthy ; and although the
eastern blasts in March can bite keenly, yet the
lack of dampness in the soil renders the country

at all seasons of the year one of the healthiest in the land—a fact which ancient races of men, whether Celtic, Roman, Anglo-Saxon, or Dane, discovered when they formed settlements here. The face of the country has been wondrously changed since the beginning of the present century, when the whole of the wold district was a vast down, forming huge sheep-walks and strays for cattle, as well as one of the favourite haunts of the bustard, till Sir Tatton Sykes discovered the capabilities of the soil for turnip and corn growing, and set the plough to work with astonishing results. What the wolds have lost in verdure and picturesqueness they have thus gained in richness.

It must be noted that Nunburnholme lies at the extreme edge of these wolds. It is this position that makes the view from the summit of Totter-downhill, just referred to, so strikingly varied, alternating as it does between long miles of level plain bounded by distant hills, the rich and wooded valley just below you, and the wavy sea of characteristic wold country beyond it.

The Rectory house itself, like so many of the old-fashioned parsonages of the country, shows traces of enlargement at different times. Immediately before Mr. Morris's arrival two wings had been added to the old house by his predecessor, which quite altered the character of the building from what it was thirty years before, when John Keble visited his friend, Charles Dyson, a former rector, and whose illustrious name figures in one of the parish register

books. There was nothing of any special interest
about the interior that needs description, except my
father's study, which was a room characteristic of
its late occupant; it overlooked the lawn, and a
peep of the road to the neighbouring village of
Burnby could be caught from it. Such traffic as
there was along this road added a measure of life
to the prospect. The furniture of the room was dis-
tinctly old-fashioned and absolutely unique. A quaint
old folding-down oak table stood in the centre of
the study; at this my father invariably wrote, seated
in a curious high-back chair, always in exactly
the same position, and did his work. He had the
window on his left hand, for he had the greatest
objection to be in a room with his face to the light;
his reason for this being lest the light should try
his eyes, of which he took the greatest care, frequently bathing them in cold water, always wearing
a green shade at night, never trying them needlessly,
and invariably using candles in preference to any
other kind of artificial light. These precautions
seem to have had the desired effect, for he retained
his sight wonderfully well, even to extreme old age,
though few could have used their eyes more than
he. His library was never an extensive one. The
chief part of it was arranged in his study, partly in
a carved old oak bookcase, and partly in recessed
shelves; it consisted mainly of books and treatises
on subjects connected with natural history, with a
certain number of antiquated volumes of divinity,
genealogy, classics, and other subjects. Nearly

THE RECTORY, NUNBURNHOLME.

covering the walls were a number of quaint prints
and pictures, mainly relating to family history;
conspicuous among these was a large genealogical
tree, giving the ramifications of the Orpen family for
many generations. In another "coign of vantage"
was a map of England deftly worked on canvas
some time in the last century. Standing on the
chimney-piece might be seen a row of handsome
vases in blue and white china; he had a great liking
for old china, as well as for old oak, and in his
choice of these and kindred objects he showed no
little good taste. Of easy-chairs he had none in his
study, and he seldom, if ever, indulged himself in
one in his own house, however tired he might be.
Various pieces of curious and handsome old furniture were arranged about the room, among which
were one or two small old oak chests in which he
kept some of his most valued papers. By far the
most interesting features of the study were the large
cabinets containing his valuable collections of butterflies, moths, flies, beetles, birds' eggs, &c.; the chief
part of the entomological specimens he had himself
captured, and every one of them he had set with
scrupulous care and neatness with his own hand.
Many of the Tineæ moths were so small that it is
hard to know how a pin, even the finest, could be
pierced through their delicate bodies without seriously injuring them as specimens. Not only was
this done with unerring skill, but also the wings
and antennæ of these minute creatures were set out
with the utmost precision and symmetry of arrange-

ment; all were named with their proper Latinised appellations, and all kept in most perfect order. When it is considered that there were no less than six of these cabinets, that every single specimen took both time and care to set in the way these were, and that of British butterflies and moths only there were something like 3500 specimens, it is difficult to see how the time was snatched to carry out this extensive by-work. It seemed almost as if, by some magical power, he was able to multiply two hands into four, and the twenty-four hours of the day to forty-eight. It was only by the strictest economy of the hours and minutes as they fled that he could have done what he did.

In his study there was a place for everything and everything in its place, so much so that he would often say that, if necessary, he could find in the dark, among his numberless papers, many a one that he needed. Everything about his room was a reflection of his well-ordered and methodical mind. His letters were for the most part arranged in numbered pigeon-holes, so that they could be easily referred to. Stuffed birds were conspicuous by their absence; such as he possessed were arranged in another part of the house. Prominent on a wall of his room were two cases of marine shells and foreign creatures of queer shapes and kinds, among which were half-a-dozen scorpions, and a huge spider with outstretched legs, measuring not far short of six inches across. On a small side-table, also of ancient make, were arranged his

paraphernalia for the setting of entomological specimens, which had been made to suit his own ideas.
In writing he always sat with his back to the fire,
and on his left hand stood what looked to be a
large, dark-coloured waste-paper basket with a cover
to it; in this he kept papers which he needed for
more immediate use or reference; and beyond this,
but within easy reach, was a revolving book-stand
which had belonged to his father, in which were kept
papers and books that had to be frequently resorted
to. On the upper shelves of the bookcases were
stowed away innumerable pamphlets and printed
papers of the most motley description, which he
had collected through a long course of years.
Standing in front of the window was perhaps the
most remarkable piece of furniture of all. This
was a curious long-shaped trunk, covered with hide
of some sort; it had belonged to his grandfather
when he was in America, and was probably of a
kind in common use about the middle of the last
century. This was packed as full as it would hold
of papers, letters, circulars of his books, &c., which
no one knew how to find but himself, though to
himself all seemed perfectly clear. Besides these
there were numerous piles of tracts and leaflets
which he made use of in his parochial visitations;
all were neatly arranged and ready to hand when
needed. On his table, or not far from his hand,
might be seen his well-worn Greek Testament
and Prayer-Book, which contained numerous inter-
lineations or notes. On the first page stood the

words, in his neatest handwriting, "Open Thou mine eyes, that I may see the wondrous things of Thy law," followed by a slightly altered and abbreviated form of the well-known Collect for the Second Sunday in Advent.

Such, in some sort, was the room wherein the chief part of his widespread work was accomplished.

It would have taxed the ingenuity of a stranger, on entering this study, to determine in what direction, mainly, lay the interests of its occupant. Tastes entomological and genealogical would probably at first sight, from a general survey of the surroundings, have been thought the most strongly marked in him. It will be seen later, when we come to speak more personally of him, how far such a surmise would have been correct.

"No admittance except on business" was practically the rule of entry into his "sanctum." It was as though he could bear no interruptions in this inner recess. He had the greatest dislike to the presence of anything which might tend to disarrange the order of his papers, and never would he allow any one to dust his room but himself, except on certain rare occasions, which he cordially disliked, and were made as few and far between as possible. Frequently was he seen, in the middle of a morning's work, to dart out of his room in his shirt-sleeves, carefully holding a duster, which he shook violently on the terrace outside, but always so that the wind carried the cloud right away. Only one person ever ventured to disturb his papers and furniture; this was his youngest brother Charles, formerly a Fellow of Oriel College, Oxford, and afterwards Professor of Latin and Greek in the University at Baltimore, who paid periodical visits to England; and when, on these occasions, he came to Nunburnholme, one of the first things he did was to rush into the study and, in a fit of playful mischief, turn everything upside down that he could lay hands on, and put the place into a state of disorder. Hearty laughter always accompanied these inroads, and the two thoroughly enjoyed the practical joke; though, if the truth were known, the feelings of the one played upon were not wholly unmingled. With these rare exceptions, the room was at all times the pink of tidiness and order.

He was not long in settling down in his new home at Nunburnholme. The claims of the parish were light as compared with those of the one he had just left, but whatever had to be done he did thoroughly and conscientiously. At this time the little church was not in a creditable condition for the performance of Divine Service, and one of the first things he did was to put it into something like decent order, though it was not until 1871 that the now well-nigh complete restoration, under Mr. G. Gilbert Scott, junior, was carried into effect.

There was no organ in the church at that time, and harmoniums were only beginning to be much used. A small band of instrumentalists and singers formed the choir of Nunburnholme Church in those days, the former accompanying the voices in the singing of old-fashioned hymns with extraordinary shakes, turns, and flourishes—the pride of those who played them, but not a little disconcerting to those of musical culture. A harmonium shortly replaced the village orchestra, and Mrs. Morris, with admirable tact and skill, soon changed the old order of things to one more in accordance with modern ideas.

The changes that had taken place in Nunburnholme, as in so many other country places, had been few and far between for a hundred years previously. One of the old mediæval customs that was kept up for some time after my father came to the parish was for some of the women to make a curtsey immediately on entering the church—an interesting survival from pre-Reformation days.

The educational advantages of the parish were small indeed. There was no efficient village school in the place, and accordingly he lost no time in setting about to build one. A grant of land was obtained from Lord Londesborough, the lord of the manor, and within a short time a good school was established in connection with the National Society. It was the custom at that time for the Sunday-school to be held in the church, the day-school, such as it was, being carried on in one of the cottages.

Happily there was no public-house in the village, which was a matter of great thankfulness to Mr. Morris, and it was a remarkable fact that in three adjoining parishes—Burnby, Kilnwick-Percy, and Londesborough—to which a fourth (Warter) might subsequently have been added, the same fact held good. To this state of things he frequently alluded afterwards in his letters and other writings with feelings of the greatest satisfaction.

Although the village was practically free from temptations to the curse of drunkenness, there were other evils which had to be reckoned with. The parish being purely agricultural, such evils as existed were those which ordinarily beset country villages. To one of these he paid special attention in the year that he came to Nunburnholme. This was the system that prevailed all over the East Riding of hiring farm servants. As a magistrate and as a parish priest, he knew only too well the evils that attended that system, and in this year he published a pamphlet dealing with the subject and suggesting remedies. Nothing could be worse than the state of things in those days in connection with this matter. The servants were engaged by the farmers annually at Martinmas, and their engagements were binding for one year only. For a week at Martinmas the young people were allowed to go to their homes for a holiday, and nothing could exceed the scenes of wild excitement that took place on these occasions, especially in the market towns, where the young servants of both sexes assembled on the hiring days, and, amid surroundings of the utmost disorder and unseemly conduct, gave free expression to their hilarious feelings.

With such displays of unbridled barbarity before him he was the last man to remain passive. He spoke of what went on as the " crying evils of this scandalous system. A system of unmitigated badness—a very gehenna of corruption. Many are led astray without any actual bad intention by the influence of the company they are in—' good company,' as they hear it called, but the worst of company if judged by its consequences. How many then first begin what becomes a habit of intoxication ! And do even their masters lose nothing in their property from such a habit ? Do they lose nothing in the county rates raised to keep up the prisons filled with prisoners who have learnt their first and last lesson of crime amid those very scenes ? Do they lose nothing in the contamination of their own children or of themselves by bringing a polluted stream among them ? Does not the whole neighbourhood suffer ? "

As a remedy for these evils he proposed the establishment of a register office for farm servants in every market town, and that farmers should take no servant into their service except from such offices, and none from them without a character obtained there, furnished by their former master or mistress, or from the clergyman and schoolmaster of their parish, if they had not been out to service before.

Owing to the difficulty of getting the farmers to combine, this proposal was never carried into effect ; though in later years he was instrumental in hiring a room in his own market town of Pocklington, to which the female servants could resort for the purpose of being hired by the farmers' wives—an example which was afterwards followed in other towns in the Riding. Thus, by degrees, the Martinmas hirings were accompanied by more orderly proceedings, and in time he lived to see an altogether improved state of things.

Among other pamphlets which he published this same year in which he took up his abode at Nunburnholme were the following :—" Account of the Battle of the Monongahela River," " Account of the Siege of Killowen," and " A Letter to Archdeacon Wilberforce on Supremacy." The first of these was drawn from an original document written by one of the survivors of the battle. The events preceding the battle are given in the form of a diary, which no doubt describes accurately what took place. A list of the officers present, with those killed or wounded, is added at the end.

The " Siege of Killowen " was from an original manuscript in the library at King's Inn, Dublin. The siege took place in 1688, the fortress being defended by Mr. Orpen, an ancestor of my father's on his mother's side.

The " Letter to Archdeacon Wilberforce " was addressed to him just after he had joined the Church of Rome, with the following apology :—" I have given you my name as its writer, and as I am quite sure that you will be ready to say that, ever since I came into the archdeaconry, no clergyman has acted with greater and more uniform respect towards you than myself ; so in now presuming to offer a word of warning to one so entirely my superior, though you may think me presumptuous, you will not, I am certain, attach to my doings any more grave objection."

It happened that one of the last official acts that the Archdeacon had to perform before he severed his connection with the Church of England was to hold his Visitation at Pocklington. On this occasion he stayed the night at Nunburnholme Rectory, but there was nothing in his manner or words to show that he so soon was about to take the step he did. It was remarked, indeed, by those who were present with him then that he seemed in particularly good spirits ; and, as an indication of this, it happened that, as he was walking in the garden with the Rector, the Archdeacon suddenly said he would like to try and jump the little stream that ran close by, and there and then he took a short run and cleared it at a bound.

The life of an English clergyman in a small country parish is generally passed quietly and peaceably enough, without anything occurring to interfere with its serenity and seclusion. As far as his parochial duties were concerned, the life of the rector of Nunburnholme was of this description. The demands of his parish upon his energies were, do what he would, only light as compared with other larger parishes, although he was one who would never admit that even a small parish did not give a clergyman much more to do than was generally supposed, provided he was determined to do his duty thoroughly. Even two or three hundred people scattered over a wide area, with no resident squire, and no inhabitant above the rank of a farmer, gave a parish priest scope for a considerable amount of work at all events; and for one like my father, who was never idle for a moment, there was perpetually something to be thought of, especially when he considered not even the most seemingly trivial thing as beneath his notice. No matter what other works of a literary kind he might be engaged in—and they were often many and exacting—yet he seemed perpetually to have every man, woman, and child in the parish in his mind and subject to his anxious care. He made it a rule to visit every house once a quarter at least, though practically his parochial visitations were of much more frequent occurrence. He kept a careful record of every visit he paid, as well as a communicants' register. Not a day passed without a visit or visits among his parishioners or to his school, and he had a most extraordinary faculty of impressing people with the feeling that each one to whom he addressed himself was the one in whom he was more interested than any other. To every one he had something kindly or useful to say, and nearly always something which he wished him to do. He was a great believer in the value of tracts' and leaflets, of which he distributed countless numbers; and in writing on two occasions to two of our leading Church newspapers on this subject he remarked :—

"I remember a clergyman once saying to me

that he did not believe in tracts. I do, and I have reason for doing so, for I know that my people—by far the most part at all events—read them and are glad to have them, and, I cannot doubt, with more or less profit.

"What is a tract but a poor man's book? He cannot read—for he has not time, as the rich have—large folios, quartos, or octavos; nor are they within his means to buy, nor could he understand them for the most part if they were. But a tract he not only can but does read, and as numbers of them have been written by the very ablest and best men in the country, they are worth reading. I can truly say that I have read very many of them myself with pleasure, and I hope with profit. It seems to me simply cruel not to make all the use one possibly can of them."

In one instance at least the giving away of a few tracts had a far-reaching result. This was in the case of the late Mrs. Smythies, the philanthropic founder of the Band of Mercy movement, whom he had the pleasure of meeting some forty years before she died. He handed to her on that occasion a few leaflets of the Royal Society for the Prevention of Cruelty to Animals, and begged her to read them. She did so, and from that time forward became an ardent supporter of the good cause of humanity to animals. In alluding to this incident the editor of the *British Workman* remarked:—"Little did the esteemed rector of Nunburnholme dream of the widespread influence in years to come of his little gift and few kind words."

His one great aim in life was to do what good he could, and, as far as he was concerned, to leave the world better than he found it. To one thus impressed and determined, every day brought more work than he could possibly get through, even in so small a parish as Nunburnholme.

His literary labours were of the most varied kinds imaginable, for there were few subjects that could be named in which he did not feel some interest.

For the first three and a half years of his residence here the "History of British Birds" was in course of publication, and naturally absorbed a considerable amount of time. His business transactions with Mr. Fawcett of Driffield were at this time, and for many years afterwards, very numerous, and meetings between the two took place frequently. The railway from York at that time did not extend beyond Market Weighton, and consequently the fourteen miles from Nunburnholme to Driffield had to be driven or walked; it was not seldom that my father did the latter. His walking powers were so extraordinary that many people used to remark upon them with expressions of astonishment; a distance, therefore, of that kind was nothing to him, except for the time it took to cover. On one occasion he walked from Driffield to Nunburnholme before breakfast, and when he reached home he was neither hungry, thirsty, nor tired. His pace was terrific. He had but little flesh to carry, not weighing more than ten stone and a half, and was wiry and nimble to a degree. He was the most merciless companion to walk with, as the writer of this memoir has reason to remember; for, no matter how quickly you walked, he would walk quicker, so at least that he might always be a foot or two ahead of you. These powers of walking he kept up till within a comparatively short time of his death; and when quite advanced in life his parishioners would sometimes remark that Mr. Morris was still "as lingey as a lad."

His conversation when walking would generally turn upon his favourite topics of natural history, and the sight of some insect or bird or flower would often lead to an interesting bit of information or anecdote connected with it. The beauties of the country had a wondrous fascination for him, and he had a remarkably quick eye for them. Although he walked apace, but few things escaped his notice; and many a letter or article was planned out in his mind on these walks within the confines of his own parish, and his productions of this nature were often made fragrant by the breath of country air that pervaded them.

He was not long in scouring the whole neighbourhood around Nunburnholme for entomological specimens, and there was scarcely a wood round about that he had not tried at night with sugar, and by day with the net, for moths or butterflies. Though not a favourable district for the purpose, he nevertheless generally captured specimens that he was glad to add to his collections.

The days at Nunburnholme were never long enough for carrying into effect all that the rector had in his mind, and, although living such a quiet life, he did not know what it was for time to hang heavily on his hands; he used to say that if he had to kill time, time would soon kill him.

He was not an early riser, being seldom up before about a quarter to eight. Breakfasting at nine, he was ready for his morning's work about ten. The post generally brought him a considerable correspondence, and every letter was at once answered. In the early days at Nunburnholme the postal arrangements were of the most primitive description. An elderly man, who in his way was a great character, walked over each morning from Hayton, through which the mail-cart from York passed, and deposited the daily budget at the Rectory somewhere between half-past nine and ten, generally approaching more nearly the later limit than the former; he called again on the return journey at noon. Postmen's uniforms were quite unknown in those days; our old friend always wore a tall hat, and, strange to say, never carried a letter-bag, so that it was impossible to distinguish him as a postman at all. There was probably no other postman in England to compare with him. What he lacked in letter-bags he made up for in pockets, which seemed to be studded about his capacious coat in various directions; indeed, so thoroughly well pocketed was he that, no matter how many letters and book-packets might arrive by any given mail, they were all carefully stowed away out of sight about his person. There was, no doubt, some method in the arrangement of his pockets, but what the law was that guided that arrangement no one was ever able to discover.

Frequently there would arrive by post natural history specimens, both living and dead—bird-skins, eggs, caterpillars, moths, butterflies, &c.—which correspondents had sent to be named, or as presents to the 'naturalist of Nunburnholme.' One morning, never to be forgotten, on the arrival of the old postman a look of distress mingled with amusement sat upon his well-known countenance. A box full of caterpillars had somehow given way in his pocket; the creatures had thus made their escape, and were seen crawling about him in various directions when he made his appearance at the Rectory door, to the no little entertainment of all who were lucky enough to witness the scene.

On another occasion, which the writer well re-members, a small box arrived by post one day, which was opened at the breakfast-table, when out flew a fine specimen of the 'Camberwell Beauty' butterfly. No letter accompanied this present, only a request that the receipt of it might be acknow-ledged to "An old woman," Post Office, Lockington.

It was sometimes a matter of great difficulty to get all letters answered by twelve o'clock. On such occasions the postman, to do him justice, was accom-

NUNBURNHOLME CHURCH.

modating, and never grumbled at waiting a few minutes. This in a measure atoned for his tardiness at the other end.

The afternoons were for the most part devoted to parochial visitations, together with a call at the school, or a walk to see some neighbour; although it was impossible to say at what hour of the day he might not have been seen writing in his study. In the evening, indeed, even the drawing-room was for him always converted into a study; that is to say, he seldom ceased writing, except for short intervals, all through the evening, even up to well-nigh midnight; and as he always wrote with great rapidity, it can be imagined what a vast amount of work he thus accomplished. It was more like a perpetually running stream than anything else; time, place, or circumstance seemed to make but little difference to him. He was exceedingly fond of music, and was never tired of listening to it. In the evening he generally requested that some member of his family would play or sing, and he had the faculty of attending to the music and writing at the same time.

The summer of 1857 saw the completion of the "History of British Birds," the latter parts of the work having been hastened as much as possible in order to make way for the production of other works which his printer had in view. Needless to say, the conclusion of the work cleared the ground for the author for increased activities. Toward the close of 1859 material was prepared for publishing a collection of "Anecdotes in Natural History," and in

E

due course Messrs. Longmans brought out the book,
which formed a small volume of anecdotes of animals,
gathered from various sources.   What gave rise to
the publication of a book of this kind was this.   He
had undertaken to give a lecture before the members
of the York Institute on the subject of Humanity,
and intended illustrating the lectures by anecdotes
of the various animals spoken of ; but it was soon
found, as stated in the preface, "that the pleasant
part of the subject would have to be omitted, to
make way for that which was of a contrary character.
The thought then occurred to me that I might publish the former as a separate work, and the following
pages are the result."

. This series was but a first instalment of that large
store of similar recorded instances of the sagacity of
animals which he accumulated in later years.   A
thousand and one stories of this description were
actually supplied by him month by month for several
years in one publication only ; and had he undertaken to supply some editor with five times the
number, there can be little doubt that he would have
proved himself equal to the task.   In fact, he used
to say that he could fill a whole shelf with similar authentic anecdotes.   A second and illustrated
edition of the "Anecdotes" was subsequently
brought out by Messrs. Partridge.

IV

HISTORY OF BRITISH BIRDS

ALTHOUGH comprising but a small portion, comparatively, of his many-sided labours, there can be no doubt that the work by which the name of Francis Orpen Morris was mainly made known to the world was the " History of British Birds." Until this work made its appearance the author's name had been but little heard of. It is a book that has had a wide circulation among all classes, and has contributed in no small measure to the greater interest that is now taken in ornithology generally, so that it will not be unfitting if some allusions are here made to it.

The treatise was first taken in hand when the author was at Nafferton. It would have been impossible for him, with his limited means, to have undertaken a work of this kind on his own responsibility. Living at that time in the small market town of Driffield, hard by, was a man of remarkable enterprise. Benjamin Fawcett, who had a great capacity for work and business, and was in fact, in his way, a genius, started for himself in Driffield in 1830 as a bookseller and printer. He was a man of great independence of character, and took his own line in almost everything he did. He first made himself a name by bringing out illustrated books for children, as well as a new kind of copy-book with pictorial covers, the designs and illustrations being all engraved by himself. These were published at extremely low prices, and had a large sale.

It was about the year 1848 or 1849 that Mr. Morris first had business transactions with Mr. Fawcett. This was in connection with a small work, brought out in parts, entitled " A Bible Natural History ; " the illustrations were by Mr. Fawcett, and it seems to have been a success, though the sale was not a very extensive one.

It will probably never be known for certain whether the idea of publishing the "History of British Birds" originated with Mr. Fawcett or its author ; it is, however, beyond doubt that the matter was very fully discussed between the two, and the venture ultimately was made. It was arranged that the work should be brought out in monthly parts, four species of birds being described in each part. Mr. Morris was to be responsible for the whole of the letterpress, while Mr. Fawcett undertook the artistic and other work connected with the production of the book. After long debate it was settled that the price of each part should be fixed at one shilling. This important decision proved to be a wise one. To that determination may be attributed in great measure the future success of the undertaking. The lowness of the price was a matter which was much commented on afterwards, and helped the sale of the work enormously. It was brought out in royal octavo, the full title being, "A History of British Birds, by the Rev. F. O. Morris, B.A., Member of the Ashmolean Society." In the case of the land-birds there was added on the title-page the words, "*Gloria in excelsis Deo ;*" "*De profundis ad Dominum*" being given as an appropriate text for the water-birds. The first part made its appearance on June 1, 1850, the publishers being Messrs Groombridge & Son, who, with proper caution, advised that at first only a thousand copies should be printed, though it was soon found that that number was not equal to the rapidly increasing demand.

At this period, and for a short time after the publication of Part I., Mr. Fawcett occupied very small premises in Driffield ; these proved inadequate to his growing business, and he removed shortly to a more suitable locality in another part of the town, where he was able to employ a considerable number of hands, and thus could produce the monthly parts of "The Birds" and other works with punctual regularity. He then decided to give up retail business, and devoted his attention to the production of books. It was here that he brought to perfection a new process, invented by himself, for fine printing in colours, for which his establishment soon became famous in the trade. Mr. Fawcett employed from thirty to forty hands, a considerable proportion being females. Every plate of "The Birds" from beginning to end was engraved with his own hand. The methods he employed in his craft were as original as the man himself; the chief part of his knowledge he picked up by degrees for himself, and to his own methods he always adhered; he was uninfluenced by others, and kept his own counsel very closely; he was seldom seen outside his own premises, his garden being his only recreation ground. Although he carried on such a large business and his name was so well known, there were many of his fellow-townsmen who had never set eyes on him. His capacity for work was enormous; he was clever in his business, and most courteous in manner.

It was certainly remarkable that two such men as the author and the producer of the " History of British Birds" should happen to be then living in two adjoining parishes in East Yorkshire, and that the entire work connected with the issue of the volumes should be carried out in so comparatively small and remote a town as Driffield.

There can be no doubt that it was something of a tax upon a clergyman's time and energies, especially in so large a parish as Nafferton, to have to supply material each month for such a treatise as " The Birds." It took over seven years to complete the work, four of these while the author was at Nafferton, and the remainder after he removed to Nunburn-holme. During the whole of that time neither illness nor other cause hindered him from per-forming month by month with regularity that part of the task that had been assigned to him. It was a labour of love, it is true, but he was the last man to sacrifice any call of duty, even the smallest, to a work of this kind. He always had so many irons in the fire that it was surprising how he found time for all. He was a great economiser of time, and being as active in mind as he was in body, he naturally accomplished much.

From the very outset the work took with the public. On June 12, 1850, less than a fortnight after the publication of Part I., Messrs Groombridge wrote to the author and said :—" The work is progressing very well ; we have requested Mr. Fawcett to forward us another supply, and hope to get it into a good circulation." As time went on the sale quickly increased, so much so that they were continually reprinting the different numbers at Driffield. The reasons for its success were not far to seek. It was the first work of the kind that had been produced at a price that placed it within the reach of all classes ; the drawings were carefully made, and were coloured by hand ; the letterpress was ample in quantity, and the whole was written in a popular style. Indeed, the great aim of the undertaking was, not to present to the world a highly scientific treatise, but rather to create, if possible, a greater taste and love for the natural history of our British birds. On this point the author always laid great stress ; as he remarked in his introduction to the treatise, his aim was " to simplify former descriptions, to adapt them to popular wants and wishes," and generally to help the ornithological student by a more methodical arrangement of the descriptions. The object in view was more than realised, and many there were, who in later life distinguished themselves in the scientific world, who confessed that this and other works by Mr. Morris were the means of first giving them an interest and stimulus to pursue those branches of study for which they had a latent bent and aptitude. There were many well-known and valuable works on ornithology published prior to 1850. The matchless genius of Bewick, who, as an engraver, has never to this day been excelled, if even approached; the many excellences of Yarrell, the accuracy of Macgillivray, had already made these men's writings deservedly famous. He was, of course, very familiar with their works, and frequently quoted them. Of all writers known to him, however, there was none that he valued more highly than Macgillivray; he always spoke of him as one who could be depended on. In alluding to him he would frequently call him "the accurate Macgillivray," or in quoting a short passage from his writings he would add, perhaps, an observation such as this: "I have only hereon to remark that Mr. Macgillivray is very seldom wrong, and this is not one of the few instances in which he is;" or again, after some brief description of Macgillivray's, such as that of the motions of the Long-Tailed Tit, he would add, "This is from the life."

The figures of the birds as they appeared month

by month were generally admitted to be life-like. Not a few of the original drawings were made by the author's old and valued friend and schoolfellow, Richard Alington, then, as already mentioned, rector of Swinhope, in Lincolnshire. Of these, the atti tudes of the Hobby, Kingfisher, Snow Bunting, Sparrow, Robin, Ringed Dotterell, Heron, Ruff, Snipe, Dunlin, and Moorhen were perhaps among the most successful.

None of Mr. Alington's sketches had more widely different opinions expressed about it than that of the Kestrel. It was a bold and clever attempt to depict this hawk in an attitude peculiar to itself. The bird was represented in the act, so familiar to every ornithologist, of hovering over its prey, the head of the bird being hidden by the extended wings. In writing to the author in the winter of 1850, just after the publication of the part containing the account of the Kestrel, Richard Alington said :—
" To those not accustomed to observe this species the attitude will appear strange, and the remark will be made, as, in fact, I have heard it, and the same, indeed, as you made upon first seeing it, 'Where is the head ?' But any one who knows the peculiarity of the Windhover's action when looking for his prey must acknowledge that, though in one of his most common, an attempt has been made to depict him in one at least of his most difficult gestures, and will therefore, I hope, take the will for the deed."

It may here be stated that the author was himself

a severe critic on the drawing of the figures which appeared in his own book. This was only to be expected in one who had all his life so closely observed the habits of birds. Some interesting notes of his upon the figures of the birds bear out my remark. In this figure it appeared to him that the front of the wing "needed a little rounding;" in that, the body of the bird was "too thick and heavy, and required tapering;" while of another he observed, "End of wing too square; also back feathers too much hollowed in near the tail. The tail is rather too short." For all things he had an accurate and observant eye; anything out of place caught his notice at once.

Not only did his friend, Richard Alington, give him the benefit of his clever sketches, but through a long course of years furnished him also with a vast number of valuable nature-notes of his own. His letters were always highly and deservedly appreciated, containing as they did many ornithological observations, made mostly in his immediate neighbourhood, which could always be relied upon for accuracy. Thus, in a letter written on November 8, 1851, he enclosed a list of all the birds he had seen in his corner of Lincolnshire, indicating by marks their different degrees of rarity, or otherwise furnishing interesting notes in connection with some species; for instance, after the Blackbird he adds :—
"Have you noticed in young birds in October and November the inclination to have a light mark round the neck where the Ring Ouzel is white?" Scarcely

a letter was written by his friend without a note or
two on some interesting point in natural history.
Many of these were found of service in the compilation of the "History of British Birds." In 1849,
when writing of the hawks seen in his neighbourhood, Mr. Alington mentions that the Peregrine
Falcon was not uncommon in the spring :—" Hobby
common ; Merlin uncommon—a specimen was shot
by myself in this parish while feeding on a lark ;
Kestrel very common ; Sparrow-hawk very common ; Kite formerly more common than it is now ;
Common Buzzard ditto ; Hen Harrier common."
How the times with these birds have changed (alas !
for the worse) since then !

Richard Alington could generally be relied on
to clear up a doubtful question. The following, as
to the flight of the Wild Duck and Teal, is a case
in point. He shall speak of it in his own way :—
" With regard to the flight of the Wild Duck
and Teal, I should say it was as nearly identical as
possible, but the latter is quicker in the stroke of
the wing—very similar to what may be observed
between the Rook and the Jackdaw. They drop,
too, upon the water more suddenly than the Duck,
all at once — possibly from this habit called a
'plump' of Teal. During flight they will sometimes (especially at sunset, when off to their feeding-
grounds) sweep down with a rush close to the
ground, and as suddenly rise again. Before settling
they will make frequent feints to do so, flying round
and round in small circles. They do not generally

fly like the Duck, in line, when moving from place to place, but in broken order." Remarks such as this prove him to have been a careful observer of the habits of birds. He was as good an entomologist as he was an ornithologist.

These common tastes made the two schoolfellows close and lifelong allies. There was no friend for whom Francis Morris had a stronger affection than he had for Richard Alington. Many were the letters that passed between the two while the " History of British Birds " was in course of publication, and for years after its completion—in fact, up to the time of Mr. Alington's death.

The author's own love for birds and frequent observations of their ways and habits are continually, and as it were unconsciously, brought out in his history of them. It is easy to see how truly his heart was in what he wrote of his lifelong feathered friends and daily companions. He had watched the graceful flight of the Buzzard, and thus describes it :—" The slow sailing of this bird, as I have thus seen it, is very striking ; the movement of its wings is hardly perceptible, but onward it steadily wends its way. You can scarcely take your eyes off it, but follow it with a gaze as steady as its own flight, until ' by degrees beautifully less ' it leaves you, glad to rest your eyeballs, and if you look again for it you look in vain." When, again, from his own garden he so often loved to watch the well-known movements of the common Flycatcher as it darted off in quest of its tiny prey, you seem to see his strong love of bird-life reflected in his description of this bird, of which he says that it is " very noticeable for a solitariness and depression of appearance, as well as for its habit of perching on the point of a branch, the top of a stake, a rail, or a projection of or a hole in a wall, from whence it can 'comprehend all vagroms' in the shape of winged insects that come within its ken. You seem to think that it is listless, but on a sudden it darts off from its stance, sometimes led a little way in chase in an irregular manner, like a butterfly ; a snap of the bill tells you that it has unerringly captured a fly, and it is back to its perch, which it generally, but not invariably, returns to after these short sorties. It has a habit of flirting its wings aside and upwards a little, while perched, every now and then. Although so quiet a little thing, it will sometimes daringly attack any wanderer who seems likely to molest its 'sacred bower,' signifying first its alarm by a snapping of the bill."

The modest and retiring little Hedge-Sparrow, or Dunnock, never escaped his observant eye. Sober though his dress be and subdued his note, he is none the less loved on that account. After alluding to the severity of the winter of 1853, when the snow lay a foot thick on the ground, he wrote of this feathered favourite in a way that showed his keen appreciation of the natural and unassuming habits of the bird. " In such severe weather," he writes, "when one would. suppose that all emotion must be chilled in the breast of the very

hardiest bird that is exposed to the damaging attacks
of the two weird sisters, cold and hunger, you will
see the Dunnock flirting about some low bush in
the splendid sunshine that succeeds the bitter blasts
which have come and gone, and warbling its unpre-
tending little lay, as if to show that an even and
quiet temper is that which will best sustain under
the most adverse circumstances of life.   Now it has
come down upon the snow, and its tiny feet move
nimbly over the crystal surface, its tail quickly
moved up and down the while ; now it stops for a
few moments, and now hops on again, and now is
gone in company with its mate, pursuing or pursued.   Or, half hopping, half walking—its usual gait—
it approaches the door in search of a few chance
crumbs, which, if you are charitably disposed, you
will have placed there for any feathered pensioners
whom the inclemency of the season may compel
to a more intimate acquaintance than they would
otherwise have chosen."

Fond as he was of music, there was none which
charmed him more than the notes of the birds.
Difficult, nay impossible, though many of them are
to describe in black and white, he delighted to allude
to them in his treatise, bringing back as they did
old associations and pleasant recollections of boyhood.   Each had its own peculiarity and charm.
Even those birds which are not generally deemed
great songsters had for him something pleasant to
give forth from their throats.   For instance, of the
note of the Great-Tit or Oxeye he said :—" I know

no bird whose voice, though monotonous, is more
cheerful and exhilarating in connection with returning spring. It begins its merry 'oxeye, oxeye,
oxeye,' which bears a strong resemblance to the
filing of a saw, about the beginning of March, and
continues it to the middle of May."

Or, again, for the note of the congener of the bird
just alluded to—the Long-Tailed Tit—he has a word
of appreciative admiration when he says :—"That
which Shakespeare truly describes as so pleasing in
a woman, a 'small voice,' goes to the heart of the
naturalist when uttered by the tiny bird before us.
It is the very embodiment of gentleness, weakness,
and tenderness. I have but lately been listening to
it in the woods of Swinhope, in company with the
Rev. R. P. Alington, my friend of the 'joyous days
of old,' in whom, as in myself, the love of nature
is inborn, inbred, and inwrought, so as that no
time nor circumstances can eradicate it. It has,
however, a second note—a louder twitter, and a
third chirp still hoarser. This is heard in the
spring."

If there was one bird-song which thrilled him
more than another, one which never failed to catch
his ear and make him stay and linger on to listen,
it was that well-known, but still matchless, voice
of the Throstle. I cannot refrain from quoting his
words in speaking of strains which gave him so
much pleasure to listen to. He remarks :—

"As for the note, that man can have no music
in his soul that does not love the song of the

Throstle. Who would not stand still to listen to it in the tranquil summer evening, and look for the place of the songster? Presently you will discover the delightful bird pouring forth his lay from the top of some neighbouring tree; you will see his throat swelling with his love-song, and hear it you may, if you choose to linger, till sable night casts her dark mantle on all around, and wraps the face of nature in the shroud. Begun with the dawn of day, the Mavis has continued his clear and liquid notes at intervals, ceasing only at midday, till now that evening has come, when he must chant his evening hymn, and remind you of your own orisons to the great Creator. The calm eventide is the hour at which he most delights to sing, and rich and eloquent then, as always, are his strains. Uninterruptably he warbles the full and harmonious sounds, which now rise in strength, and now fall in measured cadence, filling your ear with the ravishing melody, and now die away so soft and low that they are scarcely audible. If you alarm him you break the charm; he will suddenly cease, and silently drop into the underwood beneath."

The pleasant twittering of the Martin, too, was one of those homely sounds which the author delighted to describe. The note was a familiar one to him, as the birds built up their lowly home aloft, under the eaves of his roof, and in due time reared their happy family, whose small and muffled chirpings, as they lay huddled together in their snug cradle, could be heard below—sounds which were, as he remarked, "the unmistakable expression of the veriest and most complacent satisfaction."

Indeed, it may be said that the notes of all birds had an extraordinary fascination for their lifelong friend and benefactor. These he is ever careful to speak of in his history of them. Even the "curious creaking cry of the Corn-Crake," as he expresses it, had a delight for his ears ; and of the weird cry of the Golden Plover he thus writes :—

"The wild wail of the Plover's whistling note is exceedingly pleasant to those who have a relish for country sounds, and who find an additional piquancy in those that are.more wild. He that can say, 'My mind to me a kingdom is,' is in no danger of being made melancholy by any sound in nature. In the evening and at night you may hear it. It has at times a ventriloquistic power, and is very deceptive." I would fain quote more on this head, but must pass on.

Certainly one of the most striking features of the "History of British Birds" is the pleasing variety of treatment of the subject-matter with which it deals. It is no hard, dry, and scientifically formal treatise. The volumes are full of life, and contain, besides a mass of information on the nature and habits of birds, not a little of human nature also. It was this that gave the book from the first a charm peculiarly its own, and added greatly to its popularity. Those who took it up found it pleasant reading. Up and down the pages, amid a mass of bird-lore, may be found many tasteful and poetical

F

touches; here is a happy description of a country scene, there a quotation from a favourite classic, or, again, you may suddenly meet a passage betokening the author's genuine and hearty sense of humour.

As may be supposed, therefore, not a few traits in the character of the author himself may be gleaned from a careful reading of the six volumes which comprise the history. Not only is his power of observation and description of bird-life made evident, but we catch many a glimpse of the inner nature of him whose home has been spoken of as the 'Selborne of the North.' His deep religious feeling is also repeatedly brought out, and the natural kindness and humanity of his heart made plain to the reader; and not only so, but his more mundane tastes are now and again unfolded to us. His intense love of the country; its familiar sights, sounds, and fragrances; the hold that its beauties had over him; the pleasant reminiscences of the days of his boyhood, when he caught the orange-tips, chased the clouded-yellows, or threw the fly on the bank of the trout-stream—these glimpses of the author himself seem to brighten and give additional interest to the pages of the volumes. He had a sort of compassion for those whose lot was cast in the towns, as for the youth of whom he told in his account of the White Owl, when they were travelling together over the Dorsetshire Downs on the top of a stage-coach in the olden days. Sitting near him was a lady going down to Devonshire with her son from London. They passed some gleaners in a field ; whereat the lady remarked that they were the first she had seen that year. "They are the first," said the youth, "that I have ever seen in my life." Unhappy youth !

The habits of certain birds seem to have been indelibly impressed upon his memory from his earliest years, when he delighted to observe them. Of these the Chaffinch was one ; and from that fact, as well, perhaps, as from its extreme tameness and cheery voice, he used to confess that, of all birds, it was his favourite. Of its song he wrote :—"There is something very cheerful in the common notes of the Chaffinch, and as harbinging the return of spring, it is always hailed with welcome by the observer of the sights and sounds of the country." The Snipe, too, was connected in an especial way with his earliest recollections, and of this bird he says that there is none other which "gives you more the idea of a wild-fowl." Once, and only once, did he ever see one perched in a tree, and that, too, was in the old coaching days, when travelling between South-ampton and Exeter.

Rugged mountain country, as we may gather from his description of the haunts of the Ptarmigan, had a charm for him as well as homelier and more pastoral scenes. The abode of these birds, whom he calls true " Children of the Mist," is to be found in " the upper parts and summits of the highest moun-tains, where utter desolation reigns around, and Nature is seen in the most wild and savage beauty."

His graphic picture of the scene I must, however, leave to the reader of the book itself.

From time to time, in the course of writing their history, he could not forbear giving vent to his feelings against those who would persecute and wantonly destroy these happy feathered creatures in all their natural beauty. A more determined and formal crusade against bird murder was vigorously carried on by him in later years, to which allusion will be presently made, but it is not without interest to notice in passing with what fervour and feeling he now and again defends his friends against their enemies in the pages of the " History of British Birds." In the account of the Tawny Owl, for instance, he characteristically and touchingly begins his article thus :—

" Here is another victim of persecution ! Were it not for the friendly shelter of the night and the fostering care of some few friends, where is the Owl that would be able to maintain a place among the ' Feathered Tribes ' of England ? Their passports are invariably sent to them in the form of cartridge-paper ; a double-barrelled gun furnishes a ready ' missive,' their ' congé ' is given with a general ' discharge,' and the unoffending, harmless, nay, useful bird is ordered for ever to ' quit.' His family are not permitted to hold their own, but are themselves outlawed and proscribed ; their dwelling is confiscated, a ' clearance ' is effected, and if there are a wife and children, ' alack for woe ! ' They are carried into captivity. You have my pity, at all events, ' Bonny Brown Owl,' and, believe me,

I would that the expression of it might do you a kindness, but I have sad misgivings. You are a marked bird—they have given you a bad name, and the proverb tells you the fatal consequence."

The nomenclature of the various species described in the volumes formed rather a striking feature at the head of each article. Not only were the scientific Latin names in each case given, but the local or dialectical appellations were, as far as could be ascertained, also added. In the editions subsequent to the first the ancient British equivalents were also inserted, though, it must be confessed, many of these were not a little difficult to attribute and establish with any degree of certitude. The nomenclature of our native birds was a subject that always had a great interest for the author. For the old traditional English names of our common birds he had a remarkable affection. In one sense, he seemed almost as fond of these as he was of the birds themselves ; in this, as in so many other ways, he was most rigidly conservative. "One is often led to wonder," he said, when writing about the common Wagtail, "and doubtless the same remark would apply to other lands, how the most trivial names of antiquity keep their place in the vocabulary of the country, while modern inventions last but for the day or for the hour, and are then consigned for ever to the 'tombs of all the Capulets.' We may soon be lost in speculation as to the time when each of such old names were first assigned, and who it was that gave it, what combination of circumstances first procured for it the honour of durability which bids fair to be perpetual, and through what succession of changes has it been maintained. These considerations make us smile at the vain conceits of some of our modern self-styled naturalists. Do they really think, dogmatically as they may lay down the law to their own entire satisfaction, that their whimsical combinations will ever be adopted by the people of the country—that the old will be displaced to make room for the new? They are fondly mistaken if they entertain the notion. The name of the favourite and elegant little bird before us—no case of *lucus a non lucendo*—will ever remain one of the 'old standards;' no 'weak invention' will ever supersede it in the idiom of the nation. The Wagtail will always continue a Wagtail, not only in nature, but also in name." These common, time-honoured names of our British birds he preferred to all others, just as he himself gloried to bear the old title of parson in preference to the more recent appellation of clergyman.

Many were the literary contributions which he received while the work was going through the press. Next to those of Richard Alington, there were none which he prized more highly than those of another old friend, Hugh Edwin Strickland, whose sad and untimely death was such a shock to him ; his life was sacrificed to the cause of science, he being killed by a passing train in a railway cutting near Retford, whither he had gone to examine a geologi-

cal formation. His loss is feelingly alluded to in
the "History of British Birds." He and my father
had secured places next to one another the first day
of the meeting of the British Association in Hull in
1853, over which Professor Sedgwick presided. Not
twenty-four hours after they parted company his dear
and valued friend was no more. "Alas !" he wrote,
"that the words of Professor Sedgwick, near whose
right hand he sat, and whose place in the chair he
had fitly and worthily occupied from time to time,
so eloquently and feelingly, and as it were foreboding-
ingly, uttered on the afternoon of the same day in
his concluding speech, that possibly some of those
then present might not meet together at the next
anniversary, should so soon and so fatally be fulfilled ! . . . On one only other occasion in my life,
when another valued friend, W. V. J. Surtees, was
most unfortunately drowned at Oxford, have I ever
had such a shock as the sudden account of his
death."

Among those who frequently communicated with
him during the course of the publication of the
book, and gave him many interesting facts, may be
mentioned the names of Mr. O. S. Round, Mr. J.
Gatcombe, Mr. W. F. W. Bird, and Mr. Arthur
Strickland of Burlington Quay, Yorkshire, a name-
sake, oddly enough, of his friend just alluded to.
Of Mr. Arthur Strickland he used to say that there
was no one of his acquaintance who knew more
about birds, whether English or foreign, than he.

Although the work had been so many times

reprinted, the sale having in course of years reached a very large figure, it was not until 1870 that a new edition was given to the public. This second edition appeared in the early part of that year ; many additional facts were given, and corrections made upon the earlier edition ; the volumes, too, were of larger dimensions than the former ones, though in size and outward appearance the author himself always preferred the original shape of the work, and when he took up the book to read or refer to, he generally chose the first edition.

A third edition, newly revised, corrected, and enlarged, made its appearance in 1891. This edition was published by Mr. John C. Nimmo. Its chief features were the addition of twenty-nine new British species, together with the insertion of appropriate but brief poetical quotations at the end of each article. This latter adjunct, though a task of some difficulty, was one which fulfilled a long-cherished wish of the author ; indeed, he had the idea in his mind before the publication of the first number in 1850.

As a kind of natural supplement to the " History of British Birds," there appeared at the beginning of 1852, from the same pen and the same printer and engraver, the " Natural History of the Nests and Eggs of British Birds." This work also, like the " Birds," came out in monthly parts, and extended to three volumes, uniform with the greater work. The plates were cleverly executed by Mr. Fawcett on tinted paper by a plan, I believe, peculiarly his own. Only in certain cases were the nests of the birds figured, and these must have presented great difficulty to the engraver ; indeed, it was thought by some critics that it would have been better to have omitted them altogether on this account.

The sale of this work, although much more restricted than that of the "Birds," was, nevertheless, considerable. Three editions of it went through the press in the author's lifetime, the last of these having been revised by him only the year before his death.

It was while the treatise on "Nests and Eggs of British Birds" was in course of publication that it was determined, by an arrangement with Mr. Fawcett, to bring out the "Natural History of British Butterflies" in monthy parts, so that for a time material for no less than three separate works had to be prepared for the press month by month. This would sorely have tried the energies of many men of less industrious and methodical habits than the author. To him, however, to all outward appearance at least, it seemed to present no serious difficulty, even while he was with all faithfulness and diligence discharging the manifold duties of his higher calling in life. It was only at odd times, so to speak, that he devoted himself to his literary work ; but opportunities were quickly seized at all hours, and the most made of them. No minutes were lost. A very considerable proportion of the "British Birds" was written in the evening, and that of the last three volumes mainly in the drawing-room of Nunburnholme Rectory. By a remarkable power of abstraction, he appeared to be able to work nearly as easily in a room where there were a number of people joining in a general conversation, or when music was being performed, as he was when alone in his study. He frequently was in the habit of suddenly changing his work, being strongly convinced that such a change was as good as a rest. He certainly felt it to be so himself, and often advised it to others.

While the work was in course of publication her Majesty the Queen, through the intervention of Prince Albert, was graciously pleased to accept the dedication of the volumes, and the monthly parts were regularly sent to her Majesty as they appeared. On its completion a copy of the entire work was forwarded to the Queen for her acceptance, and the following letter was subsequently received :—

"WINDSOR CASTLE, *Nov.* 16, 1857.

"SIR,—I have had the honour of receiving your letter of the 13th inst., with the accompanying box containing a complete copy of your interesting work on British Birds.

"I have not failed to submit it, according to your wish, for the acceptance of her Majesty, and I have now received her Majesty's commands, in returning you her best thanks for this kind attention, to assure you of the pleasure with which she adds this valuable work to the royal library.—I have the honour to be, Sir, your very obedient servant,

"C. GREY.

"THE REV. F. O. MORRIS."

Previously to this Prince Albert had subscribed for two copies of the book, and it was probably one of these that he afterwards presented to the library of Wellington College, in which institution he took a deep interest. In a letter written in 1852 the Prince expressed himself as greatly pleased with the work, adding that the manner in which it was got up was "highly creditable to the town of Driffield."

It is hard to say whether the author of the book was more gratified by communications of this kind than by those which he received from quite poor working men, some of whom assured him that they denied themselves their pipe and beer in order to be able to take in the parts as they appeared from month to month. He received letters from people of every class, from the highest to the humblest, expressing the pleasure which the "History of British Birds" gave them as they took it in.

If, however, it gave pleasure to the thousands who read it, not less was the pleasure which it afforded to the author himself to write it. Frequently, years after its completion, would he take up one or other of the volumes and pore over its pages. Beyond a few exceptional passages, the style of the writing was unstudied and natural. One of such exceptions was in the case of the last pages of all, which give the account of the Stormy Petrel. On the writing of this article evident pains was bestowed. To no part of the volumes did he more frequently turn than he did to these last pages. He seemed to linger repeatedly with a pardonable fondness over

these farewell passages, and in giving a longer
description than usual he was evidently loth to quit
his well-loved themes.

Let me quote a single paragraph from what he
so graphically says of the haunts of this tiny sea-
bird. After contrasting the northern winter with
the "blaze of glory of the sunny South," he adds :—

"But on again, driven backwards and forwards
from one to the other, the lone and wandering sea-
bird travels, and now as it were borne on the wings
of the tempest, the gentle breeze of the hot climate
turned into the icy hurricane or tornado of the low
latitudes, the Stormy Petrel, whose name betokens
the habitual current of its life, nears the land, and
skirts and skims along the weather-worn cliffs of
the true Land's End. Wild is the scene on many
a winter's evening, each storm different from every
other that has gone before it, and yet one and all
alike. Here are low dense clouds laden with the
evening gale, and there lurid skies pregnant with
tempestuous blasts ; to seaward an endless desert
of water ; towards the shore, and breaking over the
watery waste, spray, foam, and air mingled as in one,
and over all the blackness of approaching night.
There is a brief lull, as if the tempest were taking
breath, and girding up its strength for a stronger
effort, and a frightful stillness prevails for a short
space, the sky scowls and blackens more angrily,
and low clouds whirl and wheel about in uncertain
eddies, all betokening a savage burst of the out-
poured fury of the elements ; but while other sea-

birds scuttle off to seek shelter, if any may be found, the wee Petrel still stays, and awaits the utmost violence of the storm."

Thus the pages well-nigh end, though not without a final strain of praise to the Creator so fittingly added as a climax of the whole history of the feathered tribes —"O, all ye fowls of the air, bless ye the Lord ; praise Him, and magnify Him for ever."

V

BRITISH BUTTERFLIES AND MOTHS

THE first volume of the "British Birds" was barely completed before the "Nests and Eggs of British Birds," as a natural sequel, was taken in hand, and ultimately completed in three volumes; but of all the literary work to which the author's name was attached, there was none which it gave him greater and more unfeigned pleasure to write than the "Natural History of British Butterflies." He used to confess that it was the work which he himself preferred to all his others, not excepting even his "History of British Birds;" and the reason was not far to seek, for there was no pursuit that gave him greater delight than entomology; in him it amounted almost to a passion. It was a taste which no time nor circumstances ever altered in the least; as he once wrote of himself, he was "born an entomologist." For every work of the Creator that came under his notice he had an admiration, and took it for granted that those for whom he wrote shared to some extent at least his own feelings. "Who can behold," he said in his preface to this work, "a rich sunset, a storm, the sea, a tree, a mountain, a river, a rainbow, a flower, without some degree

of admiration and some measure of thought ?"
These and every other wonder of Nature he loved
to study and become better acquainted with ; but
to no department in the wide and varied field of
Nature were his mind and heart more devotedly
given than to this of which we speak. Let us hear
his own words, quoted from the first pages of his
favourite treatise. He says :—

"If there be one branch of natural history
which is to me more captivatingly interesting than
another, it is entomology ; one, moreover, which
is so easy of full gratification, so productive of
friendly feeling with others, so amalgamative of the
high and low together in perfect amity, so singularly
pleasing and delightful in itself. I trust, indeed, that
I have not forgotten, do not forget, and never shall
forget that I have high and holy duties to perform,
to which all else must be subordinate and give way.
As a servant of the Church, a minister of the Gospel
of Christ, I willingly sacrifice natural wishes to the
cause of duty. It is but a few brief moments that
I snatch for that which is naturally most pleasing
to me. Knowing, however, that these studies are
innocent in themselves ; that they may, with many,
prevent other pursuits which, if followed, would
assuredly cause risk of most serious danger ; that
they add to the amount of human happiness ; and
that, if used as they always should be, they infallibly
lead from the works of Nature up to the God of
Nature, in feelings of the holiest admiration and
most humble worship, I encourage others to follow

them, so far as it may be right for them to do so, and have undertaken, at the request of another, to write the following 'Natural History of British Butterflies,' and to supply particulars which I have felt the want of myself."

Like the "Birds" and the "Nests and Eggs," the "History of British Butterflies" came out in parts, the first number making its appearance in the beginning of 1852, while the other two works, therefore, were also in course of publication. From the first it was favourably received by the public, and had a large sale. It went through six editions in the lifetime of the author, the proofs for the last, or seventh, edition having been carefully revised only a few days before his death; this, indeed, was the concluding stroke of literary work he did. Fitting was it that these last touches of his pen, which through his long life was never at rest, should have been given to the work which, of all others, it gave him the greatest delight to write. His earliest years were in no small measure brightened by this absorbing pursuit; it was his chief relaxation amid the activities of an exceptionally industrious life, and the happy days he had spent in this branch of Nature's field were among the pleasantest recollections of his declining years. The figures for the work were accurately drawn and engraved by Mr. Fawcett, and, like the rest of the illustrations in the author's volumes on natural history, were coloured by hand.

It was impossible to follow the descriptive portions of the "History of British Butterflies" and not see

that his heart was in his work. Besides the full
account of the insects themselves, the caterpillar,
chrysalis, localities where found, dates of appearance, with other useful information, there are to
be found interspersed through the volume, as was
the case also with the "Birds," many passages, not
strictly technical, which tell of incidents and scenes,
small perhaps in themselves, but bringing back by-
gone days on which the author loved to dwell, and
on which now and again—may we not say pardon-
ably ?—he was tempted to moralise.

In no other of his works do we seem to see so
much of the author himself as in this one. Not
only were the figures of the butterflies almost entirely
drawn from specimens in his own cabinet, but he
also carries us off with him to the woods, commons,
glades, and sunny banks, or even, it may be, to chalky
seaside cliffs and mountain-tops, favoured spots—
"localities," as he calls them—where the various flies
of many hues had been captured. Here in his
schooldays the "Wood-White" flitted airily across
his path ; there the "Red Admiral" flaunted his gay
uniform, or the "Purple Emperor" sailed majestically
high over his head. If he had occasion to remember
a particular summer, it more probably than not fixed
itself in his memory by reason of a superabundance,
or otherwise, of some particular butterfly or moth,
as was the case in 1826, when the "Large Meadow-
Brown," always a common insect, appeared in such extraordinary profusion everywhere. If some sheltered
inland nook or rugged cove clung to his recollection,

G

it was to him almost sacred ground, as being the haunt of this or that rare "Blue" or "Fritillary." It well-nigh seemed as if all the country were mapped out in his mind's eye, not so much by counties, nor according to its physical peculiarities, but rather as a large hunting-ground for his butter-flies ; indeed, he says as much in his description of the "Brimstone" butterfly (*Gonepteryx rhamni*).

"If," he observes, "the imagination chooses so to please itself, it may look upon our own country as a sort of epitome of the northern hemisphere of the world, as to its natural productions, and thus we shall find that on the south coast, from Torquay to Hastings, are our tropics ; in the midland counties our temperate zone; in Scotland our Arctic regions; and John o' Groat's House will answer to the North Pole. Correspondingly hereto are our butterflies localised. Excepting in the case of some chance wanderer, driven by we know not what storm or tempest, or 'favouring gale,' the races are for the most part distinct, and those which flourish in one district would perish at once in the other, through the difference of climate."

For each and every species he had an intense admiration, and with some of the brighter-hued or more beautifully marked kinds it seemed, when looking at them in his cabinet, as if the very light was never strong enough to show off their glories.

His own collections, to which he so frequently makes reference, were admirably arranged. In this respect at least, if not in extent, there were few, if

any, private ones in the country to surpass them.
Naturally, having many visitors to see his cabinets
of insects, he delighted in showing them to his
friends, and of almost every kind that was noticed
he would have something to say of interest. Of all
his butterflies there were none that he prized more
than his specimens of the " Large Copper" (*Lycæna
dispar*), now no more to be found in this, or perhaps
any other, country. In noticing it in his treatise he
remarked :—

"Long the tenant of the watery wastes which
formed the fen districts of Cambridgeshire and the
adjoining counties, this fine insect has at last dis-
appeared from what was for ages its secure fastness
and its safe stronghold. . . . Time was, and even
abundantly within our own recollection, when it
might have been considered a beneficial improvement to induce a stream of water where none before
existed, or to deepen it where it did into a navigable
canal, and the engineer who successfully completed
the work might say, with a laudable satisfaction—

'Impellitque rates ubi duxit aratra colonus ;'

but now the converse is a just subject for boast, and
even over the loose surface of the most treacherous
morass, the iron way conveys with speed and safety,
and to any extent, the mercantile, the physical, and
the intellectual wealth of the country. The entomologist is the only person who has cause to lament
the change, and he, loyal and patriotic subject as
he is, must not repine at even the disappearance

of the 'Large Copper' butterfly, in the face of such
vast and magnificent advantages. Still, he may be
pardoned for casting 'one longing, lingering look
behind ;' and I cannot but with some regret recall,
at all events, the time when almost any number of
this dazzling fly was easily procurable, either 'by
purchase' or 'by exchange,' for our cabinets. A
goodly 'rank and file' from some individuals, of
which the figures in the plates are taken, I now
consider myself fortunate in possessing, for the
existing number of indigenous specimens is no
more again to be added to by any fresh recruits :
'*Fuit Ilium et ingens gloria*'—

'The light of other days has faded, and all its glories past.' "

In such-like happy and unstudied expressions he
loved to speak about the various species under
consideration one after another. He treated of
them, not as scientific hardnesses, but rather as old
friends surrounded with endless reminiscences ; and
he himself spoke as one to whom every country
sight and sound was dear.

In some of his descriptions you seem to have
not only the picture of the familiar insect before
you, but also a refreshing bit of country setting with
it. Here is an instance that bears out my remark :—

" This butterfly ('The Gatekeeper'—*Hipparchia
megæra*) is to be seen flitting in its zig-zag manner
along the banks, which for the most part it frequents,
in July and August. It is fond of settling on walls,
whence one of its English names, seeming to take

delight in those situations which are the most sheltered, and from which the most heat is reflected. The shadow of your approach disturbs it, and you see it flit off, and settle again at some little distance, or continue its irregular flight along the bank."

Once more, in speaking of the locality for finding the " Lulworth Skipper " (*Hesperia Actæon*), which in former years he used to catch on the Dorsetshire coast in company with his old friend, Mr. J. C. Dale, of whom mention has been already made, he thus describes it :—

" A charming scene, where you will be fain to wish that you could for ever watch the glorious ocean, dashing up from its dark depth against the steep cliffs, which there present an aspect of the utmost seclusion and the most lonely retirement. Wild must all around be in winter, but this small butterfly rejoices in the settled summer, more fortunate than some of its class who are tempted out to woo the beautiful spring ; often their reception is cold and chilling, and their day-dream of happiness is blighted, like the contemporary delicate flower that has peered out too soon from its sheltered nook, and must again hide its head for a season till the skies are more propitious and the sun shall shine undisturbed upon it."

Passages such as these—and there are many of them—seem like the artist's lighter touches to give additional life and warmth even to such a sunny subject as that of which this volume treats. The author, however, was not content merely to write, as far as he could, accurately and pleasantly of the British Butterflies ; he also desired to make his book one of practical utility to the entomologist in pursuing his special line of study. Accordingly at the end of the volume he added what he termed the *Aphorismata Entomologica*, which consisted of four-and-twenty closely printed pages giving full and minute details as to the formation and arrangement of an entomological collection. The catching and killing of specimens, the setting of them, methods of capture, flowers and trees frequented by moths and butterflies, even the kinds of pins to be used in setting—these and many other similar mysteries of the craft of entomology were entered into and explained at length. A couple of pages of illustrations of some of the entomologist's apparatus were also added. On one of them was depicted an ingenious net which he invented for catching the "Purple Emperor" butterfly, an insect which generally flies about the tops of tall trees, and so cannot be reached with an ordinary net. This "castle in the air," as he termed it, was made as light as possible, the handle being constructed like a long fishing-rod, of bamboo ; this was kept from bending unduly by means of stays coming from near the top to a double cross-tree, somewhat after the manner of the royal-mast of a man-of-war.

He playfully ended his *Aphorismata* with a bit of advice that savoured strongly of his own principles. "Lastly," he observed, "in common with all who wish well to their collections, or to their country, I deprecate frequent 'changes in the cabinet.' 'Let well alone' is a good and wholesome proverb, applicable both politically and entomologically."

Although forming a natural continuation of a treatise on Butterflies, it was not until 1859 that the " History of British Moths" was taken in hand. The authorship of this work involved greater difficulties than any to which he had hitherto given his attention. For a long time it had been his wish to bring out a " History of British Moths" with coloured figures of every species, but his printer, Mr. Fawcett, had always shrunk from the task; he accordingly decided to undertake it on his own responsibility, employing his own artists. It was arranged that it should appear in monthly parts, as the "Birds" had done; and seeing there were about two thousand British species to be figured and described, the magnitude of the undertaking was even at first sight considerable. One great difficulty in preparing the work lay in this, that, as every species had to be figured, specimens of each must be obtained for the engravers, and many of these were so rare that it was hard to obtain the loan of them; one was in this private collection or museum, and another in that; one here, and one there. Like his other works on natural history, this one was written for all classes. Indeed, he had himself no taste for books that were worded in highly scientific language; such treatises seemed to him to deter from, rather than invite to, science. In his introduction to the "Moths" he states his views on this point thus :—

"I have both seen and heard enough, and too much, of the evil caused by some, who, in the vain and empty desire to be thought scientific themselves, have debarred their readers from becoming so. They may please those whose own nature leads them to take *omne ignotum pro magnifico,* but I know that they have not had, and do not gain, the goodwill and thanks of the many whose approbation I would rather win. They get nothing but contempt from that class which is the largest, and for whom I have written and still write. . . . If science has to do with facts, my works, as any one may prove for himself, may justly lay claim to a more scientific character than appertains to many that have preceded them. In writing for one's own countrymen, words and language need not be employed the sole effect of which will be to conceal the meaning professedly intended to be conveyed. It is only those who are more or less ignorant themselves that think nothing can be considered scientific which is not couched in language beyond the comprehension of the readers whom it ought to be its object to enlighten ; they who are wiser will be content to convey information in words that may be at once and readily ' understanded of the people.' "

The general plan of the work was simple in the extreme. Minute descriptions of the insects themselves were for the most part avoided ; it was thought that the figures, when accurately engraved and coloured, as these were, would be a sufficient guide. Some description, however, of them was in each instance given, together with that of the caterpillar and its food, the approximate date of appearance of the perfect insect being also stated. Special attention was paid to the list of the localities, and in the case of rare species, the exact dates of appearance were, as far as possible, added; even when a species is common, a few places widely separated were named as localities where the insect might be found. In addition to the scientific Latin names of the insects, the common and well-known English ones were also given. On this point, as was the case with the "Birds," the author held strong opinions, which he fully expressed. Cherished reminiscences of former days and innate respect for the things of the past were, as I have already said, deep rooted in his nature; old scenes and old names had a charm for him that could never be resisted; and, therefore, the older nomenclature of his beloved butterflies, moths, birds, trees, flowers, and everything pertaining to the country, could on no account be given up. I shall best make known his views and feelings by citing his own words in the introduction to his treatise. He there says :—

"While giving the Latin names of the several species, I have preserved all the common English ones for those who, like myself, will ever take a pleasure in them. That is a praiseworthy rather than a censurable feeling which makes the in-

habitants at large of our villages and towns cling
to the country names of the natural objects around
them. It is a feeling which I for one would altogether encourage rather than at all despise. I know,
at the same time, that nothing can be done in
natural history without scientific terms, and that
these must be given in the words of an obsolete
language in order to their communication among
the nations of the world, whose tongues are so
various and even their idioms so diverse. This, I
say, I know ; but I know also, as one who has had
the benefit of a classical education, that, though
these passwords will do for the learned, they will
not do for those who have had no opportunities
of becoming so, and that if you would gain the
hearts of the people to the studies you love yourself,
you must make yourself at home with them in the
outset in the words you employ. Nay, more ; if
you would have them wholly with you, you must
let them see and feel that you yourself are one of
themselves in taste and feeling. Who that knows
anything of the ' Pleasures of Memory' would
change the common English names of our wild
plants for those of a more pretentious character,
and make, as it were, his own youth no part of
his present existence ? Who would not leave the
humble daisy to be a daisy still ? Who that has
ever been a child would wish the heart's-ease to be
other than the heart's-ease, the buttercup than the
buttercup, the lark-spur than the lark-spur, the
mouse-ear than the mouse-ear, the foxglove than

the foxglove? . . . Do not fear that these names
will ever give place to others; they will last as long
as the mother earth that bears the plants themselves: the nation will no longer be itself when
the rose, the leek, the shamrock, and the thistle
cease to be household words. . . . As it has been
in the days before us, so do we find it to be yet,
and so will it be after we are gone, with the well-
known English names of our common butterflies
and moths. By these will they still be known
when the fancies and conceits which in vain try
to supersede them have sunk into deserved oblivion.
The gay science numbers some of all classes in
her ranks—the nobleman's or gentleman's son at
school or at college; the apprentice lad of the great
city, who may one day rise to be Lord Mayor of
London; the country clergyman in the quiet parsonage of the sequestered village; the decent tradesman of the country town; the hardy husbandman
in his neat cottage; the mechanic whose head and
hand are busy; the gallant naval or military officer,
the defender of the land; many of England's fairest
daughters, and many of her hardiest sons. These,
be sure, will ever continue to keep what they have
already preserved so long."

The passage here given has been taken at some
length, for it is a highly characteristic expression of
the mind and sentiment of the author on a subject
that for many years specially interested him; it is,
indeed, a bit of himself in his happiest mood.

As an argument against those who would advocate

the adoption of an exclusively Latin nomenclature, even by those who have never learnt any other than their mother tongue, he gave an amusing illustration of the absurd mistakes which are sometimes made with regard to the Latin names. He was describing a moth called *Vespertaria*, when he remarked :—

"Staunch Churchman as I hereditarily am, I exercise the widest tolerance towards those who are not so happy as to be within the pale of the Church. You may imagine, therefore, with what feelings I one day last year received the intelligence that a brother entomologist had recently captured and killed some two hundred *Presbyterians*. It was, in fact, made a matter of boast. I expressed the thought that it might yet prove not to have been the case, but my informant stood me out that the deed had been done. I could, as a magistrate for the East Riding, have issued a warrant for the immediate apprehension of this second Claverhouse, but I concluded that, after all, his own reflections would be a sufficient punishment; so I left him to them, and went on my way without further thought of 'Bonny Dundee,' or of the retributive justice which deeds like his might merit and demand."

The engraving of the plates was in the first instance entrusted to a skilful artist in London, who, it was generally admitted, did his work admirably. After the completion of the eighth part the illness of the engraver caused an unavoidable delay, and ultimately the engraving was placed in the hands of Mr. E. Brown of York, who performed what had been assigned to him with great care and ability.

It will give some faint idea of the labour involved · in completing this work on British Moths when it is stated that it was begun in August 1859, and was not brought to a conclusion until November 11, 1870, the issue of the four octavo volumes thus extending over a period of eleven years. The task which the author set before himself was, however, in the end faithfully carried out.

When he was engaged upon his " History of British Birds " and other works his friends used frequently to inquire how he could possibly manage to do so many things at a time ; but, as he said in the preface to the fourth volume of the " British Moths," they put the question " in the most profound and utter ignorance of all that I had on my hands in one way and another, namely, in addition to the ordinary, and I hope anything but neglected, duties of a large and laborious parish, my former one, and to say nothing of various worldly cares of a most perplexing and harassing character, the providing the 'writing materials' every month regularly for five separate works, the 'British Birds,' the 'British Butterflies,' the *Aphorismata Entomologica*, the 'Bible Natural History,' and the 'History of the Nests and Eggs of British Birds.' But thank God for good health, and for that which, as I have said before, I have always contended is far before even good health, as a worldly blessing, a good spirit.

" I may here mention also, what I had thought of
doing long ago, that every part of the former works,
from first to last, the engraving, printing, tinting the
paper, colouring with the hand, and writing, were all
executed in a small and obscure Yorkshire town,
and a still more remote and sequestered Yorkshire
village. I may also add that no one, I believe, has
yet been able to say what the plates were engraved
on ; even in London ' the Row' were at a loss
to tell."

From end to end the issue of the monthly parts
of the " Moths" was only accomplished in the face
of most serious difficulties and well-nigh insuperable hindrances. In the first instance it was arranged
that the engravings should be on wood, and an
engraver was engaged, together with a young artist
to draw the figures. Differences then arose between
these two, the result of which was to bring the work
to a standstill, and to cause considerable delay. In
the end, however, this proved a gain, for it would
have been found impossible to have engraved the
small moths on wood with proper effect, and in consequence of the change being at once made from
wood to stone, a saving of upwards of £700 was
effected in the cost of the plates. Before long there
came further delays through illnesses of both engraver and colourer, and the latter found that he
could not carry out what he had undertaken ; then
both engraver and lithographer were changed. As
before mentioned, it was a matter of the greatest
difficulty to obtain specimens of some of the rare

moths ; of one in particular there was but a single specimen in all England, and this, naturally, the owner did not like to part with. Many attempts were made to have a copy taken, but they all proved fruitless. After this, again, the printer was changed more than once, and endless trouble arose on that head ; but when it came to the third volume the difficulties increased manifold, and this is what the author himself said of them in his preface to that volume :—

"I have only to say again to my readers in explanation of the delays that have taken place in the bringing out several of the parts of this work— in fact, latterly, ever since I have had to describe and figure the small moths—that if they will read the preface to the second volume, with the account of the difficulties therein recorded as having occurred up to that time, and will then multiply them by ten, and that ten by ten again, they will then possibly be able to imagine a tenth part of those which have come in my way since."

Nevertheless the work was persevered with, and carried through to the very last letter.

VI

PERSONAL

THOSE who knew Mr. Morris only from his writings on natural history would for the most part look upon him as one to whom birds, and any other of God's creatures, were specially dear, as one who found in them friends and companions, and devoted a large portion of his care, time, and energies in shielding and delivering them from the attacks of those who cruelly or thoughtlessly persecuted them. This was, indeed, most true of him, but judged by this alone a very imperfect idea would be formed of what he really was, even though, as I have already pointed out, much more is to be found in his writings on natural history than merely information on the matters professedly dealt with in them. Something, nay a good deal, of the author's own tastes and character are to be gleaned, besides, from a perusal of the pages of his volumes. Still, even with these passing but frequent glimpses of the man himself, which seem to form one of the special features of his style as a writer, something more remains to be said.

The question may be asked why all this ceaseless work and activity in channels that lay outside his more ordinary course of duty. The answer is soon given. The key to all his actions of benevolence and philanthropy lay in this, that he looked upon life as a great reality; with him, it was not only to be lived, but to be spent in the service of Him whose creature he was. He regarded himself, as he did his fellow-men, not only as clay in the hand of the potter, but as instruments, under God, of endless possibilities. Throughout life he acted upon the principle, *Laborare est orare*. To one thus impressed every moment was of account; the maxim of his favourite classical author, though taken in a very different sense from that intended by the poet, was his also—"*Carpe diem, quam minimum credula postero.*" It was only those who were near to him who knew how deeply he realised the value of time and opportunity.

Possessed of an active body and a no less vigorous mind, his great aim through life was to employ them in the service of his Master, in doing what good he could in the world during his short stay in it, and each morning as it came filled him with the desire to make the most of its precious hours. In point of physique he seemed marked out for an active life. Of medium height, and of spare, wiry, and upright form, he looked like one who could do a good day's march without fatigue. To many he appeared to have not a little of the strict officer about him; and, indeed, those who so judged, judged rightly. Still, beneath a somewhat reserved manner, that at times made itself felt, there was ever beating the kindliest of hearts. Although striving as much as lay in him to live peaceably with all men, he was the last man in the world to have, or to wish for, peace at any price. He looked upon fighting in a good and righteous cause as a solemn duty, and when once he was convinced that the position he took up was worth contending for he would never give it up. If at times the weapons he used were thought by some to be too sharply pointed, he would justify his words by the circumstances of the case ; and he seldom saw fit to modify the language he used in attacking any evil, of the wrongness of which he was thoroughly convinced. His methods naturally raised up many adversaries against him, which he for the most part looked upon as a good sign ; as he said in one of his letters, he regarded it as an honour to be abused by certain people. "Woe unto you when all men speak well of you," was a warning of which he for one most fully felt the force. He had a keen insight into character, and was quick, as we say in Yorkshire, in "reckoning a man up."

Sometimes, no doubt, matters of discussion assumed an importance in his eyes out of proportion to their real worth ; but then the point in dispute involved some principle, and therefore had to be fought out to the end. Even in his younger days this was noticeable ; instances of it might be given from the time soon after his leaving college, when he kept up a frequent correspondence with his old friend, Mr. J. C. Dale, mainly on entomological

questions. Occasionally he would cross swords
with him on some knotty point ; and in such cases,
if the destinies of countries hung upon the issue,
the matter in dispute could not have been carried
on with greater animation and more dogged determination than by these two.

In all things, and especially in those that pertained
to his clerical work, he had a stern sense of duty.
His parochial visitations were made with scrupulous
regularity, and he kept a record of every visit he
paid, as well as of other details of work that he performed in the parish, so that no part of it might be
omitted. Though never losing sight of the main
object of such visits, he delighted in discussing all
manner of topics with his parishioners; he thus
knew his flock thoroughly, and although he went
in and out among them so much at all seasons, his
manner towards even the poorest was noticeable for
its extreme consideration and courtesy.

Having spent nearly the whole of his clerical life
in Yorkshire, he understood the ways as well as the
speech of the people. The quaint Yorkshire words
and expressions that he daily heard, especially in the
earlier days of his clerical life, greatly interested him.
He delighted in a Yorkshire story, and could tell one
with good effect. He frequently alluded with enjoyment to touches of the dialect which he had heard,
which would have been puzzling to a stranger, as
when he went to visit an old dame at Nafferton who
had seriously injured herself. Asking her one day
how the accident happened, she replied, " Ah wer

just cumin thruff t'deear, an' ah chipp'd mi teea i't' pooak on t' fleear" ("I was just coming through the door, and my toe tripped in the sack on the floor"). Or of another parishioner who, though occupying a very small house, somehow contrived to take in a lodger, and on being asked how she managed, replied in truly idiomatic Yorkshire, "Well, sir, you see, he meats hissen, an' ah weshes him" ("He finds his own food, and I wash for him").

In taking these rounds no weather stopped him, and, until his latter years, it was with difficulty that he was induced to wear a greatcoat or carry an umbrella with him. During these walks he kept his eyes about him, and any creature, whether bird or beast or creeping thing, in distress or suffering that came before his notice found in him a ready friend and helper. It almost seemed, not that he would not, but that he could not, pass by a suffering creature of any kind without at least attempting to better its case. This was made evident in the smallest matters. Occasionally, perhaps, of an evening, when deeply occupied with his writing, he would suddenly make a start almost as if something had hurt him. This was only a moth or a fly in the candle, which he made a dart at in his endeavour to save it from imminent peril. Over and over again he would try to seize it, and if successful he would take it to the window and carefully put it outside ; or if the unfortunate insect met its fate in the light, the distressed exclamation, "Oh, dear !" always ensued, betokening genuine regret that he had not been able to save the

tiny creature's life. Or if a large moth found its way
into the drawing-room, or a bat or a bird into a bed-
room at night, there was quite a lively scene. Up
he would get and rush off for one of his disused
butterfly-nets, and give chase to the animal or creature, whatever it might be. To all entreaties to let
it alone he was utterly regardless ; he would never
rest until he had caught it and put it out of reach of
danger. Even in the middle of the night, if anything of this kind happened, he at once got up, went
downstairs for his net, and did his utmost to catch
the intruder, and that even at the risk of disturbing
the slumbers of the whole household.

Few people would credit the amount of trouble he
took on behalf of all creatures, great and small, and
with regard to birds in particular. Let me give one
more instance. It would be about midsummer 1863
that he had occasion to drive with two ladies from
Driffield to Nunburnholme. In order to obtain at
first hand reliable statistics for a letter he was about
to write on the subject of small birds, in connection
with the damage they are supposed to do to crops,
he determined to count every field and every bird
he saw by the roadsides along the whole distance of
fourteen miles; that is, twenty-eight miles of hedgerows. The ladies, it is true, gave him some assistance ; otherwise it would probably have been impossible to perform the task. But the calculation was
made, and the results of his observation were as
follows:—*Fields*—Fallow, 1 ; beans, 1 ; potatoes, 1 ;
tares, 3 ; clover or seeds, 17 ; turnips, 26 ; corn, 46 ;

grass, 58—total, 153. *Birds*—Buntings, 2 ; Green-Finches, 8 ; Yellow-Hammers, 53 ; Sparrows, 195 ; Brown Linnets, a flock of about 30, as nearly as could be ascertained—total, 288.

The question was sometimes asked as to what particular school of Churchmanship he was attached. Those who made the inquiry did not, for the most part, receive the answer they expected, for he had a deep-rooted aversion to partisanship in Church matters, and never liked it to be thought that he belonged exclusively to any party ; accordingly to the " Evangelical " he seemed more than not a High Churchman, and *vice versâ*. He once explained his views as follows :—

" For myself, as far as mere names go, I am not, never was, and never will be either a Low or a High Churchman ; unless, indeed, I am both. If to take my stand on the one great and main doctrine which alone gives all others their importance is to be a Low Churchman, then I am such in the very deepest depth. If to desire to see all things done reverently, 'decently and in order,' 'according to due order,' in the Church is to be a High Churchman, then I acknowledge myself to be a High Churchman, and a very High one.

" It is always painful to me to see any common book laid on the Bible ; but I would make one exception in favour of the Prayer-Book, only as denoting that it rests solely on the authority of the Book of Books, namely, on the great Truth of Truths it contains as the 'Church's One Founda-

tion.' On the Bible and the Prayer-Book, but in
no 'metaphorical sense,' I take my stand—that is
my Churchmanship."

His faith was as deep-rooted as it was simple
and child-like, and to one thus impressed it was
distasteful to adopt practices that seemed to savour
more of party spirit than of religion. And yet he
was entirely for doing everything connected with
his clerical duty according to Church rule as he
understood it. On such a subject, for instance, as
Evening Communion, he never could bring himself
to adopt the practice; his reasons for not doing
so might fall short of those of others. For him it
would be enough that the custom of having Holy
Communion after Evening Service was not in
accordance with the usage laid down in the Book
of Common Prayer, and he had never been accustomed to any other usage than that.

Although the services in his own church were
conducted in the most simple manner possible, yet
there was a reverence in his manner of performing
them that often struck strangers. He never could or
would intone the prayers; it is probable he never
once did so throughout his clerical life, but there was
a richness and a softness in his voice which made
it an exceptionally pleasant one to listen to.

He invariably preached from written sermons; indeed public speaking and extempore preaching were
alike distasteful to him through a natural nervous-
ness which he never overcame, but which he often
regretted. His sermons reflected his own simple

and firm faith in the great verities of Christianity;
on these all his teaching was based; from them
sprang the motives of his own religious life. "Ἐν
τούτοις ἴσθι" were words often quoted by him, which
he endeavoured to act upon himself, and did what
he could to impress upon others also. His sermons
to country folk were written in the plainest language;
this was a rule which never varied, and it was one
to which he attached great importance. In nearly
every sermon he delivered, nothing could be simpler
than his thoughts and the language in which they
were clothed, and although he never waxed eloquent,
his words could not fail to gain one's attention and
go straight home. It was noticeable how largely
his sermons consisted of words of one syllable. As
an example I may perhaps be pardoned if I quote
a short passage from one he preached on 1 St.
John ii. 18. He was speaking of things done for
the last time, and drawing some simple lessons there-
from. "It is not truly," he said, "that the fact of a
thing being done for the last time makes in itself
any real difference to us, for many and many things
have already been for the last time without that
being of any consequence. But the thing that does
concern us is this: when we have done this or that
or the other for the last time, when we have eaten
and drunk for the last time, looked our last look,
spoken our last word, lived our last, even to our
last end, how will it be with us? where shall we
be? how shall we be? what will become of us?
shall we be saved? shall we be lost? Have you

thought of this ? Do you 'think on these things'?
. . . Do not live as if you were never to die. Live
for death. Live for life, for real life, for a blessed
life ; for life eternal."

In delivering his sermons he stood perfectly
upright, never placing the manuscript on the desk,
but holding it in his hand. Being written in his
small handwriting on ordinary-sized note-paper, it
would have been next to impossible to have read
it had it been any distance from the eye, while
to have bent down at all to read would have
been quite "against rule" with him ; and it positively irritated him to see any one holding himself
badly, while he took pains to avoid anything of the
kind in himself. Frequently, after a long sit at his
writing-table, he would suddenly get up, perhaps
rush out of doors and violently throw his arms
backwards and forwards for some time—an exercise
which tended, as he supposed, to expand the chest ;
and he had a theory about it that it was beneficial
to the lungs.

In the latter years of his life he found a difficulty
in composing altogether new sermons, and so he
generally contented himself with rewriting, adding
to, and improving his older ones. He used to relate
that when first he went to Nafferton as a young
man, comparatively fresh from college, Archdeacon
Wilberforce asked him if he found any difficulty
in writing sermons, to which he replied that he
did not in the least. "Wait, then," added the Archdeacon, "till you are as old as I am, and then

perhaps you will find a difference." Certainly the
last thing that he thought about in his preaching was
anything approaching to oratorical effect, though
he by no means valued lightly powers of speech
in others; his one aim and object in all his utter-
ances in the House of God was to benefit those
who heard him.

His great dislike to party signs in things ecclesiastical, to which brief reference has been made,
was well known, and showed itself in various ways.
Some of his practices might have led a stranger
to suppose that he sided with one party, and others
with another. On the question, for instance, of the
observance of Friday he held opinions that would
seem to attach him to the more strictly "Church"
party, while his views as to the way of keeping
Sunday would bring him more or less under the
category of a Sabbatarian. In 1890 he wrote
several letters to one of the leading Church papers
on the observance of Friday, and shortly afterwards
published a leaflet headed "Every Friday," in which
he gave some very plain reasons for a due regard
being paid to that day, and showed what the
Church's rule was in this particular. As another
instance of his avoidance of anything that seemed
to him to savour of party spirit, it may be mentioned
that, if he had a collection in his church for foreign
missions, he would always divide it equally between
the two great Missionary Societies of the Church.

It must not be supposed that no other music
had charms for him but the solos and choruses of

the birds. He had a strong appreciation for that made by human voices and fingers, and yet his ideas on music generally were strangely different from those commonly accepted. For the violin he had no liking; even when played by the most skilful artist, he never could divest himself of the idea that the violin did anything but squeak. He would admit that the squeak might be toned down under the influence of a good player on a good instrument, but that, under the most favourable conditions, the squeak was always there. He thought the harp the finest of all instruments, and the guitar, especially as an accompaniment to the voice, the next. Of the guitar he used to say that it is the easiest of all instruments to play a little on by ear, and the most difficult of all for the display of skill in pieces of music; that it is always admired when heard, and calls forth exclamations of pleasure and delight. He enjoyed hearing it played with the piano, and considered a duet of two guitars really charming.

The guitar was the only instrument he ever attempted to play himself, and this he only did by ear; but he was extremely fond of it, and constantly throughout the day, but only for a few minutes, he would take up his instrument and play snatches of Italian melodies which had been taught him in his younger days by an Italian who visited this country and whom he had befriended. These airs he never forgot; nor did he seem to wish to increase his *répertoire*, but played the same tunes over and over again hundreds and thousands of times. Frequently, in the course of a hard morning's work or after a long walk or an afternoon's visiting in his parish, he could be heard in his study or elsewhere singing these airs to his own accompaniment on the guitar; these seemed to refresh his mind, and enabled him to go back to his writing with redoubled energy. His ear for music was accurate, and the tone of his voice had a peculiar combination of softness and depth; of musical training, however, he had received none. It would have made a musician smile to look at his guitar and see the devices that he adopted for learning to play by note, which he once attempted, but soon abandoned as hopeless, or not worth the trouble. He had the name of every note, written on pieces of ivory, inserted below each fret, which gave his guitar a singular appearance.

Although by no means a practised vocalist, in his earlier days at Nunburnholme he would sometimes enjoy singing a song, but do what he would he could never manage to join in part-singing, unless it was that he sang the treble an octave lower. He appeared to have little appreciation for music that "had not an air in it," as he expressed it. The choicest harmonies and modulations of themselves made little or no impression upon him. The well-known and simple old English songs and melodies were those that delighted him most, and to these he was never weary of listening. No music ever appealed to him so strongly, he said,

as that which he heard performed at the funeral
of the Duke of Wellington in 1851.

Unless he found it necessary to do so for some
special purpose, he did not often read new books;
his old favourites seemed to satisfy him. Of these,
like the old airs, he never grew weary. Sir Walter
Scott's writings he always enjoyed. These, together
with Miss Edgeworth's tales and the "Vicar of
Wakefield," were among his earliest mental companions, and often quoted. Of poems, "Gray's
Elegy" was one which seemed specially to har-
monise with his tastes. For Charles Dickens' works
he had no great partiality. To him and his supposed lack of appreciation for entomological studies
Mr. Morris playfully alluded in his "History of
British Butterflies," when he said :—

"The unfeeling and heartless manner in which Mr.
Charles Dickens relates the gratuitous destruction by
the robbers of poor Grimaldi's 'Dartford Blues,' in
revenge, as it would appear, for the rest of the intended
plunder having been timely removed, must for ever
lower him in the estimation of every high-souled
entomologist. True, indeed, it is that he uses language not altogether inappropriate in treating of the
loss—language which, did it express the feelings of his
heart, might be accepted as displaying some degree
of commiseration for so lamentable a calamity; but
the acute perception of the entomologist will at once
tell him that the sympathy is but feigned, the pity
but a mockery, the pretended commiseration a mere
delusion, betokening an utter want of feeling on a

subject which ought instinctively to call forth the deepest emotion. 'Tis easy to see through the hollow speciousness—'*Hic nigri est succus loliginis* ;' which translated into plain English is — Mr. Dickens, I am quite sure, is no entomologist."

His sense of humour was very keen, and few men enjoyed a good story more than he. This appreciation of the ridiculous would often appear in his conversation, and he always seemed to take delight in telling anything of an amusing nature that he had seen or heard. Needless to say, this feature in his character made itself seen in many of his writings. Even in his "History of Birds" we find passing evidences of it ; as, for instance, in his description of the Eagle Owl, which he prefaced by an allusion to an incident recorded in Scrope's "Days and Nights of Salmon-Fishing" of the worthy gentleman who trolled for a day in the vain attempt to catch a wooden pike stuck at the bottom of a pond, and then declared to the host, who inquired if he had caught it for dinner, that though he had not succeeded in doing so, yet that it had "run at him several times."

Frequently in his letters to the newspapers he would introduce his subject by recording something he had recently seen or heard that had amused him, as when he sent a story to one of the papers about a foxhound, and embellished his account by stating that he had just sent his pamphlet about fox-hunting to an old Oxford friend who, though he was not before aware of it, was a fox-hunter of long standing.

After jokingly passing a favourable criticism on his own production, he instanced the case of a clergyman he had known very well in former days who had passed a somewhat similar criticism, but seriously, on one of his own sermons. The said clergyman had to preach for some missionary object in a neighbouring parish, and, speaking of his sermon afterwards to a mutual friend, he observed, "Ah, it was indeed an excellent sermon, a most excellent discourse. The points, you see, were so well put, the argument was so sustained throughout, and the whole so well done. A proof of it," he said. "A proof of it! I went to church meaning only to give five shillings to the collection, but it was so powerful, so weighty, so convincing, I was obliged to give ten shillings. I was indeed! I was indeed!"

As another phase of this same faculty, it may be added that he enjoyed light and diverting passages with those he knew in various callings in life. He used to record, for instance, how he once went into his tailor's shop in York as if in a state of great annoyance, and requested that he might at once see the master of the establishment. Mr. H., who was as polite and competent a tradesman as any in the city, soon appeared, whereupon Mr. Morris, with the blackest looks that he could command for the occasion, said that he was sorry to have to make a great complaint with regard to the last coat that had been made for him ; indeed, he could not understand how Mr. H. could have sent him such an article as this one proved to be. Mr. H. expressed the utmost astonishment that any complaint of this kind could be made ; adding that he had never had such fault found with his workmen and cloth before. He assured his customer that the coat was made of the very best materials, and strictly in accordance with orders. "That may be all very true," said Mr. Morris, "but still my complaint holds good. In fact, the long and short of the matter is, that I simply cannot wear the coat out !" When the ensuing laughter had subsided, another order was, of course, promptly given.

It has been already remarked that he always took a hopeful view of things ; but he did more than this : he regarded everything that happened as "for the best," and his natural temperament was cheerful and sanguine, even to a fault. Whatever evils happened, he was perfectly confident that in the end good would come out of them. "Whatever is, is best" was a dictum in which he thoroughly believed, not as thereby excluding the exercise of active energies for good in any single individual, but as being content, after all has been done that can be done, to leave the outcome in the hands of a higher Power than our own. This hopeful and trustful frame of mind often gave him heart and courage to overcome many difficulties that would else have seemed ready to weigh him down.

Those who have read even small portions of his various writings can hardly fail to have noticed traces of a strong personality underlying them. As we may often see much of a man's chararacter from a single letter that he may have written, so in this case, not only from the facts he actually recorded, but also, and perhaps even more, from his style, we seem to see much of what the author felt and thought. A man's style is the man himself, and certainly a leading feature in Mr. Morris's style was, that his own tastes and traits of character were so clearly revealed in it.

As in conversation he had the happy knack of telling a simple story with good effect, so in writing he would occasionally preface the narration of a plain fact by an introduction, or garnish it by light touches, that seemed to interest you more than the particular thing that caused him to take up his pen. Thus, for example, in writing to one of the natural history journals about a pair of Wild Ducks which had built on the top of a straw stack near a neighbouring farm-house, he spins out quite a long story, filling nearly three times as much space as that required to relate the fact itself, and in it you see something of the man. It was on a Sunday, "in the cool of the day," after his Evening Service at church was over, that he was sitting in his garden. He alludes to the recent restoration of the little church, and of the advantage of evening over afternoon services, as well as that of preaching in words that plain folk can understand; then he approaches more nearly the point that he wishes to come to, and he does this in a way so happy and so like himself that the *ipsissima verba* of his telling will, I hope, bear repetition, for they were written nearly twenty years ago:—"I was sitting down, as I have said,

after having walked about my garden like Isaac of
old.   I had watched the Flittermice hawking by the
beckside, my Wood-Pigeons had cooed their last coo
to each other in our shrubbery close to me, and the
daylight was now but scant.   The next to appear on
the scene was a large Brown Owl, which, after two
or three turns over the lawn, went off to prowl somewhere else.   He was followed by a Heronseugh sailing away down-stream to his fishing-ground.   And
this brings me to the subject of these few lines,
namely, a Wild Duck—the next to come between me
and the sky and my star-gazing, wending her or his
way overhead in the opposite direction."   Then he
goes on to say that he has no doubt that this was one
of the pair of Wild Ducks which had built in the
neighbouring stackyard ; and the curious part of it
was, that the situation was half-a-mile from any water,
except, indeed, a trickling rill.   How well we can
picture him on this summer Sunday evening, his
work for the day over, enjoying the delights of the
balmy air and all that surrounded him, hatless, I will
answer for it, and alone—alone, but in company that
he delighted in ; for he could say, as John Henry
Newman, in his Oxford days, did when, in one of his
solitary walks, he was met by a friend, who tauntingly
alluded to his seemingly lonesome ways.   To this
gentle thrust on the part of his friend Newman made
answer, " *Nunquam minus solus quam cum solus ;* "
and yet there were few who enjoyed the society of
congenial friends more than my father.

The frequency, and not seldom the aptness, with

which he introduced quotations from his favourite authors into his writing was quite remarkable. It seemed almost impossible for him to write even an ordinary letter without making use of inverted commas. A line from a Latin classic, a passage from Shakespeare, a saying of Mr. Thornhill's, or of some other character from his old friend the "Vicar of Wakefield," a sentence of Sir Walter Scott's—with these, and such as these, his writings abounded.

In many ways his style reflected his own simple and rustic tastes. Even such a thing as his quiet appreciation of hearth and home is occasionally made clear to us in what he wrote. Thus in the descriptions he gives in his "History of British Birds" of the flight and song of the Sky-Lark, which I will presently quote for another purpose, he ends one of his passages in a way that opens out to us something of his thoroughly English feeling on this head.

At times his language bore evident traces of haste. Now and again, when thoughts seemed to come more quickly than he could formulate and transcribe them, the sentences and parentheses tumbled over one another in such a way that the original construction of the opening part of the sentence became well-nigh lost in the apparent confusion. Thus, for instance, when describing a visit to Northamptonshire in search of the "Purple Emperor" in his "History of British Butterflies," he finds himself landed in the following involved sentence :—"The next day, in the same wood at Barnwell Wold, near Oundle, Northamptonshire, during my absence in successful search of the 'Large Blue,' of which more anon, Mr. Bree most cleverly captured one, by acting on the principle— an invaluable one, as I have always found it, long before its enunciation by the late Sir Robert Peel to the students of the University of Glasgow at his installation as Rector, in the best speech, by the way, if I do not make my sentence too long, that he ever made—namely, whatever you want to do that is within the bounds of possibility, determine that it shall be done, and you will be sure to succeed."

I will now revert to the passage just alluded to, in which he describes the unbroken song and soaring of the Sky-Lark. It is a happy and characteristic example of his style, and therefore may not be thought out of place here. The length of the sentence is evidently in this case constructed de- signedly as a kind of faint parallel to the uninter- rupted singing of the bird. He says :—"As to the flight of the Lark, it is indeed, like the poet's, a 'lofty' one, continued upwards higher and higher as the spring advances, and the sun, towards whom he soars, gets higher in the heavens, up and up into the very highest regions of the air, so that the eye is literally oftentimes unable to follow it ; but if you watch long enough, as perhaps this equally long sentence will enable you to do with your mind's eye, you will again perceive the songster, and downwards in measured cadence, both of song and descent, but rather more rapidly than he went up, he will stoop, nearer and nearer he will come, until at last, suspended for a moment over the spot which contains his mate, for whose delight no doubt he has been warbling all the while his loudest and sweetest notes, and whom he has kept all along in his sight, slanting at the end for a greater or less distance, probably as danger may or may not appear to be nigh, he drops with half-closed and unmoved wings, and is at *home :*—

'A charm from the skies seems to hallow us there,
Which, search where you will, you'll ne'er meet with else-where.'"

It is remarkable how the subject of nomenclature, scientific or other, seemed to have interested him all through his life. So early as 1837 he wrote a paper for the *Naturalist* on the present nomenclature of British ornithology, giving explicit suggestions for a remedy, and from that time onwards the question "What's in a name?" seemed to him to be one that always needed a careful and thoughtful answer. Allusion having been made to this else-where, I need not dwell further upon it, except to add that he had the greatest objection to adopt any abbreviation or alteration in men's names or place-names; he could never bring himself even to make use of such common shortnesses as Dick, Tom, or Fred in addressing people ; with him they, even the poorest, were always Richard, Thomas, and Frederick. Neither would he, under any circumstances, shorten a place-name ; Scarborough, for instance, would never be written Scarbro', nor Yorkshire, Yorks. Nor would he ever omit to cross a "t," dot an "i," or make a needed comma ; while such mutilations as "exam" for examination or "photo" for photograph he could, under no circumstances, put up with, even in others. It may seem to some hardly worth mentioning these trifles, but as straws show the course of the wind, so are these minute details highly characteristic of his ways. He was always for doing whatever he did thoroughly ; no half-measures satisfied him. In times of pressure he must have been tempted, one would suppose, to adopt ordinary abbreviations in writing ; but if he were so, he never appears to have given way to the temptation.

The even flow of his periods was sometimes needlessly broken by reason of an inordinate fondness for excessive punctuation, especially in the matter of commas. Phrases and sentences which were in themselves perfectly plain and simple would now and again be studded over with a number of superfluous commas that rather irritated than assisted the reader ; on this subject the writer of these pages has had many a diverting discussion with him, but he always stuck to his commas—I had almost said his "point."

VII

THE PROTECTION OF BIRDS

ALWAYS favouring the protection of our native birds, and using many endeavours on their behalf, it was not until about the year 1867 that Mr. Morris commenced that determined and systematic agitation for his friends in feather which was carried on for so many years, and was ultimately crowned with success. Few people would credit the unwearied labour that he ungrudgingly expended on behalf of the birds, and the difficulties and discouragements that were thrown in his way. This labour of love would have been deemed a life's work for some.

His suggestion for a tax on guns was practically the opening of his campaign. It was just before the close of the parliamentary session of 1867 that the "Rector of Nunburnholme" presented a petition to the House of Commons praying that a heavy tax be imposed on the possession of a gun, and that the law of trespass be made more stringent, with the like object in view, namely, the protection, within certain limits, of all our native birds. Among other reasons he set out the following :—

"That birds perform a most useful part in the

economy of Nature ; that if they are unduly destroyed insects increase in similar proportion, and
do vast damage to the produce of both farms and
gardens ; that birds are ornamental as well as useful,
and give great pleasure and instruction to naturalists
and others that observe their habits ; that, owing to
the indiscriminate and untaxed use of guns, they are
recklessly destroyed in great numbers every year ;
that many important and useful species have in this
way already become extinct in Great Britain, and that
others have become more or less rare, and will in like
manner be exterminated if some means for their
protection and preservation be not adopted. . . .
That such a tax [on guns] would bring in a. very
large revenue to the exchequer ; that its enactment
would at the same time do away with a vast amount
of poaching ; that it would be the means of saving
many lives which at present are sacrificed every year
by the incautious use of firearms in every one's hands
ad libitum, as well as otherwise."

Letters innumerable to the public journals he
wrote upon this subject through a long course of
years. It may be said, indeed, that his mind was in
a state of perpetual motion with regard to the preservation of birds ; for no sooner was an Act of
Parliament passed with the object of fixing a close
time for them than he quickly saw in it something
that needed amendment ; and to carry his views, if
possible, into effect, he would vigorously and at
once apply himself.

It was in October 1869 that the monthly paper

called *The Animal World* made its appearance. Among the contributors to the first number were the Bishop of Gloucester and Bristol, William and Mary Howitt, Frank Buckland, Frances Power Cobbe, and Francis Orpen Morris. For many years no signature was more frequently seen in the columns of this periodical than that of F. O. Morris, and his very first contribution to its pages was headed " British Birds," in which a strong appeal was made for their protection. He quoted the words of a correspondent who stated that on one Sunday morning in this same year he had counted from a railway-carriage no less than thirteen shooting parties along one side of the railway between Stratford and Tottenham stations alone, one shot being fired from the railway at a robin perched on the telegraph wire ! Another correspondent gave a graphic account of the miserable shooting matches in which linnets and sparrows were the unfortunate victims. The principal actors in these tragic scenes were would-be " sportsmen " of the Jones, Brown, and Robinson type ; other interested parties being innkeepers and betting men of the lowest type. A third correspondent who had travelled in many parts of the world no less graphically described various other kinds of slaughter, especially the way in which the trustful sea-birds which follow ships at sea are shot and captured in the most heartless and barbarous fashion. He related how that he once asked one of these people what particular pleasure it gave him to shoot a poor sea-bird thus, to which he made reply, "The instincts of a sportsman"! "Bah!" replied the writer; "I should like to know what the brave fellow who, with nothing but a single rifle and a stout heart, goes to seek the man-eating tiger in his lair, or even the man who will walk twenty miles through swamp and bog for snipe, or the chance of some, thinks of such sportsmen!"

For three years not a month passed without his writing in the pages of *The Animal World*, some of his communications extending to great length.

He was never at a loss for a text for a letter, but would have doubled or trebled the amount he wrote could he have found the time. The powers of the poetic art were sometimes called in to aid him in his appeals and give them greater eloquence. In the number for March 1870, for instance, appeared the touching and graceful lines entitled "The Small Birds' Appeal," beginning with the words, "All day we flit across your view." The sonnet was written by his friend and neighbour of many years' standing, the Rev. Richard Wilton (now Canon of York), the rector of Londesborough. Besides communications on British birds, other subjects of his letters were "Inculcation of Humanity in Schools," "Dog Kennels," "Transit of Cattle," "Petition to Parliament in favour of a Land Birds' Protection Bill," "Association for the Protection of British Birds," "A Tax on Guns," "The most Humane Mode of killing Insects," "Horses and Grass," "Steel Traps," "Lecture on Humanity," "The Last of the Swallows."

These, with many others, might be quoted to show the diversified channels in which his sympathies were exercised in the cause of humanity to animals.

A few years later he drew up another lengthy petition to Parliament, which was first published in *The Animal World*, with a view to inviting suggestions for improvement in the form of it. He argued that luxuries should be taxed before anything else ; that gamekeepers are luxuries, and that therefore they should be heavily taxed. The amount suggested for such tax was £20. Then he would have had a prohibitory law passed against the use of iron traps, thus doing away with an untold amount of cruelty. He instanced the case of a farmer in a district where weasels, &c., had been destroyed, who had killed in one instance in his stack-yard upwards of 2500 rats between the previous autumn and that spring; of another who had killed 600 in a short space of time; and of a third who had destroyed 80 under a small bean-stack not much bigger than a hay-cock. He argued, further, that "the *battue*, being an un-English sport, and only of French origin, as its name imports, should be made of use, as a foreign luxury, for the revenue of the country, and that a license of £20 be paid for every one engaging in a *battue ;* and, further, that all game shot at such should be distributed in equal proportions between the poor of the parish in which the shooting takes place and the county hospital of the same. That much Sunday desecration is caused by the capture and sale of small birds; that, therefore, this should be prohibited by law, and a fine of £5 imposed on any person found guilty of the practice. That a similar fine be imposed on the use of loaded guns on Sunday. That a license of £1 be required for every cage of less than one foot square. That a license at a cost of £5 be required to be obtained by every one dealing in live birds. That a license of £10 be paid for the use of clap-nets. That a heavy license-duty be paid for the use of guns of bore beyond a certain width." Such were some of his *desiderata* in the way of legislation.

Among the chief breeding-places for sea-birds that frequent the east coast in summer are the lofty cliffs between Scarborough and Bridlington. Here in the months of May and June the sea-fowl may be seen in myriads, and the sight is one that will repay those who visit the locality. Ever since 1830 a systematic destruction of these birds had been going on. It was about that year when the first steamer came to Scarborough, which was hired by parties of twelve to thirty "gentlemen," who shot countless numbers of sea-birds under the cliffs. From that time onwards things proceeded from bad to worse, until in 1867 the birds were becoming so reduced in numbers that it was absolutely necessary that something should be done, if they were not to be exterminated altogether.

News of what went on constantly reached the ears of the bird-friend who dwelt at Nunburn-holme. One of his correspondents told him that in that same year he had witnessed wholesale destruction of the birds ; on one occasion he saw two boats "literally laden with birds, the boatmen sitting on them, and the birds heaped up in the bow and the stern above the gunwale." It was after hearing such-like sad tales of bird murder that he wrote, in April 1867 :—

"It is a most heartless thing to shoot the parent birds in this disgraceful manner, the effect of which must be to leave their young to perish miserably of starvation. . . . They deserve a better fate, for if their young be taken in a boat they may be seen to follow it for hours in the vain hope of aiding or rescuing them, often losing their own lives in consequence at the hands of those who ought to know better. And, lastly, many poor families of the neighbouring villages used to earn an honest livelihood in summer by collecting the eggs for sale, which might then be seen brought in panniers on donkeys both for food and sale as specimens, their endless variety of colour and markings being most remarkable and interesting ; but so few are now left that it is hardly worth their while to run the risk of collecting them. Like the black-headed and other Gulls, the Guillemots come in numbers early in April almost to the day, staying a short time about their nesting-places, and then disappear, re-turning again in the beginning of May with the Puffins and Razor-Bills, when they all stay together to rear their young *silice in nudâ*, if but permitted."

Not only on the Yorkshire coast was this pitiless slaughter of the sea-birds perpetrated ; the tale was the same in other and widely distant parts of the country. At the Bass Rock, the Isle of May in the Firth of Forth, Ailsa Craig in the Firth of Clyde, the Pembrokeshire coast, and many other places the same destructive work was wantonly carried on at this time; that is to say, about the year 1867. A correspondent told him that on Ramsey Island, off St. David's, 1400 birds had been killed in one week during that summer. With such facts as these before·them, it was generally admitted by the public that it was time that something should be done on behalf of the birds.

For years after this he interested himself in the passing of Acts for the protection of birds, and his frequent letters to the *Times* and other papers contributed in no small degree to influence public opinion upon the question. It must, however, be borne in mind that the movement, in an organised shape, originated with the formation of an association for the protection of sea-birds at Bridlington. The inspiring cause which actually set on foot the movement in Yorkshire was the account of a meeting of the British Association at which the subject of the sea-birds came up, and one speaker denounced the people of Bridlington as atrociously cruel in their treatment of the birds. This inaccurate statement caused the vicar of the parish to make inquiries. He found that the blame lay, not with his parishioners, but with " cheap trippers " from a distance. He, however, at once determined to establish an association for the protection of the

persecuted birds. This association was formed in
October 1868, at a meeting held in Bridlington
Vicarage, Yorkshire, under the presidency of the
vicar of the parish, the Rev. H. F. Barnes (now
Canon Barnes-Lawrence), an old friend of my
father's, and an ardent defender and champion of
the cause of the birds. Mr. Harland, of the same
place, worked energetically as secretary. The tales
of cruelty that reached the ears of the good people
of Bridlington were heart-rending in the extreme.
" Sportsmen " (!) from the West Riding made descents upon the coast in the neighbourhood of
Flamborough Head, where the birds were known
to breed in countless multitudes, and slaughtered
these beautiful and harmless creatures wholesale,
when, where, and how they listed. It was a thing
of no concern to these people whether it was the
breeding season of the birds or whether it was not.
At them they went, and brought them down in
the midst of their graceful flight, or as they rode
upon the wave, in hundreds and in thousands. It
mattered not even to these contemptible shooters
whether the birds had young in their nests or not ;
the piteous cries of the young birds bereft of their
parents, and starving for lack of the attention they
needed, moved not the hearts of their tormentors.
Boat-loads of the mangled remains of these interesting sea-birds were made away with, while others,
wounded and bleeding, were left to die a lingering
and agonising death in the waters. At one time
the rate of slaughter had reached such a pitch

that there was a likelihood of several species being practically exterminated in a short time from that part of the coast. It was indeed full time that something should be done to stay the murderous cruelty of the thing.

Under the direction of the first promoters of the association for the protection of the birds subscriptions were invited and circulars drawn up giving some particulars of what went on along the coast. Influential support was quickly given to the movement, which grew apace. Public opinion was stirred on the question, and ultimately Mr. Christopher Sykes, the popular member for the East Riding of Yorkshire, undertook to introduce a Bill into Parliament, which he shortly afterwards did, and carried it triumphantly through the House of Commons. Mr. Frank Buckland, Mr. J. E. Harting, and others "aided and abetted" the passing of this much-needed measure, while the part which Mr. Morris took in the movement was mainly with his pen. His numerous letters to the *Times* and other papers appeared in rapid succession, and told strongly in favour of the remedial measures being applied.

No movement of this kind could be set going without raising opposition in some quarter or another, and the name of F. O. Morris was sometimes held up to something, perhaps, worse than ridicule by the boatmen about Flamborough, who fancied that one means of their livelihood would be lessened if the birds were protected by law. It was

said at the time by those who wished to raise a
laugh at the expense of the protector of the sea-
birds, that if only the said boatmen could have
induced him to enter one of their craft there was
no telling what they might have done with him !
Even thus, however, he might have caused them
some little trouble and disappointment, for he was
both lithe of limb and an excellent swimmer withal !
As a matter of fact, he wished them no harm whatever, and in a little book he brought out upon
the subject, called the "Sea-Gull Shooter," he made
this plain when he said at the outset :—

"I should be sorry indeed if a single word in this
small book should be, or even should be considered
to be, of the slightest injury to any of my good friends
the boatmen of our Yorkshire coast. Coming of a
naval family myself, I cannot but love the sea, and
everybody and everything connected with it, and
therefore that would be the very last thing that I
could or would wish to do.

"On the contrary, I am sure that the more our
sea-birds are preserved the better it will be for those
boatmen who may be engaged to take out the visitors at our watering-places to see that wonderful
and most interesting sight, the birds in their native
home, 'the stupendous cliffs of Speeton,' as
Waterton well calls them—Crow Shoot, 410 feet;
Jordan's Leap, 436 feet; and Speeton Beacon, 444
feet, sheer down to the sea. But if the birds, besides those that are killed, are frightened off by the
shots that echo against and from those weird head-

K

lands, the beauty of the scene is lost, the happiness of the wild creatures that build in them is destroyed, and the object in view is itself done away with."

While the Bill was before Parliament an influential meeting was held at the Hanover Square Rooms in support of the measure. This meeting Mr. Morris attended, and was called upon to second one of the resolutions. On this occasion certain points were finally settled which facilitated the progress of the Bill, and those who attended the gathering were soon gratified by the announcement of the passing of the measure in the House of Commons. In the Upper House the Duke of Northumberland took charge of the Bill, and, with some modifications, it passed the House of Lords, and became law in time to give the sea-birds a taste of the protection of which they stood so much in need before the close of the summer of 1869. A remarkable degree of interest was shown in the passing of this Act, the first of the kind, it was said, since the reign of Henry VIII. It may be added that some time before the formation of the association just alluded to a letter appeared in the *Times*, with the signature " F. O. Morris," drawing attention to some gross acts of cruelty to the sea-birds on the Yorkshire coast. He wrote from Norwich under date August 21, 1868, having attended the meeting of the British Association there that year. This is what he said :—

" On coming to the reception-room here from

a very interesting discussion on the connection
between the Game Laws and the destruction of
British birds of the Hawk kind, when the destruction of the Gulls at Flamborough Head by cockney
shooters (sportsmen of course they are not) was
warmly commented on, I have just read in the
Times of this morning the letter of your correspondent, 'A,' of Glasgow, on the destruction of the
Kittiwake. The facts he states were fully corro-
borated coincidently by the speakers to-day, and
will, I trust, be thought sufficiently bad ; but I am
sorry to say there is worse in the background. I
can assure you that it is the truth that one of
these unfortunate birds was picked up alive on
the beach near Bridlington, some half-a-dozen
miles from Flamborough Head, with both its
wings—the 'plumes' of which your correspondent
speaks—torn off, and another was picked up in
a field alive, with its bill tied so that it could not
feed."

And again, on October 13 of the same year, he
wrote once more to the leading journal with an
urgent plea for the protection of the Sea-Gulls,
stating that a movement had been set on foot in
the East Riding for their preservation during the
breeding season ; also that a petition would be sent
round to ask the members to support the Bill when
before the House. He further asked the favour of
the insertion of some graceful and touching lines
on the birds' behalf "from the pen of a gifted
friend," though, as he put it, "plain prose is

ordinarily, I am aware, the staple of your columns."
The lines were headed "A Plea for the Sea-Birds,"
and the first stanza ran thus :—

> " Stay now thine hand !
>   Proclaim not man's dominion
>   Over God's works by strewing rocks and sand
>   With sea-birds' blood-stained plumes and broken
>   pinion."
>   —RICHARD WILTON.

A perceptible increase in the number of the birds
along the rocky coast around Flamborough Head
soon followed the passing of this much-needed and
humane Act of Parliament. The very birds themselves seemed, as it were, to know that the law was
now on their side, for they became more trustful
in their ways as they were more secure from danger.
Their lifelong and devoted friend would not, however, have been himself had he for a moment
rested satisfied with what Parliament had granted.
No sooner was the Sea-Birds Act passed than he
proceeded to take steps to have a like benefit extended to all British birds.

In the February following he formulated a short
circular in connection with what he styled an
"Association for the Protection of British Birds,"
in which he drew attention to the widespread
feeling that existed showing that something should
be done to prevent the otherwise inevitable and
speedy destruction of many species. Letters had
come to him from all sides urging him to continue the campaign further. The following from

an officer of the 54th Regiment may be taken as a specimen of many similar communications :—

"I have from time to time read with great interest your letters on bird preservation. Pray agitate the small bird question once more. I was at Eastbourne last summer, and for the first time, and the last, I hope, in my life, I witnessed a bird murder. There was a grand sparrow match advertised between Mr. A. of Blank, and Mr. B. of Somewhere ; the match was twenty-one birds, H. or I. traps, for £20, eighteen yards' distance, bounds forty yards.

"The match was duly shot. A lantern-jawed man attended with twelve dozen sparrows and three dozen linnets. The birds were so thickly packed in cages that they must have been either silly or stunned before being put into a trap about the size of a quarter-pound cigar-box. The noble sportsmen each stood ready, one with his gun at the shoulder, pointed at the trap (the bore of the gun being wide enough to admit an ordinary thumb), the other with the gun at the hip, so that the latter shooter's style had a latent semblance of sportsmanship. The match being over, Jones, Brown, and Robinson, and other sportsmen present, shot handicap matches, and the whole fifteen dozen birds were shot at.

"This is a short account of one of a hundred *per diem* probably, and unless a stop is put to it the small birds must be annihilated. They are captured wholesale by the bat-fowlers, and in the neighbourhood of London small birds are almost wholly disappearing."

Not only by word, but by deed also, did he endeavour his utmost to protect his feathered friends from their persecutors. It was a year or two after this time that he was one day coming home from a long walk, when he fell in with a bird-catcher in the very act of setting his traps within the limits of the parish of Nunburnholme. This was a case not to be passed over, and he at once proceeded to the spot. Argument was of no avail whatever. The bird-catcher had two stuffed linnets, one of which he placed on the top of the hedge, and the other on a thorn-bush near it. But let us hear the incident related as it was first told :—" He was in the act of lining his twigs, and had his decoy bird in a very small cage, and another larger one to put his captives into, all covered over with a thick dark cloth, when I came up. I soon told him that if he did not decamp I should stop if it was till ten o'clock at night, and frighten off every bird that came near. He began to talk very big, but when he found that that was a game that a just indignation would enable me to play at as well as himself, he drew in his horns, and seeing that my foot was pretty firmly set on the ground, he soon 'packed up his traps' and sheered off, muttering and spluttering as he went. This I did not much mind, but kept my place till he was well out of sight, and remained near some time longer to prevent his return. It was the very spot that I had often remarked as the one in the parish resorted to by these birds, and the very time that was in the height of the breeding season. But what cared he for that?" This was by no means the only occasion when he interfered in this kind of way; indeed, it is not too much to say that it was impossible for him not to interfere whenever any act of cruelty came before his notice.

To those who knew anything of what went on along our coast, it was evident in the course of a year or two that the close time as laid down in the Act was by no means a sufficient protection to the birds, although it had worked untold good for them. One or two species of the Herring-Gull, together with Cormorant, for instance, returned to breed at Flamborough Head, which they had not done for years, though the former was once very abundant there.

For several years prior to 1874 a policeman had been appointed to take down the number of persons found shooting sea-birds about Flamborough and Speeton; it was ascertained that in the first two weeks only of August 1874 eighty-nine persons were stopped by the said officer, and of these, twenty did not carry the ordinary gun license. At Flamborough alone three hundred and thirty-six birds were brought on shore in that short time, and the number destroyed altogether was, at the lowest computation, upwards of a thousand. This was stated by Mr. Morris in a letter he wrote to the *Times* on October 26, 1874.

He added :—"One of these would-be sportsmen laid a wager that he would shoot eighty sea-birds within an hour, and he had the discredit and disgrace of having succeeded in doing so. In fact, the very tameness of the birds, through the unwonted protection extended to them for the summer months, proved in the end an element of danger to them. As was truly stated, 'they trust in our humanity, and suffer in consequence.'"

It was in consequence of the inadequacy of the first Act for the protection of the sea-birds, and of the fact that the land-birds needed as much protection almost as those on the sea-board, that Mr. Morris continued unremittingly to move for further measures, though it would need an entire volume to give anything like a full account of the part he took in this movement. What added so much to his labours was the circumstance that legislation on the subject was effected piecemeal. First there was the Sea-Birds Act, the close time specified therein being too short for the purpose designed ; then the extension had to be authorised by the magistrates in Quarter Sessions. When, after much urging, this had been accomplished, there then came Mr. Dillwyn's Act repealing the former one and going back to the original close time, so that the agitation for an extension of the close season had to be undertaken a second time ; indeed, the changes were so frequent that the matter never seemed at rest.

He did not consider that agriculture would suffer

by reason of such protection, because he would allow birds to be shot after the close time was over in certain cases. As he said in his evidence before the Committee of the House of Commons on this question, "What I would like to see would be this: a close time for every British bird during the breeding season; such close time to last from the 1st of March to the 1st of August. If thought necessary, the Bullfinch to be allowed to be shot by persons holding a gun license, in gardens only, up to the 1st of April; some birds, to be specified, never to be allowed to be shot at all for the next twenty years, or longer, if then found to be required, such as the Bee-Eater, the Roller, the Hoopoe, &c. All birds useful for food, or increasing in undue numbers, to be allowed to be shot by persons having a gun license during the remainder of the year. All other kinds of birds useless for food, of which a large number might be specified, such as the Golden-Crested Wren, Cole-Titmouse, Marsh-Titmouse, Wren, Willow-Wren (the several species of), Redstart (both species of), Whinchat, Stonechat, Swift, and many others, only allowed to be shot for scientific purposes, and with a license obtainable for a limited period, by persons of fixed residence, &c. No nests, eggs, or young birds to be allowed to be taken in the breeding season, except in the same way, for scientific purposes, and under the like restrictions."

In all the controversies on the subject, there was no bird that he defended with greater persistence and vehemence than the Sparrow. It was mainly in defence of the Sparrow that he and others gave evidence before a Committee of the House of Commons on Bird Protection in 1873, presided over by the Hon. Auberon Herbert. In a statement that he subsequently handed in he gave a mass of evidence in favour of this bird, and among other facts he observed :—"This is the twentieth year I have been rector of Nunburnholme, and in the whole of that time I have never but twice, at intervals, known the Sparrows do me any harm that I should not feel ashamed to complain of."

To many it appeared a small matter to agitate and legislate for the protection of our native birds ; to him, who knew what a vast amount of cruelty was perpetrated every year upon these beautiful creatures of God's world, it seemed anything but small ; nay, it would have appeared to him absolutely wrong not to have espoused a cause which cried so loudly for help. It was not in him to pass in silence such accounts as a short one that I will quote which was sent to him from Suffolk in 1885. A gentleman and his sister were standing on a lonely beach one day, when the only human being in sight was a man who approached them from a distance with a dog and gun, dealing destruction as he came along. As they approached him a pair of small Gulls flew past over the sea. He shot one, and it fell into the water out of reach. Its mate hovered pitifully over it, and soon shared the same fate. The man laughed and looked at the dead birds. The two then went up to him, and asked, "What use will those birds be to you?" He stared, and said, "None." They added, "What do you do with them when you have shot them?" "Let 'em be," he answered, grinning. Accounts like this distressed and moved him to the quick.

VIII

LATER WORKS AND FRIENDSHIPS

WE must now look back a few years from the point
to which we were brought in the last chapter. The
year following the publication of his "Anecdotes
on Natural History" Mr. Morris was found com-
piling another volume of a similar kind, entitled
"Records of Animal Sagacity and Character." This
small work would need no special notice but for the
fact that it contained a remarkable essay, inserted
as a preface to the volume, giving the author's
views on a speculative subject of no little difficulty,
and one to which he had from time to time given
a good deal of thought. This was the future
existence of the animal creation. In this essay he
gave the opinions of several well-known writers,
among whom was Bishop Butler, and after formu-
lating his own ideas, he came to the conclusion that
there was at all events much in favour of the notion
that the spiritual life of animals, if such it may be
called, was not brought to an end at the time of
their bodily death. The most that could be urged
against the idea is only, as he said, in the words of
Sir E. Lytton Bulwer, that they have "no warrant

of a hereafter." "I dare not, and do not," he wrote, "affirm that they have ; but I do say, 'Why should it be thought a thing incredible that God should raise the dead in the case of the animal creation any more than in that of men ?—God, in whose hand is the soul of every living thing and the breath of all mankind.'" The author's mind is well reflected in the following striking passage :—

"It is therefore of God that there is something solemn in the death of every living creature. No one can watch without any emotion the eye glazing in death of a faithful dog, the mild look of a dying bird, or the expiring throb of a wounded animal. Who can avoid the thought that something is going away which he cannot bring back, nor any power of his then stay, even for a while, the departure of ? And if it be some long-known and favourite com-panion, conspicuous, perhaps, for fidelity, affection, and sagacity, whose bodily life is ebbing away, who is there who can resist the thought that he is not parting with the dying creature for ever, but that the same Creator who gave the spirit, and now commands it to return, will one day restore it, and bid it live again, or rather will never allow it really to die ? It is repulsive to our natural feeling to think that anything in the nature of spiritual life can be annihilated."

He referred again to this subject in a characteristic sermon he preached in York Minster on May 9, 1886. This sermon was afterwards published under the title of "The Curse of Cruelty." After giving out his text, "Thou, Lord, shalt save both man and beast" (Ps. xxxvi. 6), his introductory words were:—"It seems to me hardly possible that any one could be cruel to a dumb animal if he believed in the future existence of that creature after death. It is most likely that very few persons of those here present have ever thought of such a thing. The idea of it is now put before you, and I imagine that many would be at first disposed to deny the possibility, and many more the probability, of it. But it is certainly not impossible. On the contrary, it is probable, and there is good reason to believe that it is so." Such were his thoughts on this interesting though difficult question.

It was, however, against the practice of vivisection that this sermon was mainly directed, and to this reference is made elsewhere in these pages. There can be no doubt that the idea in his mind of the possibility, if not the probability, of their future existence added to the extraordinary kindliness and gentleness of his feelings towards all dumb animals, and caused him to regard them from a higher standpoint than he might otherwise have done. When so many subjects engrossed his attention, it was hard to say at times what was uppermost in his thoughts; certainly those which concerned him as a clergyman were never allowed to suffer.

During 1860 he found opportunities for editing a small work differing in character from those already referred to. This was a collection of hymns for

congregational use. Although the publication itself
was insignificant in outward form, and attracted but
little attention at the time, yet the subject was one
in which he always felt great interest. This little
compilation, which was styled "The Yorkshire
Hymn Book," was brought out, it must be remembered, before the many excellent hymnals now
obtainable had come into general use, and was
primarily designed by the editor for the use of his
own parishioners. In this, as in so many other
matters connected with his clerical work, he held
decided opinions, which he was never slow in his
endeavours to carry into effect. His view was, that
in the hymnals at that time procurable there were
always a considerable number of hymns that were
practically useless for ordinary village congrega-
tions. In this collection of his own he only inserted such as were to his thinking more or less of
a devotional character, and thus more in conso-
nance with the idea of worship. He was, moreover,
a great advocate, whether in preaching or in the
matter of hymnology, for the use of simple language
for country folk. For this reason he omitted from
his compilation many hymns, otherwise good, containing words likely to be unintelligible to un-
lettered people. Occasionally, however, he ventured
to alter a word of this kind to a simple one—a bold
step, perhaps—for the sake of being able to retain
the use of the hymn. Those hymns, too, that had
seemingly been written more for poetic effect than
for the main object in view were also excluded.

Under these heads he instanced such hymns as those beginning with the lines—" It was not, then, a poet's dream;" "Farewell, thou vase of splendour;" "In vain our fancy strives to paint;" "Mistaken souls that dream of heaven."

Verses which in certain hymns had equal claim to be admitted with the rest, and had been omitted in some other collections, he restored in his. Other hymns, again, which were generally restricted in their use to certain Church seasons, were made available at all times when it was found possible to do so. "Those, therefore," he said, "which are only suitable to those seasons are arranged for them, and those which are also suitable to them, though not solely so, may be selected at any time from the general list without their use at other times being precluded except at the expense of the Church system."

His interest in hymnology was kept up for many years, and only a few years before his death he contributed a selection from various sources of hymn-verses for each day of the year to the *Church Evangelist*, "for the sons and daughters of the Church." It was, too, a long-cherished wish of his that a "Book of Common Praise," as a companion to the "Book of Common Prayer," should be issued by authority, and he once, if not more than once, petitioned the Convocation of the York Province to take the matter up.

Another little work of a similar character—similar, I mean, in so far as it was intended for use in his own parish—was one which he brought out two or three years later upon the Church Catechism. The idea of it was in part suggested by his noticing the inability of children to answer some questions put by her Majesty's Inspectors, whose duty it was at that time to examine in religious as well as in secular knowledge. The ordinary questions of the Catechism were here broken up, and the whole expanded and explained by sub-questions. In those days he used from time to time, though always a difficulty to him, to catechise the children in church, and he found his enlarged Catechism of help on these occasions, for he used to confess that he never had the gift of being a good catechist, nor the patience to become a successful teacher ; so that it was also partly with the object of supplying an aid against this defect in himself, as well as for the teacher generally, that he framed this useful little manual. He also found it of great service to himself when preparing young people for Confirmation. Although possessed of no gift for teaching, yet whenever duty imposed this task upon him, his aim always was to be plain and definite in all he taught ; to the last, however, this was a work that was never congenial to him.

In face of the floods of corrupting publications that have been for years poured over the country, the question of providing wholesome literature for the masses is one that cannot but concern every clergyman, especially in these days. For Mr. Morris it seemed to have had, at all times, a special interest, more particularly with regard to literature suitable for Sunday.

In 1862 he made an attempt to start, and himself edit, a magazine for Sunday reading only. It is described in a prospectus he had printed as *The Sunday Penny Magazine;* it was to be a weekly publication, and was intended for readers of all classes. Literature was not so varied in those days as it is now, and it was stated in this same prospectus that there was not one among the cheap publications of the day, of a religious or moral character, that met the want that this one was designed to supply. There was nothing of the kind, certainly, in connection with the Church. He added in his circular : "The undertaking is in a cause which is second to none in importance, whether as regards nations or individuals."

It was emphatically not from lack of will or interest that he failed to carry into effect this cherished idea ; he was baffled solely for want of ways and means. On the subject of Sunday observance he always felt most strongly, and it was impossible to spend a single Sunday with him and not catch something of his spirit in this matter. The idea of the Continental Sunday was repulsive to him, and if ever we came to it in England he confessed he should look upon it as a bad sign.

Among his many minor works of a religious kind, one was brought out a few years later than the last-named, and was found useful for distribution among his parishioners and others. This was a small handbook called "The Paradise of the Soul;" it contained instructions and devotions for various occasions, and was mainly an adaptation for English Churchmen of extracts taken from the manual of the Roman Church, "The Garden of the Soul"— a book which Mr. Morris used to say contained so much that was good and beautiful, that it was much to be regretted that we had not something corresponding to it in the Church of England for general use.   Staunch Anglican though he was, he was ever ready to join hands with those outside the pale of the Church to which he belonged, and to stand with them on common ground whenever it could be done without sacrifice of principle.   No one deplored the unhappy divisions of Christendom more than he did, because, independently of other considerations, no one realised more fully than himself the fearful waste and loss of power caused by such divisions in the great conflict between the opposing forces of good and evil in the world.

We must again turn our thoughts back a year or two to touch very briefly on Mr. Morris's authorship of a series of volumes which it took some years to complete, though in one sense they were never completed.

New publications were constantly being produced at Mr. Fawcett's printing-house, and it was about the year 1864 that my father was engaged to write the letterpress for the most costly work Mr. Fawcett ever executed, and one which greatly extended his fame as a most enterprising and skilful engineer and printer. The publication to which I refer was the "County Seats of the Noblemen and Gentlemen of Great Britain and Ireland"—a work which has found its way into the houses of thousands of the nobility and gentry of this country. The task assigned to him was one very congenial to the author, for he had always had a taste for genealogy and family history, and his memory was such that there were few families of note in this country that he could not tell you something about. His old friend Sir Bernard Burke showed great interest in the publication of the volumes; for many years he and my father were in frequent correspondence on matters and tastes that were common to both. The custom, too, of sending presentation copies of their own works to each other was kept up for many years. In the first instance the "County Seats" came out in half-crown quarto numbers, and for some time the progress it made with the public was but slow. When a sufficient number of parts had been published, two large and handsomely bound volumes were issued; then, after an interval, two more; and again, after another interval, two further volumes, making six in all. For some time the course of the progress of the work did not appear to run quite smoothly, the publisher being changed more than once, while the title also underwent alteration. It is not easy to assign an adequate reason for the comparatively slow progress of the sale of the work in its earlier stages, but that it was not in the right hands for attaining success was plain. Accordingly it was determined to make a change in the method of publication, and ultimately the work was issued only to subscribers. This decision proved to be a right one. The Queen and several members of the Royal Family were among those who took copies, and there was but one opinion expressed as to the excellency of the plates and general appearance of the volumes. From beginning to end the drawings, which were coloured originals made on wood for the engraver, were the work of Mr. A. F. Lydon, an artist of no little ability, who had for many years been employed by Mr. Fawcett; the engraving also was executed under his direction, in the office at Driffield, though not actually by Mr. Lydon's own hand. It will give some idea of the magnitude of the undertaking when it is said that each plate as it appeared in the volumes required for its production, on an average, eight separate blocks for giving the various colours, so that about two thousand blocks in all were made, each of which was drawn by Mr. Lydon.

The circulation of the work reached ten thousand copies, the price to subscribers being nine guineas for the six volumes, so that this sale would realise not far short of £100,000. Only about a third of that sum was said to have fallen to Mr. Fawcett, out of which the whole cost of production, except possibly the binding, had to be defrayed. It is evident, therefore, that considerable profits must have accrued to those who undertook the publication of the work. At one time the sale of this and other works was so large that a difficulty was experienced in finding a sufficient number of old tea-chests—a favourite means for packing the volumes Mr. Fawcett produced—and the country around Driffield was scoured far and wide for these articles, and for some time a whole lorry-load was brought to his premises daily.

It was impossible, as has been said, that a work like this should ever be complete. One of the difficulties of the undertaking was to know where to begin, and which seats to select. As was stated by the author in his prefatory address—

" In describing the mansions of Old England, the difficulty that first occurs is to decide with which to begin where so many claim foremost attention. Here is one to which I could point where the same family has dwelt, generation after generation, for six hundred years ; and there another whose quaint Gothic architecture demands and receives our admiration. This is approached by a stately avenue of ancient elms, the *Cunabula gentis* of the cawing rooks, so well in keeping with all around, that exhibits in front a dazzling labyrinth of the most gorgeous coloured flowers. Here is one the novelty of whose structure arrests the eye, and there another the remarkable seclusion of whose situation at once engages our interest. Again we see one the vastness of whose size asserts for itself a hold on our notice on that account ; and yet again another, the present desolation of which, and decay of its former grandeur, asks a place in our sympathy for its owners in their fallen fortunes, and regret for its own mouldering state.

"In a word, these are the mansions of England, Ireland, Scotland, and Wales ; and such many of them have stood time out of mind—the Castle, the Moat, the Court, the Hall, the Grange, the House, the Priory, the Manor, the Park, the Abbey, the Place, the Cote, the Cottage—the 'ivy-mantled walls' of some, and the 'grey towers' and 'turrets high' of others, each and all suited to their various situations, and each and all characteristic of the favoured country in which we have such deep cause for thankfulness that our lot has been cast."

In one sense at least the work was a national one, for it gave a faithful delineation and description of some of the chief architectural glories of our own land, as they are the envy of other and more modern countries—those stately halls of our noblest and most historic families, whose annals and traditions have been for generations so closely bound up with the fortunes of the British Isles. Accompanying each plate was an account—often of necessity brief—of the descents of the various families to which the houses belonged, and of their own histories, together with curious and interesting legends attaching to some. Every variety of landscape and building was depicted in these volumes, commencing appropriately with the royal residence of Windsor, after which followed those of many feudal nobles, such as Arundel, Raby, Lumley, and Berkeley, with many more of lesser, though scarcely less interesting, note.

Of all the works with which the author's name was connected, there was none in which the illustrations were so elaborate as in this, and none which more severely taxed the resources of Mr. Fawcett's house of business; but the result must have exceeded the expectations of the author and producer of the work, for the sale ultimately extended far beyond their calculations.

To the year 1869 may be assigned the publication of two little booklets of a religious character. These were titled "None but Christ" and "Words of Wesley on Constant Communion." The former consisted of a number of clearly expressed, simple and practical thoughts on certain suitably chosen passages of Holy Scripture, the whole design being to quicken the spiritual life and build up the Christian in the rudiments of the faith. Among the texts selected were the following :—" I am with you alway," "Christ Jesus came into the world to save sinners;" "The love of Christ, which passeth knowledge;" "He is not far from every one of us;" "Whom have I in heaven but Thee?" "There is no peace, saith my God, to the wicked;" "Those that seek Me early shall find Me;" "Come unto Me, and I will give you rest." From beginning to end the little volume breathes a devotional and reverent spirit, and had it been made more widely known it could hardly fail to have had a greater circulation and usefulness. The writer of the little

manual made constant, if not daily, use of it himself, even to his latest years. His well-worn copy,
with numerous emendations, showed how · frequently it had been in his hands, and, we cannot
doubt, had spoken comfort to him..

The other tractate just mentioned was on a
subject which interested him deeply, namely, the
relation of the Wesleyan body to the Church of
England. For the old-fashioned members among
the Wesleyans who remained in communion with
the Church of their fathers he had every respect,
and was on friendly terms with those of them
with whom he came in contact, never compro-
mising himself, however, or deviating in the slightest
degree from his own principles. He deplored the
lamentable falling away of many modern Methodists
from the teaching of their founder, and the object
of the publication, " Words of Wesley on Constant
Communion," was designed to remind them of their
duty with regard to the performance of the most
hallowed religious act in which they could engage.
The pages consisted almost wholly of extracts from
Mr. Wesley's sermon on the subject. It was, too,
a matter to which Mr. Morris frequently alluded in
his own sermons. At the end of this little book he
added :—"There is, I believe, not one argument that
I have been in the habit of using to bring you to a
proper sense of your duty in this respect which you
do not now see that he (John Wesley) has used
before me. And why ? Because he has taken
Scripture for his text and has gone by it, and I

have done the same. And it is not of any 'doubtful interpretation,' but one that is as plain as the
sun in the heavens."

Although, as I said, Mr. Morris had respect for
the old-fashioned Wesleyans who still remained
faithful and loyal to the Church of their founder,
he regarded very differently the more modern
developments of political Dissent. To those who
advocated these principles he was most resolutely
opposed, and wrote at great length through a long
course of years in defence of the Church against
her many foes; indeed, some of his most trenchant
and telling letters and pamphlets were written in
antagonism to those who, for one reason or another,
levelled their attacks against the Church of England; on this ground he always took a firm stand,
as his writings on the subject clearly show. On
this point, however, we cannot here dwell further,
but must pass on to draw attention to other works
connected with this period.

To one who, like Mr. Morris, had such a strong
abhorrence of cruelty towards animals, there never
are lacking channels for doing good work in the
cause of humanity. He was literally ingenious in
discovering ways for giving effect to his humane
and kindly feelings towards his friends in fur,
feather, or any other garb; friends they indeed
seemed to him, and as such he ever regarded them.
Whether he benefited them most by means of his
pen or by a more direct interference in their favour
it would be hard to say. In any case, he made his

influence very widely felt on their behalf ; he was quick to seize an opportunity for saying or doing something for them, and this quite as much in what are generally deemed small matters as in those of greater consequence. He would no more have passed by without concern the suffering of an insect any more than he would that of a horse that was being cruelly oppressed by its driver.

It may have been the passing of the Education Act of 1870, which at that time increased people's interest in the training of the young all through the country, that gave my father the idea of introducing the subject of humanity to animals into the curriculum of schools, thus laying in the minds of the young principles of kindness and gentleness towards those animals with which they had or might have to do in their daily work. To this end he began to compile, in the year 1872, a series of reading-books for schools, which he called the " Humanity Series of Schoolbooks," consisting of six small volumes graduated so as to suit the six standards in elementary schools. They were probably the first series of the kind ever published, and although the volumes were not illustrated, and their outward appearance was hardly worthy of so interesting and important a subject, they nevertheless had for many years a considerable circulation. Had more attention been paid to the general external attractiveness of the books, and a few minor improvements made in the contents, there can be little doubt that their usefulness would have kept pace with the great advance of the educational movement in more recent years. As it was, they were unaltered, either in outward form or as regards their subject-matter, from the date of their publication down to the time of Mr. Morris's death. The late Lord Selborne, for whom my father had a profound admiration, showed no slight interest in this series of schoolbooks, and highly approved of the idea. It was stated in the preface that the series was intended to be supplementary to ordinary school reading-books, "and was only thought of to supply lessons on the great duty of humanity to animals, while at the same time the danger of monotony, if the lessons had been confined to that one subject, has been avoided by the introduction of other topics for the encouragement of every good word and work." Among those to whom the editor expressed his obligation for permission to make extracts from their writings was the Rev. Richard Wilton, rector of Londesborough, "my good friend and neighbour," as he called him, many of whose beautiful sonnets and poems graced the pages of volumes. The sale of these reading-books more than realised Mr. Morris's expectations, and thus to a great extent fulfilled the object for which they were intended in many of our large and populous centres, as well as in remote country villages.

It must not be supposed that the large demands made upon his time by his incessant literary work cut Mr. Morris off from taking an interest in his neighbours and the events of everyday life that took place around him. He was no recluse, but fully alive to his social duties, and endeavoured to fulfil them at all times. Of all the friendships, how-ever, which he formed through life, there was none more enduring nor more highly prized than those which dated from his school and college days. In these cases years only tended to bind the knot more tightly. There was but one thing, indeed, which was strong enough to separate these early alliances, and it is a power which none of us can withstand.

Whether it was through a natural disinclination to do so, or through the constant and increasing activities of his literary work, certain it is that from middle life onwards my father did not make many close friends; possibly, however, those that he did so make were on that account the more thought of and appreciated. Of these friends of his later years there was none for whom he had a greater regard and affection than his near neighbour and brother clergyman, the Rev. R. Wilton, now Canon of York, to whom I just now referred. The two had much in common, especially on those subjects which were nearest to the hearts of both. In religious views there were no wide divergencies between them, and in their love of country scenes and country pursuits and tastes they were entirely at one.

It was a delightful and invigorating walk over the breezy wold from Nunburnholme to Londesborough. The few hundred feet of ascent was as nothing to one who was so light of foot as Mr. Morris, even

when advancing years stole on apace. It may easily
be imagined, therefore, that the walk was not seldom
made, and this the more when it was known that
at the end of the journey a kindly and genial welcome, coupled with a lively and friendly interchange
of ideas, was always in store for him. For many
years the two friends met periodically at each
other's houses to discuss religious, parochial, natural
history, and other subjects which were likely to be
to their mutual advantage when thus hammered out
between them. When these meetings took place,
Mr. Morris, according to his methodical ways,
generally had a carefully prepared list of questions
on various topics that had occurred to him as suitable for discussion since the previous meeting. But
over and above these alternate periodical visitations,
many pleasant social gatherings took place between
the two families after Mr. Wilton came to Londesborough in 1866. These were joyous and happy
days ; and not only so, but on several occasions,
when Mr. Wilton was spending a few hours at
Nunburnholme, something was casually seen or
heard in or about the Rectory which afforded a
theme to his poetic and tasteful mind, and the
result was shortly afterwards given forth in one of
those scholarly sonnets for which his name became
in course of time widely known. Perhaps it may
not be out of place if I here quote two out of several
such sonnets, linked as they are with his friend in
ways and pursuits peculiarly his own. One was
headed, "On seeing some birds in winter feeding at

the study window of Rev. F. O. Morris, Nunburnholme Rectory." The lines flow thus :—

" Trust him, ye gentle birds, of various wing ;
    Flock to his window, flutter round your friend :
    Through these inclement days ye may depend
On his prompt hand the punctual crumbs to bring.
And oh ! remember when, in sunny spring,
    Your earliest lays to bounteous heaven ascend,
    Some grateful notes for Christmas fare to blend,
And at your patron's casement sweetly sing.
For not alone when gusts of winter blow
    He loves you, but through all the changing year ;
To his kind care thanks manifold you owe ;
    His voice secures for you a nation's ear ;
Then trust him when the air is thick with snow,
    And warble to him when the skies are clear."

The inspiring cause which kindled the poetic
fancy in the other example which I will give was
the sight of the collections of butterflies arranged in
Mr. Morris's cabinets. The thoughts evoked by the
examination of these specimens of Nature's handiwork, in all their variegated forms and colours, found
expression in the following words :—

" In ordered sequence and of rainbow dyes,
    Rank after rank they passed before my view,
    Our British butterflies—bright with each hue
Of autumn leaf, fair flower, or sunset skies,
Prismatic tints they flash upon our eyes
    From yonder Light of lights, Divine and true,
    Who lends an insect's wing its gold or blue
Or purple, which all art of man outvies.
Thus yearly have these winged blooms unfurled
    Their streaks and stains, each after its own kind,
Since first they fluttered o'er the new-made world,
    Tiny reflections of the Eternal Mind,

Tokens that boundless Beauty reigns above,
Unchanging Order and exhaustless Love."

These frequent visits to Londesborough my father thoroughly enjoyed, and not less so those which his kind friend and neighbour paid to Nunburnholme. Although not easily depressed, he must often have found such friendly intercourse a help and a solace in times of difficulty or trial. Many of these pleasant meetings Canon Wilton alluded to when writing to an old friend of his—G. M. Let one or two extracts speak for themselves. Thus, for instance, in a letter dated September 30, 1868, he makes mention of a visit Mr. Morris paid him the previous day :—

"Yesterday my friend Mr. Morris came up (with Mrs. Morris, whom my wife took possession of) for an afternoon's talk and tea with me. I wish you could have seen and joined us over the fire in my cosy study, discussing the difficulties of Darwinism ! Mr. Morris reposed in my easiest of easy-chairs, with his foot resting on the fireplace on a level with his head—*more Oxoniensi vel Cantabrigiensi*—while I leaned back in a more dignified manner in my American rocking-chair, reading aloud his address to the British Association, which perhaps you saw mentioned in the *Times*. The happiness of my companion was complete ; indeed, he told me there was nothing he enjoyed more than to hear one of his own papers read aloud to him by a sympathetic friend ! Of course we often paused to discuss interesting points ; in fact, between us we quite demolished that heterodox philosopher (Darwin).

He had nothing to say for himself. We silenced him utterly. It is no use for him to ask us to call ourselves cousins with ourang-outangs. We will not admit that we are descended from a monkey, or a frog, or an atom. But seriously, we had a very interesting talk, and Mr. Morris is able to throw much light, from his peculiar studies, on this question of the day. . . . Other subjects of theology and literature were discussed, as well as a good Yorkshire tea, and so ended a pleasant evening."

When the Nightingale made its way to the valley of Nunburnholme, which it did in the summer of 1868, this, as a matter of course, demanded a special visit from the rector of Londesborough, who records it in his happy way when writing to this same friend at a distance. On this occasion the start was made at nine o'clock in the evening, with the moon shining and wild roses in bloom—fitting accompaniments for the party who went, as he expressed it, "to pay their respects to the new-comer."

And again, in another letter, Mr. Wilton wrote of one of these many friendly calls :—

"Mr. Morris has just been up to see me, and has done me good with half-an-hour's pleasant chat. He wants me to go down with my dear wife and meet a few friends at his house on Thursday evening. It *is* a descent, I assure you, into the pretty valley of Nunburnholme. You go down an immensely long steep hill, quite a mile from the top to the bottom. It is called most appropriately 'Totterdown.' Fortunately we have the steadiest

M

horse in the world, or at least on the Wolds, a steady man, and a patent brake. I am contemplating one or two papers to be called 'Walks on the Yorkshire Wolds.' My first walk will be to Nunburnholme, and the subject the pleasures and advantages of natural history. I am at this moment surrounded by all Mr. Morris's 'British Birds,' 'Nests and Eggs of British Birds,' 'British Butterflies,' and 'British Moths' (a famous confusion they make in my room), and think I shall be able to write an interesting paper on this subject, which is so congenial to my own tastes."

For a number of years after he came to Nunburnholme my father used to see a good deal of another friend of long standing whose tastes accorded with his own. This was the Rev. George Rudston Read, the rector of Sutton-on-Derwent, in the East Riding. Mr. Read was a keen entomologist, and had an excellent collection of butterflies and moths; this alone would have sufficed to form a bond of union. Many were the "field-days" which the two friends had together in the neighbourhood of Sutton-on-Derwent, while the capture and interchange of entomological specimens were on these occasions numerous, and not seldom some "scarce articles" passed between them. These moth-hunting visits were known to Mr. Read's family as 'camphor-days,' and frequently exciting chases and catches took place by day and night. On one occasion, when "sugaring" at night in Langwith Wood—a noted locality for insects—Mr. Read and my father

were suddenly pounced upon by some of Lord Wen-
lock's keepers, who at first took them for poachers.
It is true they had nets, but no guns! Great was
the disappointment of the keepers when, instead of
being about to seize, as they thought, two "old
hands," they discovered a couple of country parsons,
and magistrates to boot, in pursuit of game indeed,
but game which keepers had never before heard of
as liable to be hunted by anybody, and of a kind
which they no doubt thought it the height of folly
for any one in his senses to take any trouble about.
These, however, were not the only times when the
two entomologists met.

From time to time they sat together on the magis-
terial bench at the Pocklington Petty Sessions. On
these occasions Mr. Read would sometimes bring his
son with him, then a boy of some ten years of age.
These days are still well remembered. Occasionally,
when an unimportant case was brought on which did
not require special attention, Mr. Morris left it in the
hands of his brother magistrates, and himself wrote
letters as fast as he could—an occupation for which
he seemed at all times ready, not to say eager. One
day, during an interval of this kind, and wishing
at the same time to amuse his young friend, Mr.
Morris drew a life-like sketch of the boy's father,
net in hand, giving chase to a butterfly, and in the
midst of his wild excitement he depicted him in the
act of coming to grief over a thorn-bush. Needless to
say this diversion had the desired effect, and sent the
boy into a fit of laughter before the assembled court.

In the eyes of every entomologist Mr. Read's collection of butterflies was famous from the fact that it contained one of the very few specimens captured in England of the scarce Swallow-Tail Butterfly (*Papilio podalirius*); this valued insect was caught by his brother, W. H. Rudston Read, Esq., when a boy at Eton in 1826, and from it the drawing was made for the figure in Mr. Morris's work on British Butterflies.

IX

CORRESPONDENCE

To few private individuals could it have fallen to have carried on a correspondence at once so varied and extensive as was the case with my father. Not only from all parts of the country did he receive communications, but from people of all sorts and conditions. To every letter he replied by return of post, except on Saturdays, when he rarely, if ever, posted a letter, unless assured that it would be delivered the same day; for he had a conscientious objection to the Sunday post, and under no circumstances would he receive or despatch a letter on that day.

Every letter that he received upon any point bearing on natural history he scrupulously preserved. Of these, many of the most interesting have been already made public, either in Mr. Morris's books and pamphlets or in the newspapers; it will not, therefore, be necessary here to allude to many of them; indeed, out of so varied a collection it would be impossible to do so. Such as are here given must be regarded as typical of others. Some seven or eight years before his death he took it into his head to try and ascertain the actual number of letters bearing on natural history only that he had received. Having counted up to thirteen thousand, he gave up the task, no doubt thinking it a great waste of time to proceed further with it merely for the sake of gratifying his curiosity. Of his own letters, the most interesting were some of those which he wrote for publication to various journals and magazines. Those which he penned to private individuals were for the most part brief, and devoid of those features which would entitle him to be called an entertaining letter-writer; this may have been due to want of time and care, but more probably it was owing to a lack of that rare power which is needed to make an interesting writer of letters.

Of the thousands of letters on points of natural history which he accumulated, there were few better worth preserving than those addressed to him by Thomas Edward, the famous naturalist, of Banff. Many of these were inserted in the pages of the *Naturalist* from time to time, and some were afterwards introduced into Smiles' interesting life of that remarkable man. Many of Edward's letters were written to Mr. Morris when the "History of British Birds" was going through the press in monthly parts, and they nearly always contained facts which could be, and very often were, made use of. I cannot but give one or two here which Mr. Smiles had probably not seen when he wrote Edward's life; the first of them turns upon a history of a spider which Edward had kept for a long time experimentally without food. He writes :—

"BANFF, *November* 28, 1852.

"You will see by one of the printed slips of paper which I have taken the liberty of enclosing along with this, that I have in my possession an animal which has lived for a considerable length of time without food. The fact of which the printed paper already alluded to is a copy was published in the *Banffshire Journal* about seven weeks ago. Since then I have been almost worried to death about the affair. I have had the honour of being denominated an 'ass' for supposing that any creature could live so long without food. I have likewise had the pleasure of being branded with the laudable title of 'fool' because I could not, and cannot yet, swallow the dogmas of certain individuals here, who argue strongly that the whole empty space within the case is replete with invisible insects, on which the spider has lived ; so that, according to these gentlemen, instead of lacking, he has had an abundant supply of food. Again, other of my opponents say, and affirm their saying as a positive and undeniable fact, that the spider can and does, when deprived of other food, draw nourishment from the air, confined and free, and thereby sustains life by invisible means. What is meant, I suppose, is that this animal can suck food from the elements, and breathe, as a pump does, water from the earth. If so, what is the use of the sucker ? With respect to the invisible theory, I have likewise no faith in it either.

"My opponents belong to the class generally termed gentlemen. Their story is believed. I am a poor man, and am discredited in consequence. From these circumstances I have at last come to the conclusion of soliciting the opinions of as many eminent naturalists on the subject as possible, and with this view I have ventured to address you first. Will you, therefore, be so kind as to intimate what you think of the matter? Do spiders live, or can they live, on invisible insects? Do spiders, or can they, draw nourishment from the atmosphere so as to enable them to sustain life without any other food?

.   .   .   .

"I may add that the spider has changed his skin *three times* during his confinement, and each time has *increased in size*. This fact my friends laugh to scorn by stating that such could not have been the case if the animal had not been supplied with an abundance of food.

"Hoping that you will grant my humble request at your leisure,   THOMAS EDWARD.

"*P.S.—The spider is still alive.* My notion is, that the food of this creature consists of the blood or juice of animals, and not moisture drawn from the air.—T. E."

To this letter Mr. Morris wrote a speedy reply, with a characteristic request that the spider might have his freedom. He received shortly the following from Thomas Edward :—

"BANNF, *December* 6, 1852.

"MY DEAR SIR,—I beg to return my most grateful thanks for the kind manner and promptitude with which you have answered my letter referring to the spider.

"I am sorry, very sorry, to say, however, that I cannot in the meantime comply with your feeling request—that of giving him his liberty.

"I wish to ascertain, if possible, how long he will, or can, live without food.[1] That he feels *no pain* from the want of food as yet I do think, from the circumstance that he has shown no symptoms of it as far as I can, or have been able to, detect; and I can add that he is frequently, very frequently, looked at both *night* and day.

"My intention is to give him his freedom, and to supply him with food also, whenever he becomes restless and ventures to wander about the case, which in my opinion will be the sign of his feeling 'the keen demands of appetite.'

"Again begging to return my best thanks for your kindness, I remain, my dear Sir, your most obedient servant, THOMAS EDWARD."

Thomas Edward was a man of action and endurance as well as of observation. A few years later he sent my father a long account of an evening

[1] It was reported that the creature lived in this way for a whole year.

spent in a wood near Banff moth-hunting; he described the place as a most romantic and secluded
spot, close to the side of a river, and right well he
tells his tale. This communication was inserted in
the pages of the *Naturalist*, which Mr. Morris at
that time edited, and in it the "Scotch Naturalist"
alludes to his extraordinary passion and fondness for
all living creatures in these words:—"I have, and
it would seem that I have been born with it, a most
inordinate, and perhaps unexampled, either in this
country or in any other, predilection for everything
of this kind, whatsoever be the number of their feet
or legs, or whether they have any or none at all;
all is one to me providing they are of Nature's
handiwork." Accordingly one summer evening he
proceeded with his collecting-box and other apparatus to his hunting-ground. He was alone, as was
his wont on such occasions, and he rejoiced in the
freedom of his nightly excursion, which refreshed
him after his daily task was done, for he was by
trade a shoemaker and had to work for his bread.
He had a delightfully natural way of describing
all he saw and did. After relating the manner of
his movements in capturing his specimens, this
ardent lover of Nature graphically proceeds with
his narrative:—

"So on I went, and at the same time listening to
the doleful and melancholy wailing of the Owl, the
spinning-wheel-like *birr, birr* of the Night-Jar, and
the occasional barking of the fleet and lightsome
little Roe, the pride of our lowland woods, as they

now, too, had stealthily crept out of their secret retreats to pursue their night's peregrinations, and now and then all the while boxing another culprit. In this fashion time, as it always does on such and similar occasions, passed rapidly—too rapidly, but pleasantly—away ; nay, flew unconsciously as it were, so that the shades of night were now fast settling down, but yet I thought not of home or giving up the chase. I still could in some measure see the objects of my solicitude and search as they passed between the branches of the trees and betwixt me and the sky, or dropped from the luxuriant foliage overhead, or darted like an arrow or shadow by, or lightly fanned the tops of the long and waving grasses and graceful ferns—all pursuing their little joys." After taking a number of good specimens, Edward was proceeding happily and carelessly along, thinking to himself how fortunate he had been, and whistling some of his favourite old Scotch melodies, when he was suddenly brought to a standstill. Something very large and extraordinarily long appeared before him in his path, moving along towards him. "Well," he writes, "if every limb did not shake like an aspen leaf, and every bone in me did not crack and quake with downright fear, as I beheld the hideous-looking beast. The whistling, as you may easily guess, instantly ceased, and, coming to a standstill, I could not help wondering, as I beheld the moving mass drawing slowly, it is true, yet steadily, towards me, what in the world the creature could possibly be ; what grizzly apparition or midnight monster or unearthly thing it was, and how, or by what strange means, it had come there. What was to be done ? or what could I do ? I was totally unarmed—not so much as a sixpenny blade upon me. 'Tis quite true I possessed a good *piece*, but what of that ? It was, and unluckily too, nearly two miles off, and could not, therefore, be called to my aid."

At one time Edward thought of taking to flight, but his courage got the mastery of his weaker feelings, and he determined to stand it out, come what might. Accordingly, in order the better to prepare for action and see what the beast really was, he says :—

" I would now and again take another sly peep at him, to reconnoitre, as it were, to see if anything like *horns* or a *cloven foot* stood in the way ; when lo and behold! instead of one, I beheld—beheld what ?—why, no fewer than three—three large and full Badgers and not devils, each a short distance behind the other, and the foremost only about sixteen yards from where I stood."

The rest is soon told. Edward, who wished to capture one, if not all three, of the Badgers, gave chase, for on seeing him they instantly turned and made off at the best speed they could, two of them quickly disappearing down a steep declivity. The third animal Edward came up with, and in a sudden frantic endeavour to administer a stunning blow with his foot, he himself fell down with terrific force upon the hard path below, receiving thereby a bump on the back of his head as large, according to him, as a turkey's egg. Thus his moth-hunting expedition was brought to a speedy end for that night; but adventures such as this in nowise daunted him in his enthusiastic researches in the domain of natural history.

It would seem that this animated description of Edward's encounter brought back to my father some vivid recollections of his school-days in connection with these animals, which at that time were pretty commonly met with ; for, on Edward's making the assertion that, though Badgers can bite desperately, they cannot run fast, Mr. Morris added the following note of his own :—"Can't they ? Some of my schoolfellows will have with me, I entertain no doubt—at least I can answer for myself—a considerable amount of difference of opinion about this. What a tale I could unfold of school-days !"

Thomas Edward's communications were always to be depended on for accuracy of description, as well as being most interesting reading, but we cannot here dwell longer on them.

The agitation connected with the passing of the Bird Protection Acts naturally brought Mr. Morris many communications from those who sympathised with him, and they came from people of all classes. Occasionally he was roundly abused by some 'sportsman,' so called, who wrote, perhaps wisely in these cases, under cover of an incognito. By no means always, however, were his anonymous correspondents on the side of the enemy. I will

here quote one epistle from a well-wisher, and I
will do so *verbatim et literatim,* only suppressing the
place-names ; it was written apparently towards the
end of July 1874, and is as follows :—

"Sir, as regards Preserving the Gold finch or
commonly called the Red Cap Which I ham a ware
that the Bird Catcher is not allowed to catch untill
the first of next month. Well Sir is the Public
allowed to distroy them ? I answer No. Very
well then what is our County Police doing when
they are allowing the Nests to be taken in all directions. The first nest that I New of being taken
Was at W. by a labrur and brought to P. when
they all died but one And then down to M. Which
is one of the Principle Breeding places in this
district, And a place besides in the Vilage and
allow Nests to be taken. And I believe there is a
Cage hung with five young ones in and the old
ones feeding them through wires, And men coming
to seek Bird lime to Catch the Old ones with and
then to B. where it should be looked after at once
Because last year there was about 30 Birds Caught
a Week before the 1 of August, And it will be
the case again if not looked after, Because they
have got some Allready. The most birds is bred
at E. I have no dought they would be eight pairs
of Red Caps Breed there, And every pair having
two Nests, And every nest a average of 4 Birds,
And all these makes to B. Paster Joiny the Mill,
and the Catchers lay waite for them. Therse are

the men Places for Red Caps which should be looked after at once, yours truly a fancier."

Another letter from a correspondent in Wiltshire, written in 1873, on the same topic as the foregoing, though expressed in a way better calculated to satisfy one of Her Majesty's Inspectors of Schools, gave a long account of the ways of certain bird-catchers near Bristol. After advocating a tax on clap-nets, the licensing of bird-shops, with other precautionary measures, the writer went on to express his opinion of the Act which had recently been passed for the protection of birds. In the schedule of names he held that it was desirable to give various designations for the same bird, and in support of his opinion he instanced a case in point. He had a garden, and in the spring the Bullfinches made raids upon it, doing no little damage. Mentioning this to a neighbour, he was met with the remark, "There is none gets into mine; I keep the door looked, so that neither bulls nor cows get in"! He was reminded that it was the birds that were meant. "Oh," he replied, "you mean the 'Tawney Hoops,' not the Bull—what do you call them? Oh, finchers; ay, just so"!

When it was said, as it was so commonly, that the damage done by birds was a "serious loss to farmers and gardeners," and that to protect the birds was only to do so at other people's expense, such letters as the following from a large market-gardener came as most welcome and valuable testimony to Mr. Morris with regard to the great usefulness of birds, and out of such evidence he always contrived to make capital for his friends the Sparrows and other small birds:—

"HESTON, HOUNSLOW, *December* 22, 1879.

" MY DEAR SIR,—Knowing the great interest you take in birds must be my excuse for troubling you with this letter. I have seven acres of garden ground, on which I cultivate fruit for market, and for the last twenty-five years have used all the means in my power to protect all kinds of birds, and the result has been that I have had better crops of fruit than my neighbours and my trees more free from blight. I am in the habit of feeding the birds all through the winter, but, alas! this year all my little friends seem gone, and the food that I give them remains for a long time untouched. A pet Robin who has for three years come when I called it, and perched on my finger, and eaten from my hand, came to me the other day with a broken leg, having been caught in a trap, and the next day a tame Blackbird came without a tail and his leg broken. Both died very soon after. Surely there ought to be a law to protect birds from cruelty as well as animals, for I feel convinced that neither farmer nor gardener can do without them. I beg to remain, dear Sir, yours very truly,

" F. E. TRIMMER."

Every naturalist must deplore the way in which our rarer birds are being gradually exterminated, when many of them, if left to themselves, would breed and become an ornament to the country; they sorely need all the help that Bird Protection Societies and Acts of Parliament can give them. As a matter of course it gave my father the greatest satisfaction whenever he heard of the increase of any of the more uncommon kinds of birds, although such news came rather after the manner of angels' visits, the reports sent to him being for the most part of the contrary telling. It can be imagined, therefore, with what pleasure he received such an account as was sent him in 1881 by his friend, Mr. A. F. Astley, which he had from an acquaintance who owned a good part of Achill Island, in the west of Ireland, and was a great protector of the birds in that region. His facts are such interesting ones that I venture to quote some of them. He writes :—

" I am glad to say that the Choughs are increasing here. I saw two large flocks of from twenty-five to thirty-five last week. They are very susceptible of cold, and appear to suffer in a severe winter. Achill is in the direct line of the Gulf Stream, and the winters are warmer by several degrees than any part of Europe except the south of Spain and Italy. To this fact I attribute the large number of Choughs we have. . . . I have had several of them as pets which were taken from an old castle in which they had built for many years. I have had one now for the last five years. He flies about the place during the day, but always comes in to sleep in the kitchen

N

at night. He is a most interesting pet, and knows me perfectly. . . . He will not leave the house on a wet day, and is equal to a weather-glass. The favourite food of the Chough in a wild state is the grub of what is commonly called here the 'Daddy-Long-Legs.' I have shot one some years ago for my Eagle, and found its craw full of them. I watched mine the other day near the hall-door, and saw him draw eight or nine from the grass in a few minutes. . . . If he sees me he will try to feed me, and often puts a piece of bread to my mouth, as some Parrots will try to do. Several of those I had flew away at last with the wild ones. The best plan is partly to clip the wing the first year.

"I have now three Peregrine Falcons a year old. . . . They breed in the same cliffs as the Choughs and Eagles. We have still a good many of the latter. I do not shoot them. I had an Eagle for twenty-five years. She was much attached to me. She laid when nineteen years old two eggs, and the following year four. I put goose eggs under her, and she brought out two. One of them died; the other, with care from us, lived, and grew to be a fine goose. It in turn laid, and I put fertile eggs under it which it brought out. The Eagle adopted the new brood, and taught them all to eat meat. It almost seems to be incredible, but they have been seen by hundreds doing so."

And again, in a subsequent letter, the same correspondent added :—

"We have still several Golden Eagles in Achill—

some time ago I saw three at once over my house. They are seen mostly in couples. The Wild Swan (Bewick) frequents our lakes. I counted one hundred and ten in one flock the year before last. Last winter the most I saw at once was fifty-four. The Eagles killed one of them."

Out of such a number of letters it is not easy to make selections when so many seem to claim notice. At best I can only hope to cite a few typical ones which must serve as examples of hundreds of others. Many are those which record deeds of kindness towards friends in fur and feather. Here, for instance, are two from a lady correspondent in Devonshire which contain some interesting facts. She says :—

" I live in a detached country house, and make a practice of feeding various birds from the windows. On the lawn we often see Wood-Pigeons, Magpies, Jays, Rooks, and two kinds of Woodpeckers, all close to the house. One Rook, who is an almost constant attendant, has apparently lost part of the upper mandible of the bill ; the lower part has, in consequence, grown prodigiously, curling upwards towards the forehead of the bird, who has, of course, much difficulty in feeding. He takes up grains of Indian-corn with his head placed on the ground sideways. I believe he roosts here always alone, and does not resort to any rookery. . . . A pair of Nuthatches often appear close to the windows, upon the ledges sometimes, and take nuts placed there for them ; they also come into the bedrooms and sitting-rooms in search for nuts. I have had poles placed against the windows, close to the glass ; on these I nail Turkey figs, Brazil nuts cut in halves, cocoa-nuts and chestnuts, sometimes slices of apples. All these are highly appreciated by the Nuthatches, and also the various Tits, who appear to prefer them to the bones usually offered to them by kind friends. Chaffinches and Robins also claim their share. Outside our window (on a stand) I have placed a parrot's cage, replenished with these and other delicacies ; in this all the smaller birds can regale themselves undisturbed by the Sparrows, who are unable or unwilling to pass through the wires. During some late severe weather a hen Chaffinch, that had been constantly fed by the servants, came into the passage every evening, and allowed itself to be taken up and put into a basket to sleep.

" A few years ago, when riding under a large holly-tree, hearing a lamentable squeaking over my head, I looked about, and saw a large mouse suspended on a horizontal spray of bramble by a thorn run through its tail, no doubt done by a Butcher-Bird. I released the mouse, which ran away, none the worse apparently.

" I have omitted to mention that the Cole-Tits watch the various windows, and, on their being open, fly in on to our hands, and take pieces of almond from our fingers."

And again the same correspondent subsequently wrote :—

" I have placed nuts in little baskets close to the

glass of the windows, which the Nuthatches fetch away. I have closely watched the manner in which they take the nuts up in their bills. They seem to have a little difficulty in this if the nut is large, and I observe that they moisten the shell of the nut plentifully with their tongues, so as to make it adhesive apparently, and more safely carried. I have bored holes in a log of wood and placed nuts therein, also almonds. Sometimes these are broken and eaten on the spot, but more often carried away or buried on the lawn. Numbers of young nut-trees are growing in my garden, evidently planted by them. I once saw a Nuthatch, after burying a nut, bring a fallen leaf and fix it over the spot, probably as a mark.

"Some months ago a member of my family saw a rat on the lawn 'stalking' a Blackbird. At last it sprang on the back of the bird and killed it by biting it on the head."

Sad to say, a large class of the letters which reached him had tales of cruelty to unfold in various shapes and forms; for correspondents knew that they would find in him a ready sympathiser, and never did he turn a deaf ear to any appeal of this kind that was made to him. He always took action upon it, and that promptly, in some way or other.

The letter which I will next quote is an example of many more of a similar kind that he received. It came from a correspondent of many years' standing, and had to do with the suppression

of sparrow and starling matches, which cause so
much disgust in the minds of every humane person.   The letter was written in 1880, and ran
thus :—

"Eleven years ago I had the pleasure. of corresponding with you, and communicated to you the
full and accurate account of the murder of twelve
dozen sparrows and three dozen linnets at Eastbourne, which, after being packed in cages until half
suffocated, were put one by one by a lantern-jawed
man into a small spring trap like a quarter-of-a-
pound cigar-box, and so 'shot up' into the air, and
'shot-down' by noble (?) sportsmen, eighteen yards
off, with a large-muzzled gun, one of whom covered
the iron trap with his gun before the string was
pulled. You quoted my letter in one of yours to
the *Times* afterwards, and, as you remember, the
Hon. Grantley Berkeley took up the running, and
from the combined labours of all who joined you
in condemning bird murder, and your own and
Mr. Berkeley's influence, the 'Gun Act' was passed.
Read enclosed advertisement No. 1 :—'A big day's
shooting, at which twenty dozen starlings at least'
are advertised to be shot to-morrow, and they
will be dead, I fear, after you have received this
letter. See advertisement No. 2, which announces
that 'J. Spurgeon, Hackney-Wick, will be on the
ground with twenty dozen starlings and forty dozen
sparrows.' Literally for heaven's sake, stop this
infamous massacre of one of our prettiest and
most domestic home birds. Starlings are being

domesticated even in London. Outside my bed-
room window in the suburbs there is a large tree,
which is a great nuisance as regards making the
room dark, but which is the comfort of my life.
It is a kind of early club or breakfast-house for
birds of all kinds, and from daylight onwards the
chatter of the sparrows and low pipe of the starlings
and twittering of other birds is delightful. And
these hallowed precincts were threatened. A man
came to me one evening at Christmas, and, I must
say, very civilly asked leave to net my ivy for 'a
sparrow-shoot' on Boxing Day. He was astonished
when I told him he should not do it for a hundred
guineas. Now comes the question, Where do these
starlings and sparrows for matches come from?
Stolen! For I say that a man has no more right to
come into my premises and take my birds than I
have to go into his garden and take his flowers, and
we all know what a row 'the working man' makes
if his rights are infringed. Sparrow and starling
matches mean beer, betting, cruelty, and drunkenness, as much as Hurlingham matches mean
cruelty, betting, tea, champagne cup, idleness, and
flirting. All these so-called sports are lowering
our national character. The monstrous over-pre-
serving and murderous battues have caused the
general public to look with perfect indifference to
the abolition of the Game Laws, though their overthrow is brought about by men who know little
of the subject, and who promote their cause more
from spite than principle. A short law is now

wanted, making the setting of any snare, or using any engine-net, or other instrument for the capture of birds on any lands, common or private lands, without the consent of all parties who shall be owners, lessees, and occupiers, or in or upon any public road without the consent of adjoining owners, lessees, and occupiers, . . . punishable with fine, or imprisonment in default. Why should not boys be punished for stealing my birds as much as for stealing my fruit? There is a great deal of mawkish sentimentality about punishing boys and village lads for trespass. . . . The police in many rural districts are shamefully negligent about shooting in season without a license—particularly on a Sunday—and out of season, bird-snaring out of season, common firing, and other offences. . . . You may use this letter as you please; only don't publish my name, as it is very well known, and I am afraid my dogs may be poisoned, or some other spiteful action done against my pets of land and air. I will tell you what I will do, and it is this, namely, if you will have a small council of such men as yourself, Mr. Grantley Berkeley, Mr. Frank Buckland, and others whom you know, I will do all the work quick enough."

The following was sent to my father by a lady in Shropshire, and shows how much can be done with animals by kindness, even in cases where we might least expect it. It forcibly reminds one of the many similar feats performed by Mrs. Brightwen, and told in her delightful volumes, showing how

"Wild Nature" may be, as she expresses it, "won by kindness":—

"I see, in your book on 'British Birds,' you state that the Kestrel is easily tamed. Our bird was taken from a nest last year, and put into a cage out of doors, for a few days only, until fledged. He was then turned out, and flew across the park into the woods, and was seen no more for some days, when he returned, found his way into the house, and has never voluntarily left it since. We often turn him out, and see him a mile or more from the house, but soon after find him searching for an open window by which he may reach the dining-room, where he lives by preference, perching on a picture-frame, but always coming on to my husband's arm when called, even though with thirty people at dinner, and through the glare of lamps and candles. He invariably twitters a sort of soft song when we speak to him. He is a grand bird, in perfect plumage. . . . I have a white rat, who lives, as all our pets do, entirely loose in the house or garden, perfectly free to leave us if they choose. The rat was given to me as old and worthless two years ago, then quite wild. He gradually became extremely tame, and during a severe illness I had last year he took it into his head to sit on my pillow to guard me. Ever since then he has continued to sleep there; he runs upstairs with me, and follows me to bed, sleeping always on the bolster or pillow by my head. He is very plucky, and defended himself during one whole night when he was shut up accidentally in the same room with a large and savage cat. He was found sitting up, with teeth and claws ready, and was perfectly overjoyed when his human friends took him up. Though six months have elapsed, nothing will induce him to enter that room again. Our dogs are perfect friends with him. He uses his left paw always when drinking, 'ladling' the water up to his mouth, even from the bottom of a tumbler, and is quite 'left-handed.'"

The following account relating to one of the same species of bird is curious, and interested Mr. Morris greatly at the time. This bird was brought to him by a neighbour one evening in the winter of 1873, and gave rise to an interesting correspondence. Shortly before Christmas in that year a large annual party was given at Nunburnholme, to which several of the neighbouring clergy and others were invited, and among them a young clerical friend and his wife, who lived some six or seven miles off. On his arrival he said that he had brought the rector of Nunburnholme a Kestrel which had flown to his window only a short time before he left home. He thought it must be a tame one, as it seemed quiet and showed no inclination to fly away. Without delay Mr. Morris opened the basket, and found the bird to be very tame, for it suffered him to stroke it without its attempting to bite or claw him. It was, however, very light in weight, and before attending to his other guests he, with characteristic humane feeling, procured the poor bird some food, which it ate readily.

And now comes the curious part of the story. For in the *Times* of that very day, which was received the following morning, there appeared an advertisement for a Kestrel Hawk that had strayed away, and the owner offered a reward of a sovereign to any one who would restore the bird to him. The address given was Eaton Terrace, London. Hardly supposing it possible that this could be the same bird that had flown two hundred miles northwards, Mr. Morris nevertheless thought that he would write to the advertiser in the hope, at all events, that the bird might be his. This accordingly he did, but no reply did he receive to his letter. Thinking it just possible that, in case some servant had been, through carelessness, the cause of the loss of the bird, the letter might not be delivered, the letters A. B. C. only being given for the name, it was determined that a second letter should be written. This time the following reply was received :—

"Eaton Terrace, S.W.,
December 30, 1873.

"My dear Sir,—I am much obliged by your letter. The first was not received.

"The Hawk lost belongs to me, and is one that I have had for two years, and should be very sorry to part with. It would know me if I could see it. Perhaps you would be kind enough to send it to me, and if it is not mine I shall nevertheless be glad to find it a good home, as I can easily do if I do not keep it myself. I am writing in haste to save the post.—I am, my dear Sir, yours faithfully,   C. C. B."

The Hawk was accordingly sent off by train in a hamper, with "refreshments" for the journey, most of which it consumed, and at the same time an invoice was forwarded by post to the supposed owner. What followed will speak for itself :—

"*January* 1, 1874.

"MY DEAR SIR,—I am very much obliged to you for sending the Hawk. It is not mine, but one of the same species, and has evidently been a pet of some one who has been as unfortunate as myself. We will keep it ourselves (that is to say, Mrs. B. and myself), and you may be assured it will be taken good care of, as we now understand the ways of Hawks, so that our kindness will not be made to take the shape of cruelty. We yet hope to get the other one again as a companion to it, and I have two more at the Royal Military College, Sandhurst, where I have an appointment, so that altogether we may hope that the poor little thing will be happy when it has ceased to be strange," &c., &c., &c.   "C. C. B."

After this came the last chapter, or rather the last but one, in the history of the bird :—

"*January* 11, 1874.

" MY DEAR SIR,—The welfare of small birds must seem to many people a very trivial matter, and those who take an interest in them be looked upon as being foolish, as there is no money or gain to be made out of them ; but I am sure, from your kindness, you will not think us troublesome in writing to tell you that we recovered our lost Hawk the day before yesterday, and that he was as much delighted to see us as we were to see him. After being lost about ten days he alighted on a window-sill, and was taken in by some workmen, who treated him kindly, and brought him to us in consequence of a second edition of hand-bills we had printed a few days before. Although our perseverance might be much ridiculed, it has been well rewarded, and our ' Peter' has found in ' Pauline' a very amiable wife, so that the curtain descends on a happy conclusion of the drama. The bird was caught about a mile and a half away," &c., &c., &c.   "C. C. B."

Altough the conclusion was thus far a happy one, the end was not yet. After writing a short note to say that the Hawks were going on satisfactorily, and that people would hardly credit their romantic history, the gallant captain (for such he was) wrote yet another after little more than a month, giving the sad news of the death of " Pauline." His last words were :—"One consolation is, that it was not neglected, and was never during its illness out of our sight and immediate care night or day ; and we are now trying to find another to console our old pet, who misses his wife so much."

It may give some little idea of the extent and varied character of his newspaper correspondence when I say that five large folio volumes of about two hundred and fifty pages each are well-nigh filled with press cuttings of his letters and leaflets. Here are two pages lying open before me ; covering these two large pages are letters on the following subjects :—"Strikes and High Prices," "Railway Fares," "Pure Literature," "Nonconformist Burial Bill," "Railway Mismanagement" (2), "The American Revival," "Small Incumbencies," "Post Office Grievances," "Our Sea-Birds," "North-Eastern Railway," "Dr. Livingstone," "Farm Servants," "The Illiberals," "Altar v. Table and Table v. Altar," "Thistle-Hunting," "The Roman Church," "Ffoulkes v. Manning," "The Potato Disease," "The late Archbishop of York," "Parish Registers," "Highway Districts," "Stack-Burning," "Church and State," "The Viaduct at Stamford Bridge."

Turning over the leaves of these portly volumes, we find letters by the dozen on such subjects as these :—"Church Defence," "Gleaning," "Sunday Observance," "Badness of Trade," "The Use of the Conjunction," "Price of Meat," "Experiments on Living Animals," "Taxes on the Clergy," "The Sparrow," "Free Education," "The Evolution Craze," "The Observance of Friday," "Dairy Farming," "Foxes v. Farmers," "School Work and Manual Labour," "Robbers of Churches," "Methodists and Undenominational Education," "Fruit-Trees in Hedgerows," "Tithes," "Sale of Small Birds," "Pasteur & Co.," "Close Time for Sea-Birds," "Birds and Bonnets," "The Plumage League."

On many of these topics—for instance, "The Sparrow," "Evolution," "Church Defence," and "Close Time for Birds"—the letters he wrote would have sufficed to fill volumes of considerable size. Those which he wrote to the *Times* alone between the years 1870–1880, mainly about birds, he published in a separate volume of over two hundred and fifty pages—though subsequently to that period he must have written enough letters to the same journal to fill another volume.

The newspapers to whose columns he was so incessantly contributing were as varied in character as the matters on which he wrote. Conservative or Liberal, religious or secular, Church or Dissenting, scientific, popular, agricultural, philanthropic, humanitarian, all were the same to him for the end he had in view. Although holding his own views, religious and political, so strongly, whenever he felt that he had something to say that would interest or benefit in some way those for whom he wrote, it mattered but little or nothing what the particular colour of the paper might be to which he addressed himself. The following are some of those which may be named :—*The Animals' Guardian, Animal World, Arrow, Christian World, Cambrian Journal,*

Champion of the Faith, Church Bells, Church Evangelist, Church Review, Church Times, County Gentleman, Dietetic Reformer, Doncaster Gazette, Doncaster Chronicle, Ecclesiastical Gazette, Entomologists' Intelligencer, Family Circle, Farmer, Fireside News, Field Club, Guardian, Hereford Times, Home Chronicler, Hospital, Hour, Land and Water, Leeds Mercury, Leisure Hour, Live Stock Journal, Liverpool Courier, Manchester Examiner, Morning Post, National Church, Naturalist, Pall Mall Gazette, Public Opinion, Record, Rock, Saltburn Times, School Guardian, Scarborough Herald, Scarborough Post, Shield of Faith, Stonyhurst Magazine, St. James's Gazette, Sunday at Home, Times, Vegetarian, Weekly Churchman, Westmoreland Gazette, Yorkshire Gazette, Yorkshire Herald, Yorkshire Post, Zoophilist.

It may well be wondered what he could have to communicate to all these papers. Here, then, are some of the topics on which he wrote to one only, which I have taken by chance as it were (*The Farmer*) :—" Dairy Farming," " Fruit-Trees in Hedgerows," " Reafforesting of Ireland," " Miss Ormerod and the Sparrows," " British Birds of Prey," "Farmers and Taxation," "The Sand Grouse," " Foxes *v.* Farmers," "The Sparrow," "The Bird-Catching Fraternity," " The Cuckoo," " Tithes," " Dangers from Bulls."

It will thus be seen that it was impossible to say on what subject Mr. Morris might not be found writing to any periodical or paper in the land on any day in the year !

As a matter of course all this mass of correspondence involved him very often in lengthened paper warfares. These he carried on with the greatest animation and determination; indeed, he was truly in his element when engaged in them. He attacked abuses and evils of many kinds regardless of the consequences, and simply because they were evils in his eyes. His capacity for carrying on these pen-and-ink battles was practically inexhaustible. No amount of abuse, or ridicule, or argument made any difference when he felt he had a cause at heart that was worth fighting for, whereby some good might be done. It is probable that few, if any, among the clergy have ever written so much in this way, and therefore have had heaped upon them so much invective as he. It was, as I have before said, useless to attempt to silence him. He might at times be worsted in argument, but that only added fuel to the flames; for if he failed in making good his case by one method, two others were at once brought to bear upon the point at issue, so that his resources seemed endless.

At times, no doubt, he was hardly dealt with, and had to confront misrepresentation. The following is an example of the kind of treatment he sometimes received, and of his way of meeting it. He had sent petitions to Parliament many times on the subject of vivisection. When a petition for its total abolition was refused, he asked that, as a concession towards it, all experiments should be made in public. And yet, forsooth, because he took this

O

line, one anti-vivisectionist organ made it appear as if he was not heart and soul against the practice. It was thus that he hastened to set the matter right in the eyes of those who might else have been misled by it.

"You yourself," he wrote, "quote my own words as petitioning for the total abolition of the practice, and yet after this you would make out that this is not my one and main object, which it has been all along, as I believe is fully known, and which I have been doing all in my power to obtain, very many more times, practically, than on every day in the year, and for several years, through the post. And what is your ground for your perversion of this fact? Simply this: that if the petition is refused no concession towards it should be asked or accepted even as a stepping-stone to it.

"By parity of reasoning, if a general demands the surrender of a citadel, and it is refused, he must not ask nor accept the surrender of the walls and outworks as stepping-stones to it. If he does, he is to be told that he does not want to take the citadel.

"You knew that this was my view, for I expressed it to you in so many words several months since, and yet, after all, you have represented me as if not caring for the total abolition of the practice!

" . . . Only let the public see for themselves the practices in these deeds of cruelty, and the atrocity will be swept away at once.

"Depend upon it that our honest artisans and

mechanics will then take the law into their own hands, and will soon 'overthrow the tables,' and will make a clean sweep of those that sit at them. You will see them, as John Bright said, 'running for their lives,' and it will be well for the hindmost if they are not caught by the indignant pursuers, some to be tarred and feathered, and the others to have the cat-o'-nine-tails well laid on. *Sauve qui peut* will be the outcry of the 'vocal chord' of every one of them within the sound of Bow Bells.

"You knew all this when you wrote your review of my pamphlet, for it is a copy of what I sent you, as above said ; and yet, after this, you say I only meant a half-measure. It really is too bad."

Over and above all the correspondence which he carried on in the papers and with private individuals on natural history, as well as the other extraordinarily diversified subjects upon which he so often had something to say, he kept himself in touch through the post not only with members of his own family, but with many friends far and near besides. He had a remarkable faculty for not losing sight of or overlooking any one in whom he had at any time felt an interest. He frequently wrote on very small scraps of paper, with the worst of steel pens, and in a hand that was always small and often most difficult to make out for those unaccustomed to it ; so much so, indeed, that sometimes, in despair, his correspondents would cut out the address at the head of his letters, paste it on the back of an envelope, and let it take its chance through the post. It says something for the skill and patience of the Post Office officials that these letters somehow or other ultimately reached their destination ; but it says still more for Mr. Fawcett's printers at Driffield that they got so accustomed at last to my father's handwriting that they very rarely were at loss or even at fault with it. This refers to what he wrote for others to make out. There was another style of penmanship adopted by him which he called his "shorthand," though "short" only in the sense that it was written at "express" speed, and was intended, happily, only for his own use. Its general appearance was such as to beggar description ; it may, perhaps, best be likened to what it would be if a dozen or so of beetles had tumbled into the ink and run backwards and forwards for some little time over a sheet of paper. And yet, when he had time and occasion to take special pains, he could write in a hand of remarkable delicacy and neatness.

X

DARWINISM AND VIVISECTION

THAT would be a very incomplete record of the life
of Mr. Morris which did not make some mention of
his attitude towards what is commonly known as
the Darwinian theory of evolution, and the views
to which he gave utterance with reference thereto;
for not only did he feel strongly upon the subject,
but of all the clergy of the Church of England who
made public their opinions there was probably not
one who wrote at greater length, more outspokenly,
vehemently, and decidedly than he. When, therefore, the clergy were alluded to, as they not seldom
were, as being opposed to the tendencies of the
new ideas, it was well-nigh impossible to sever his
name from that connection, being, as he was, one
of the first and foremost in exposing what he conceived to be the extravagant and illogical deduc-
tions that had been too hastily drawn from some of
Darwin's writings by those who were carried away
by his theories. There were, no doubt, many who
deplored and repudiated the line he took, as well as
the strong language and bantering tone that he frequently employed, but there were also many others
who were wholly at one with him.

It would not here be fitting to enter at all into the details of those animated discussions in pamphlets, periodicals, and papers in which he took part; this much, however, may be said of them, and ought to be said of them, that so far as he himself was concerned there was no personal feeling in the matter; it was the unsound arguments advanced to which he so strongly and persistently objected, and not to those who advocated them. Consequently he felt that there was nothing unbecoming to him as a clergyman in taking up the position he did. Nay more, and of this I am well assured, he would as soon have thought of offering no resistance to one who, he knew, had entered his home to take from him all he had, as of holding his peace when, according to his sincerest convictions, the very foundations of that faith which he held more dear than all besides were being undermined—a faith, too, which he had solemnly promised to do his utmost to maintain and defend.

He believed that nothing in recent times had done more to unsettle the minds and the religious opinions and beliefs of many than the unwarrantable conclusions that had been drawn from the writings of Darwin. With the main point arrived at by many of the disciples of Darwinism—namely, "that all the organised beings which have ever lived on this earth have descended from some *one* primordial form"—he wholly disagreed. There were to him insuperable difficulties in the way of accepting anything approaching to such a sweeping conclusion.

His opinions were first expressed at length in the year 1868, when a paper of his, entitled "Difficulties of Darwinism," was read at the meeting of the British Association held at Exeter. This paper, which was afterwards published, with some additions, raised much comment and opposition. It was stated at the time by one of the leaders of thought in the scientific world that the objections here made to Darwin's theories had been already answered; but when Mr. Morris pertinently inquired where such answers could be found, no satisfactory reply was forthcoming to throw any light upon the question. Many, indeed, were the difficulties that presented themselves to the writer of the paper, and seemed to call for elucidation. It would be out of place here to specify them in detail, but for the most part they were such as came before his mind in connection with those branches of study with which he was more specially conversant, namely, ornithology and entomology.

To those who maintained that it made no difference from a religious point of view whether the Almighty Creator called animals and plants into existence in the way that had been for ages believed that He did, or whether the different species had been developed from some one original form, Mr. Morris argued that it made the whole difference. "Where," he asked, "is the setting forth of the doctrine of evolution in the Book of Genesis? I see no trace or sign of it; but I do see what is agreeable to the reason which God has given me which most assuredly the Darwinian doctrine is not when looked at in the light of the facts of nature, and put forth, moreover, as it is, with the most flagrant, the most palpable, the most egregious self-contradictions, the most extravagant demands, contradicted by common sense, and in direct opposition to the teaching of astronomy, which proves that in the inconceivably vast space of time which Darwin demands for his theory it was utterly impossible for life of any sort to have existed on the earth."

For the interesting manner in which Darwin, after such extraordinary labour and research, had brought his facts together Mr. Morris had, of course, nothing to express but admiration. This was one thing; it was another thing when some of the chief followers of Darwin proceeded to draw the inferences they did from those facts. It was the process of reasoning which they adopted which was the main exciting cause of all his opposition and plain speaking.

He did not, and could not, deny the existence of connecting-links throughout the whole range of animated nature; indeed, he admits this in his writings. His views on this subject had been briefly indicated in the pages of the "History of British Birds." When speaking of one of the larger Hawks (vol. i. p. 21, 2nd edition), and of its approximation to the Owl tribe, he says :—"That a real natural bond of union, so to call it, does exist from the highest to the lowest animal in the scale of creation is, without doubt, to be received as true ; but even with the materials to his hand, how short-sighted is man to trace it—how utterly blind—a mere wanderer in darkness while all around him is light!"   And again, in another place, he observes :—"The endless variety of the objects of Nature, though doubtless in the whole connected by almost imperceptible links, yet to the student of only a part, is, as it were, interrupted here and there by sudden breaks, origins of fresh series, from where again the chain goes on."

This much he granted ; but to suppose that all animated things could be traced to a mohad was in his eyes nothing but a crude fancy and an assumption the reverse of scientific.

He found it utterly impossible to deny that if the Darwinian theory, thus carried to its furthest limit, be true, then the Bible is untrue ; and when placed in these two alternatives he decidedly preferred resting his faith on the older Book. To quote his own words, this is simply what he said :—" The Book of Genesis most certainly does state that some kinds of creatures were created at different periods of time from others, in a regular order, and that the doctrine of evolution is absolutely irreconcilable with any such statement, holding, as it does, that there was no creation at all, but that all the creatures in the world, and, I suppose, planets too, came down in 'the sequence of events' (these are their own words, the words of these 'men of science,' *mirabile dictu*) from some one original monad, as they call it, the creation and the word alike of their

own creating. . . . Our philosophers are vainly
exhibiting the futility of attempting to be wise above
that which is written. 'The ways of the Lord are
past finding out.' He giveth not an account of any
of His matters."

He maintained that, as far as the great question
of the origin of species is concerned, no further
advance has been made beyond the fact that the
hand that made them is Divine, and that "whatsoever the Lord pleased, that did He in the earth, and
in the sea, and in all deep places."

In reply to those who were of opinion that scientific questions, such as those propounded by Darwin
were generally supposed to be, could only be dealt
with by men who had a special scientific training,
Mr. Morris considered that nothing of the kind was
necessary, but that any one of average ability was
quite competent to undertake a discussion on these
matters.

To give at length his own contributions to these
discussions would be to write a book ; suffice it to
say that he continued throughout stoutly to maintain the position he first took up, namely, that which
has been here already indicated. The difficulties that
stood in the way of his conceding anything approaching the demands which the ultimate outcome of the
Darwinian theory made upon his reason, to say
nothing of his faith, were to him, as I have already
stated, absolutely insuperable. Many of these difficulties he adduced in his numerous published
pamphlets and other writings upon the subject. It

need hardly be stated that these would not all be considered of equal force ; some even might be ridiculed as trivial, but many were such as carried much with them to strengthen him in the standpoint he felt himself driven to occupy.

The following brief extracts from his writings on this question may be enough to show the general drift of his arguments in dealing with the subject ; more than this need not here be touched upon. In one of the pamphlets on the subject, already alluded to, he says :—

" The result of this startling theory, if carried to its legitimate extent, is, then, that not only species but genera, not only genera but orders, not only orders but classes, all classes under which the creatures have been hitherto arranged by naturalists in all ages, were but one and the same originally, had one common source of being in some one first parent or pair of parents ; that the lion and the lamb, the hawk and the eel, the humming-bird and the spider, the butterfly and the toad, had all one single original from which they at first sprang, and that they have only assumed their present forms through tendencies which, making use of fortuitous advantages, acted upon individuals of the gradually increasing types of forms in the various ages of their existence. Nay, not only so, but that even man himself, as well as the so-called species of creatures, had one and the same ancestry."

He reasoned that it is no argument in the way of proof that because certain species supposed to be new are not really such, but only varieties, therefore "those other species to the genera of which the former were for a time commonly supposed to be additions are not true and real species. Who can point to a species described by Pliny and say that it is not a species now? His description describes it, and describes it as such as at the present day."

As to the action of the mind and will in their relation to changes wrought upon the bodily structure, strongly called into continuous operation by the needs of fortuitous circumstances, he maintained that such changes were not permanent. He observes :— "They not only are not handed down to descendants (at all events it cannot be foretold that they will be), but, more than this, they will even fail the individual who had acquired them, should an improvement in the bodily defects which had been the means of eliciting them cause them to be no longer demanded for the remedy of such defects by the substitution of an increase of other power." Many instances were cited to show how in the human frame special powers had been acquired to serve special circumstances. But these, he asserted, were not transmitted from one generation to another.

Darwin contended that new species were formed by the power of natural selection ; but, said Mr. Morris, "how can this possibly apply to the case of the vast majority of species, insects and others, whose specific differences are only distinguishable by their colours and marks ?" And, again, he asked, "How did natural selection produce lungs by variation in those lower species in the scale of creation in which there is no trace whatever of any such organ ? . . . As the condition of the world is constantly varying, should not variations of species be seen taking place in these times, as in all others, with definite regularity, if the first primordial form contained within itself the elements of perpetual change for adaptation to such varying condition ?

" Is the use of such expressions as ' natural selection,' ' modification of form,' ' acclimatisation,' ' use and disuse,' ' the law of variation,' ' divergence of character,' ' correlation of growth,' ' compensation,' and ' economy of growth,' or ' the *imperfection* of the geological record,' a sufficient substitute for proof of the assertions that a flying fish might be converted into a bird, a flying squirrel into a bat, a lobster into an eagle, or a bear, ' swimming about with its mouth open to catch flies,' become in process of time ' very like a whale' ? "

Of Darwin's two books—the one on " The Origin of Species by Natural Selection," the other on " Variation of Species "—Mr. Morris did not hesitate, after a careful perusal of them, to assert :—" I should have said that a more inconclusive, illogical book than the former I had never read, and that I should suppose there could scarcely be one more so ; but if I had said so it would only have been an instance and illustration of the truth of the old saying that it is unwise to advance too hastily to a conclusion, for I had not then seen his second work on the ' Variation of Animals and Plants.' I ask any reader of it whether, for absolute, unmitigated inconclusiveness as to the main doctrine, it is not of the two *facile princeps*. . . . His mistake, the one great mistake, the one great cardinal error, as it appears to me, which runs through the whole of his work, is in supposing that because many mere varieties had their origin in one common ancestor, therefore all distinct species are to be similarly accounted for.   His whole argument is a *non sequitur*.   It is no argument, but mere assumption, that because the whole of animated nature is joined together (including fossil species, with their '*imperfection* of record') by a series of links, even though almost imperceptibly following on to one another, therefore the whole chain has come from a single unit."

Needless to say, the views which he advanced exposed him to many attacks and no little abuse from various quarters, but of one and all of them it can only be said here that, so far from silencing him, they appeared, if they had any effect at all, to convince him more strongly of the necessity for going on unswervingly and with no less determination in the line which seemed to him to be marked out by sound reasoning ; and being so marked out, it would have been in his eyes a failure of duty not to have expressed his views fearlessly. This was the position he maintained to the very end of the chapter.

Closely connected in his mind with Darwinism was the, to him, painful and distressing subject of vivisection. It would be hard to say on which of these two topics he wrote at the greatest length.

Certain it is that, of all the forms of cruelty against which he carried on such a long and determined crusade, there was none which he held in greater loathing and abhorrence, none which, in his conviction, was fraught with more dire consequences, than that which is involved in the term vivisection. It would be impossible to describe his feelings with regard to this practice ; no words seemed strong enough to express what he thought about it, and therefore no trouble was too great for him to take in his endeavour to influence public opinion against it. He looked upon it as something infinitely worse than any ordinary cruelty ; in fact, there was nothing else to which it could be compared. How could it possibly be otherwise with him ? Towards every animal he had a kindly feeling ; nothing was beneath his notice ; for him everything had its place in the world, each its use, however humble and obscure ; all were God's creatures, all wonderful, all to be loved and cared for. To be in any way a party to the torturing and experimenting upon any one of these was in his eyes to descend to the lowest depths of degradation and cruelty. Rather would he have died a hundred deaths than have had his life prolonged, if such a thing were possible, by any discovery that might be made through the abominations of the vivisecting-room.

Column after column in correspondence to newspapers and magazines, enough to fill volumes, did he write during the last twenty years of his life, besides private letters innumerable, upon this burning subject, never deviating from his uncompromising opposition to the vivisectionists of every shade and colour.

As a matter of course, in this as in almost every other cause which he espoused, he met with much violent opposition; but this he heeded not, except in so far that the louder the cry against him and the crusade on which he had entered, the faster he drew the arrows out of his quiver. The bare fact of his being a clergyman seemed to make some of his enemies the more bitter against him. They called him an outsider, who therefore could know nothing about the matter—that he was an "ignoramus" and a sentimentalist. He was, however, always ready with his reply, and they could not thus shut the mouth of him who lifted up his voice against them. "As well," said he, in a letter written in 1881, "tell you that you can know nothing of a bull-fight because you have never been in the bull-ring hand-in-glove with the matadors and picadors, or ever even been in Spain or crossed the Bay of Biscay. As well tell you that you can know nothing of the cruelty of cock-fighting because you have never handled a 'main' of cocks in the pit, or clipped their combs, or fitted on their spurs for a 'round.' Any one who has eyes can see through it all, and only laughs at it. . . . Let them 'talk to the marines.' It is only wasting their breath!"

Of all the petitions that he drew up and had presented to Parliament, none were worded in stronger
and more characteristic language than those which
related to vivisection. His reasons against it were
clearly stated, and every argument he could think
of that would tell against it he made use of. The
cowardliness of it, its diabolical cruelty, its comparative uselessness, its exemplification of the
thoroughly unsound position that, even granting
untold blessings resulted to the human race from
it, we may do evil that good may come. He would
say that those should allow themselves to be
operated upon who, admitting that they themselves
were descended from lower forms of animal life,
believed that there was much to be said for the
notion that such animals are mere machines and
have no feelings. He held, with Professor Newman,
that vivisection "cannot be justified without justify-
ing the scientific torture of men; that to torture a
man is not wrong on the ground that he is intel-
ligent or immortal, but only because he has a
sensitive body; and the same is true of all verte-
brated animals." He entirely disbelieved in the
idea that any valuable discoveries had been made
by means of vivisection that might not have been
reached in other ways. In 1878 he drew up a petition couched in these words :—

"The Petition of the undersigned Rector of
Nunburnholme, in the East Riding of the County
of York, showeth—That licenses for experiments
on living animals were granted only on the re-

P

presentation that valuable discoveries for the life and health of man would thereby be made. That ample time has passed since the granting of the said licenses for such alleged discoveries to have been made. Your petitioner therefore prays that a return of the number of such discoveries be forthwith demanded of each and every of those to whom such licenses were granted ; and that in the meantime such licenses be absolutely suspended, and be considered as withdrawn and revoked.

"And your petitioner will ever pray.

"F. O. MORRIS, B.A., J.P."

Among the many columns, not to say pages, that he penned to the public journals on this harrowing question was a series of contributions to one of the London papers which he styled "Collectanea for a Bill of Indictment at the Bar of Public Opinion against the Perpetrators of Experiments on Living Animals." In these he quoted the opinions of many eminent men upon the subject, together with his own views, which he expressed in feeling terms. To plead for the weak against the strong was in this connection a religious duty, from which nothing could make him swerve. Said he at the outset :—"I have heard a voice from above to every one that will hear it—'Open thy mouth for the dumb ;' and it is a voice of the Great Judge—of Him who has said for all such crimes, 'Shall I not visit for these things ?' Yes ; but would that the plaintiffs in this case could speak and plead for themselves ! Could they but do so, their heart-rending cries would be heard in such a loud and bitter complaint as would echo up against the very vault of heaven, a complaint of sufferings neither the amount nor the intensity of which can be told by any but themselves. If they could be written down against those who have so vilely sinned against them, they would compose such a volume as the world has never yet seen."

In this series of papers he simply set forth facts and opinions ; not one word was said in malice, and he left the case in the hands of the ladies and gentlemen, or, as he said, a far higher title, the men and women of England, Scotland, Ireland, and Wales, for their decision as to the issue.

Most earnestly and eloquently did he plead the cause of the animals who could not speak for themselves. Hear him :—"As for you, poor dumb creatures of the hand of God, who only by reason of your want of speech are unable to tell the sad and harrowing tale of your own most grievous, most lamentable, bitter, and heart-rending sufferings, heartily, and on my knees, and with tears in my eyes, I have prayed to Him, who saveth both man and beast, that He would, for the sake of One by whom you, as well I, were made—and so ' fearfully and wonderfully made ' — that He would give a force and a power to my humble words in your behalf which they could never otherwise have of themselves."

He cordially agreed with Professor F. W. Newman in his nine reasons against the scientific torture of animals, and often quoted them. He held with him that "Christianity must be eternally and fatally disgraced if nations called Christian allow the perpetration of these heart-rending enormities under any pretence whatever."

To the medical students, who were mainly concerned in these experiments, he appealed with all his heart and mind. On them, he urged, these practices had a direct hardening of the better feelings, and tended to demoralise the whole community. He would have had the names of all those medical practitioners who favoured vivisection, as well as those who were against it, published to the world ; and the same with regard to those who had received licenses and certificates from the Home Secretary for practising experiments on living animals. The fact that the names of those who held such licenses were at first withheld from the public showed, in his opinion, that there was, on the face of it, something to be ashamed of in these experiments, and that, therefore, they ought to be suppressed.

It need hardly be stated that my father was in cordial agreement with Miss Frances Power Cobbe in her noble endeavours in the cause of humanity, especially on the vivisection question, and many were the letters that passed between them. In any matter about which he was convinced, and in any cause that he advocated, no half-measures ever satisfied him. Compromises he abhorred, and eminently so on this absorbing topic. From the first day he was convinced of the iniquity of the thing, and began his campaign against it, he never rested under it, not even up to the very last days of his life. But few knew the extent of his labour in defence of the dumb animals against those who so horribly experimented upon them, as well as the perseverance, determination, and deep earnestness with which he carried on his contest. He always preferred to call a spade by its best-known and knowable name, and for the word vivisection he thought it better to use the plainer term, "experiments on living animals." As a matter of course he was altogether and heartily at one with those societies that made for the total suppression of vivisection, and those only. In October 1878 he wrote in these words to the *Home Chronicler* :—

"In common, I am sure, with many others, I have been truly glad and thankful indeed to hear that the Victoria Street Association have now seen that there can be no truce with the experimenters, and that not one of them can be trusted. About a year ago Miss Cobbe did me the honour of writing to me to ask me to join her Society ; but I was obliged to tell her that that could not be so long as they went in for half-measures only. Now, however, that, as it appears, they are of one mind with us, the only question is, What is to be done ? and it does seem to me that the union of the two associations in one is most desirable and loudly called for. I would at once have said, if they desired that we should join with them, by all means let it be so, but for the fact that our title happens to be so much the better one ; in fact, I think, the best that could be devised, at least as to the word 'International,' for I should much prefer the plain English words, 'experimenters on living animals,' to the long Latin words, which so many have not understood. Let something be done, and that soon, for *vis unita fortior*, and *bis dat qui cito dat*. It will be to the great economy of time, trouble, and expense, and a bolder front will be presented to the enemy, with whom there must, in God's name, be no truce till the abomination is trodden under foot and stamped out."

It was a gratification to Mr. Morris when he learned that the Victoria Street Society and the International Society became amalgamated, as they finally were on April 6, 1883. For several years, and that almost daily, he carried on what he termed a "Plan of Campaign" against this, the greatest cruelty of the age. Thousands of copies of various publications, among which was one of his own entitled "A Defence of our Dumb Companions against the cowardly Cruelty of the Experimenters on Living Animals," were circulated by post far and wide all over the country, in which the practices of the vivisectionists were trenchantly dealt with.

As already mentioned, he gave a very plain and decided expression of his views generally on this question in a sermon he preached in York Minster in 1886. Well knowing the opinions of Mr. Ruskin with regard to the practice of vivisection, it naturally enough occurred to my father to send him a copy of this sermon, and in acknowledging the receipt of it Mr. Ruskin wrote :—" I am deeply grateful for your sermon. Far the strongest and clearest bit of writing I have seen on our side, and it gives me much comfort and help in my own immediate work. I have read it to the end, and may have something to write of it, but can't to-day."

For Mr. Ruskin's noble conduct in resigning his professorship at Oxford rather than continue to hold any public office in a University that had thought fit to endow vivisection Mr. Morris had a profound admiration ; though in one of Mr. Ruskin's transparent honesty, tenderness, and courage, the course which he took on that memorable occasion could scarcely have come as a surprise to those who had any knowledge of the man.

XI

VIEWS ON QUESTIONS OF THE DAY

IN politics Mr. Morris was the staunchest of Tories; he had inherited those principles from his fore-elders, and they seemed to be in his very blood. And yet he differed in many ways from the typical Tory of his earlier days, who looked upon almost every change with suspicion and aversion. His Toryism consisted rather in his adhesion to the leading principles of the creed of the party, and not in any aversion to change as such. Anything that tended to weaken the Church in her union with the State, or to the secularising of the educational system of the country, to that he was resolutely opposed. But within certain limits he not only was not opposed to change, but favoured it when he saw it meant a strengthening of the good ship of the Church or that of the State. In all political questions he took the keenest interest, and was a great reader of newspapers. Sometimes, in exciting times like a General Election, his appetite for journalistic literature was enormous, and as he read he would frequently make mental or manuscript notes with a view to answering by a letter to the paper some question that struck him, or correcting some

flagrant misstatement which seemed to him calculated to do harm to his cause and principles.

For the opinions of certain statesmen he had a
peculiar aversion, and for none more than those of
John Bright, whom he looked upon as one not only
opposed to the best interests of the Church, but as
one who was continually setting class against class.
He therefore thought it well to deal with some of
what he conceived to be the fallacies commonly put
forth by that orator, and this he did in a lengthy
pamphlet, styled a "Letter," in which he handled in a
lively but telling way some of Mr. Bright's views on
questions affecting the Church, the land, and the
factory. To give a summary of this "Letter," even
if it were possible, for it consisted very largely of
quotations from newspapers and the writings of
others, would carry me far out of my course.

It would, perhaps, hardly be straining a point to
say that Mr. Morris's political views on all great
questions might be described as diametrically opposite to those of Mr. Bright. On such a subject,
for instance, as the tenure of land and the de-
sirability or otherwise of large tracts of the country
being in the hands of a comparatively small number
of owners, he expressed himself at great length.
Although strongly in favour of small holdings for
the labouring classes, he by no means looked upon
it as an evil, but rather the reverse, that the large
estates of the nobility and gentry comprised such a
considerable portion of the land of England. He
reminded Mr. Bright of the case of the Duke of

Northumberland, which he took as an example, and showed that since he had inherited the estates he had spent hundreds of thousands of pounds upon improvements of various kinds, such as the building of churches, parsonage houses, schools, cottages, and farm-steads, drainage, the making of roads and bridges, besides establishing and supporting innumerable philanthropic institutions and charities. Adopting Mr. Bright's favourite formula, Mr. Morris says that he should " like to know" how a number of poor tenants could have accomplishsd a work of this kind.   It was one thing to create small holdings, which he considered an immense advantage to many of the poorer classes; it was another to advocate the principle of peasant proprietorship.   He was able to do something more than talk about the advantages of small holdings ; as far as in him lay he carried his views into effect.   The glebe land at Nunburnholme was conveniently situated as regards the village, and, instead of letting his land, consisting of about 120 acres, to two or three tenants, he subdivided it into allotments and small holdings, thus enabling a number of the villagers to keep cows who had not before kept them, and to grow enough potatoes and other produce for their families to last them throughout the year.

On this, as on so many other social and economical questions affecting the labouring classes, especially in country places, he thought and wrote much.   In order to strengthen his arguments in favour of small holdings, he would frequently cite cases that had come under his notice at Nunburnholme of labourers, or, as he always preferred to call them, husbandmen, who had raised themselves by their meritorious exertions to the rank of small farmers. In writing on one occasion to the *Times* on this subject, he mentioned the case of a man who had been employed at the Rectory at half-a-crown a day, and who subsequently saved enough money to take a farm of eighty acres on a long lease, which farm he had had a hand in obtaining for him. He told of another similar instance where the man had seven cows and calves, a horse, carrier's cart, and ten acres of glebe land, besides some more that he rented. Of a third from another parish where the erewhile husbandman now rented a small farm of sixty acres. A fourth mentioned held a farm of from eighty to ninety acres. A fifth held some thirty-six acres in the West Riding. On these and similar cases he remarked :—

"I may here say that all these men, as well as others to a lesser extent, have been greatly aided in their endeavours to raise themselves by allotment gardens, which had been set out for them, as much as wanted—a rood or half an acre—to each, by one of my predecessors in this living ; and not long after I came here I furthered the same object by setting apart fifteen acres of good grass land as cow-gaits, which they prize most highly, and which are the greatest possible benefit to themselves and their children. By these, and such-like means as these, and the small farms spoken of, not only the clergy, but landed proprietors, larger and lesser, will do much to better the condition of their worthy neighbours, and will at the same time largely increase the numbers of those who will have a direct plain interest in supporting them and their cause in the country. They will be public benefactors, the *agathoergoi* of our day and generation.

"These instances might be multiplied to a very large extent indeed ; but if the practice of throwing all such farms together into a few very large ones is to be carried out in a still more extensive way, no opening is left for the men I have been speaking of, and I can conceive nothing more dispiriting than such a practical non-recognition of their most laudable lives."

Whatever may have been the case in other parts of England, it was certainly not only possible but common for husbandmen to save money out of their weekly wages in East Yorkshire. As an instance of this, out of many others that might have been given, Mr. Morris mentioned one in a letter on this subject, where a farm-servant in his parish, who had died, had saved £102. In addition to this, he had been in the habit of sending money to his parents, and if this had been taken into account his savings would have amounted to £179 in a period of twelve years. For a portion of the time he had acted as groom. In this same letter, written in 1869, he says :—

"Many farm-servants about here—I am speaking of the Wold farms, nearly all of which are large, and some of them very large, and of the best class of servants—receive much larger wages than the amount I spoke of in his case. A hind will receive £50 a year, with a house and more or less of a garden rent free ; a shepherd, £30, with £1 yearly for his *fest—i.e.*, fastening money or hiring penny. A small farmer in this parish, who, like several others I could name, has risen from the ranks, told me the other day that he had had that amount as such for the last twelve or thirteen years of his service, a foreman from £24 to £25 or £26, and the other farm-servants or farm-lads from £14 to £18 or so, according to their age and the value of their services, all with their meat and house-room, except, of course, the hind as spoken of."

There was no question affecting the well-being of the agricultural labourers in which he did not take a real interest, and on many of these he wrote at great length.

Although strongly in favour of small holdings where practicable, he ridiculed the extravagant ideas of certain politicians who would extend the principle indiscriminately, and thus rob Peter to pay Paul. He gave vent to his views in a lively little treatise on the subject in which he gave a hundred reasons against what he called the "land craze." Some of his reasons might be taken seriously ; others were of a *reductio ad absurdum* character. At the head of the title-page he quoted Carlyle's well-known dictum that the population of England consisted of so many millions, "the greater

part of whom are fools"; the writer adding as a
rider, that of the remainder, many are more knaves
than fools, and as a subscript the Scriptural de-
nunciation against him that "removeth his neighbour's landmark." If, argued the writer, the whole
country were to be subdivided into patches of
ground for the teeming population, what would
happen in a district like the Wolds of East Yorkshire, where the water-supply is such a difficulty
owing to a lack of springs, many of the farmers in
a dry summer having to send their water-carts miles
in order to obtain sufficient water for their cattle?
"Many of the Wold farms," he observed, "are as
much as a thousand acres each. Each of these
acre holdings, therefore, would require a supply of
water in hot weather. How are they to get it?
They cannot have ponds at each one of their small
holdings, their space being over-stinted already.
Where is each one of them to get a horse and cart
to fetch it for him?"

On most of the burning questions of the day,
as well as many others that were not burning on
which he expressed himself, he held views clear and
decided.

With regard to teetotalism, for instance, he considered that religious principle is a better safeguard
against intemperance than merely signing one's
name in a book, but that, if a pledge had to be
taken at all, he was of opinion that it would be
likely to be better kept if it were one never to enter
the doors of a public-house than one to abstain

altogether from intoxicating liquors. As to the principle of never tasting wine or ale because some persons drink them in excess, this argument, if carried to its legitimate extent, is no more sound than to say that because some persons lie in bed too long, others must never go to bed at all.

On temperance in eating he frequently spoke and wrote almost as decidedly as on temperance in drinking, and his views, while not satisfying altogether the strict vegetarian, went a long way towards it.

When a person lives so far beyond the allotted days of man in good health of mind and body, and gets through such a vast amount of work as was the case with Mr. Morris, it is interesting to know what his dietetic rules were, if he had any. He was at all times a very small eater, especially of meat; indeed, occasionally he became practically a vegetarian, and maintained stoutly that a vegetarian diet was more wholesome than a carnivorous one. He seldom ate meat more than once a day, and then only in small quantities, and at times he would give it up altogether, though not for long periods. Though not an abstainer from alcoholic drinks, in late years he took less in that way than he did in middle life. In short, he made no hard-and-fast rules of any kind with regard to diet, but took exactly that which seemed to conduce most to his health and enjoyment. His only rule was the general one of being "temperate in all things." He maintained that the vegetarian had a splendid choice of diet, although it was commonly supposed that if, as he once expressed it, he did not "feed upon grass, like the Babylonian monarch of old, he at best varied his diet with cabbage and other such green food." It appeared to him that as a fruiterer's was a pleasanter place to visit than a butcher's shop, so the vegetarian's *répertoire* was a more inviting one than the meat-eater's.

Being once asked by the editor of a vegetarian newspaper to give a list of viands suitable for his readers from which to make a choice, he willingly did so, prefacing the catalogue of dainties by some remarks of his own which were not a little to the point. He observed :—"Just in the same way that the Almighty, our Heavenly Father, ordained that men should live out their allotted time, and not throw their lives away, by implanting within them a due fear of death, so has He made the food which He has given for their sustenance 'pleasant to the eyes,' and 'all things richly to enjoy,' that they might be inclined to eat it, and sustain and prolong their existence. Here it is that the vegetarian has the advantage over every one that is of the contrary part."

After describing the way the ordinary Englishman gorged himself with beef or mutton, which he washed down with strong ale or stronger stout—a strange contrast to the way the Frenchman dines— he adds :—"A fearful amount of cruelty would be avoided by a vegetarian diet, and the demoralisation of a whole class of the community employed in the killing of animals for food ; there would be a vast saving of expense in keeping each household, and the land of the country would be able to maintain a population manifold more numerous than the present, and, at the same time, in better health, strength, and prosperity."

His list of viands contained some two hundred and twenty items. It makes one smile to notice some few of the dishes, such as "dandelion coffee" and "burnt onions," which were included in the number given, although possibly even these might commend themselves to the tastes of some; still, it would be admitted on all hands that there were many excellent things among them, and he was fully justified in his final words when he said, "May I not add that such a variety of wholesome and most agreeable foods demands a 'Grace' of very heartfelt thanksgiving, before and after partaking of any of them, to the 'Giver of all good'?"

For many years he took a great interest in all matters affecting the education of the children in our public elementary schools, and although his views on many points were what would be termed old-fashioned, and by no means in harmony with the views of many educationalists, his opinions on the whole were in advance of most of his contemporaries.

Soon after the passing of the Education Act of 1870, it was found that many parishes were, from their smallness and poverty, unable to find funds for supporting an efficient certificated teacher, thus entailing a withdrawal of the grant from the Govern-

Q

ment. It was felt to be a hardship in such cases that the schools should suffer a pecuniary loss, when the results were, or might become, satisfactory, simply because the teacher did not happen to be certificated. To meet this difficulty, a scheme was devised under the patronage and support of the Baroness Burdett-Coutts, with the approval of the Education Department, for grouping a certain number of such schools together within a limited area, with a thoroughly well-trained certificated master over them all, whose duty it should be to visit each school during the week, to superintend, direct, and test the work in various ways, giving advice and instruction where necessary, and generally acting so as to further by every possible means the efficiency of the schools placed under his supervision. One of such tentative schemes was tried in the East Riding, Nunburnholme being one of the five schools chosen for the purpose in the neighbourhood. For five years Mr. Morris acted as general manager of these schools for the Baroness Burdett-Coutts, and engaged the services of a competent master. For two years grants were received from the Government for the schools worked under this system, and the results were, on the whole, very satisfactory. But changes came ; possibly "another king arose" in high places, and Mr. Morris was informed that the grant must for the future not be looked for. This was naturally felt to be a grievance in face of the good results which had taken place through the working of the system. Notwithstanding great difficulties at the outset, owing partly to opposition and prejudice, which any new and untried scheme of the kind would be sure to give rise to, as well as to the fact that for about five months of the year the demand for child-labour in the fields was at that time very great, yet it was found, in spite of these and other difficulties, that at the end of the first year, when the children were assembled for examination by her Majesty's Inspector, the average result, as tested by the six standards, was 1 per cent. higher than the average of all the schools of England and Wales. In the second year one of the schools, and that the worst, was closed for about four months, and without a master ; but the average in the results gained in the other four schools, as compared with that of all other public elementary schools in England and Wales, was equal in reading, 12½ per cent. higher in writing, 9 per cent. higher in arithmetic, and 3 per cent. higher on the final average of all subjects. These results must have borne a still greater contrast to the state of things educational in Nunburnholme a quarter of a century previously, when the village school was held in one of the cottages. At that time the discipline at least of the school could hardly be deemed satisfactory, if, that is, we may judge from the fact that it was customary for the master, who was a great smoker, when he felt inclined for his pipe, to give it to one of the elder boys, no doubt as a reward for good. conduct, with instructions to take it to one of the neighbouring cottages and light it for him—an order which the youngster was all too ready to obey, and thus get a few whiffs of the weed for his trouble.

It was a matter of sincere regret to Mr. Morris that this grouped-school system was so soon brought to an end. In writing to the *Guardian* in 1875 he said of it :—" The grouped-school system has worked well, and *Quieta non movere* ought, I think, to have been the motto with regard to it, . . . capable as the plan was of indefinite extension, and improving year by year." But the red-tape of the Government offices can reach a long way, in this case stretching to a remote country village at the edge of the Yorkshire Wolds, thus putting an end to a plan which was helping forward the education of the district, in which it had been tried. The result was that the standard of efficiency declined.

If in no other way, the deep interest he took in elementary education was shown in the large number of letters he wrote with regard to the question through a long course of years. Several pages of his large folio volumes of press cuttings are covered with his communications dealing with various phases and details of the subject, " School Boards," " Religious Teaching," " Payment by Results," " School Attendance," " Codification of the Code," and " Help to Voluntary Schools" being among the headings of the letters. To give even an outline of his views upon these and other topics bearing on the general subject of education would carry me beyond my limits. It may be stated, however, that he was generally in favour of children doing a moderate amount well, rather than unduly multiplying subjects, which tended only to a smattering of learning, and did little or no permanent good. Even such a subject as drawing he rather looked at askance, and doubted whether for country lads, the majority of whom would be eventually called to agricultural work, the time spent on it might not be better employed.

It is hardly to be expected that one of his time of life would have very much sympathy with the movement that took effect shortly before his death with regard to free education. He held that it was uncalled for and unnecessary ; that the parents saved far more than the small weekly fee of a penny or twopence in children's clothing and in doctors' bills through their being kept for six hours of the day in a dry and warm school ; and that, therefore, on that ground alone they would get their money's worth, independently of any instruction they received.

On many other matters connected with his work as a clergyman he was wont to express himself freely when occasion seemed to call for it, though it must be confessed his ideas did not always take a practical shape. For instance, he would say that, of all a clergyman's duties, there were few which distressed him more than the difficulty which was so often experienced in finding good sponsors for the children of the poor, even when the parents themselves are most desirous to obtain them. The remedy that approved itself to him was to have fixed and suitable persons, four in number—two males and two females at least—in every parish who would undertake the duties for those parents who might wish them to do so ; though this, of course, would only apply in those cases where the parents otherwise found a difficulty. He considered that the parish schoolmaster or schoolmistress ought to be the most fitting persons for such an office ; and others, even in the smallest parishes, might be found to act with these, and so meet what has so often been felt as a difficulty to many a clergyman, to say nothing of the parents themselves.

To come down to smaller concerns, even the prevalence of some fashion was not beneath his notice if he thought it called for comment. Among such fashions which found no favour in his eyes was the modern one of recording with minute detail the proceedings at "fashionable marriages," even down to the elaborate lists one sees of the presents bestowed on these interesting occasions. If these small particulars are given in the case of the rank and fashion of the land, why, he asked, in an amusing account he once gave, and sent to one of the "society" papers, of an imaginary wedding of a couple of plain country folk, should not the "short and simple annals of the poor" be found as worthy of a place in the columns of the newspapers "as those of dukes and duchesses, or even of millionaire manufacturers or Continental counts ?" "What," he exclaimed, "though the ceremony were performed by a country parson, unaided by a phalanx of brother priests, and among the bridesmaids were names no more high-sounding than those of Miss Dorothy Doogood, Miss Patience Primrose, and Miss Jane Little, while the bridegroom's best-man was none other than Mr. Hearty Goodman of the Manor Farm ? What though among the list of wedding-presents might be included such articles as a pair of brass candlesticks given by Mrs. Lighton, a set of fire-irons by Mr. Cole, and a walking-stick by Mr. Turnbull ? What mattered it if of the dresses no more need be said than that the bride appeared in a plain but very neatly made dress of home-spun material, while the bridegroom was attired in his best Sunday suit ?." Such was the contrast he drew, or, as he added, " *Sic magnis componere parva solebam.*"

XII

SPORT AND SLAUGHTER

ON the subject of sport my father held decided
views, and frequently expressed them strongly. To
the system of battue shooting as practised at the
present day he was opposed heart and soul ; with
him it was not sport at all, but only butchery of the
worst kind. A very considerable part of his correspondence had reference to so-called sport and
matters connected with it, such as traps and the
destruction of hawks, owls, and other birds which
did or were supposed to do harm to game ; while
against the horrors of the battue and all that accompanied it he never wearied in his warfare. To the
old-fashioned, more English, and altogether healthier
method of game preserving and shooting he raised no
objection, except that he did not think gamekeepers
the best judges in the world as to which kinds of
birds and animals did harm and which did not. It
was a real grief to him to see the way in which some
of our most interesting native birds were shot down
or trapped for the sake of partridges and pheasants.

Literally volumes of letters on this topic he wrote
to the newspapers, from the leading journal to the
most insignificant local weekly, all in the same

strain, all telling the same tale of bird murder and
cruelty. "What," he said, "makes me write is the
very strong feeling which I cannot help having on
the score of the inconceivable amount of cruelty
which it involves, through the countless thousands
of iron traps set all over the country every night of
the year for the mere preservation of the pheasants
for the slaughter. No words can describe what I
have myself seen." He had, in fact, seen a great
deal—much more than he liked to see—of the
ways of gamekeepers; but having seen and heard
so much, he could not keep silence.

It was in the spring of 1873 that he was one day
walking in a wood not far from Nunburnholme,
when his enjoyment of the scene that lay before
him and around him was suddenly brought to an
end. There, a few yards in front of him, he came
to a pole fixed in the ground, on the top of which
was an iron trap; from this hung, head downwards,
a luckless white owl, with both its legs broken by the
cruel spring. As he came near to it, its splendid
bright eyes looked piteously at him; it would have
taken a hard heart indeed not to have been moved
by such a sight. For many a long hour the poor
bird must there have hung, helpless and in pain.
There was nothing left but to put it out of its hopeless torture as quickly as possible. Its beautiful
wings were stretched out to the full, giving it the
appearance, as its would-be deliverer expressed it in
a letter written shortly afterwards, "of being cruci-
fied with its head downwards, as in fact it was."

Sights such as this, heart-rending as they were to him, gave him the text for many a letter and eloquent appeal to the better feelings of our landed proprietors who allow such cruelties to take place upon their estates. This very case of the bonny but hapless owl gave rise to a plea for this bird in the *Times*, in which the sad story was graphically told, and not without a suggested remedy. " Had the capture," he wrote, " of any and all of our British birds been forbidden by the recent Act during the breeding season, such cruelties would be prevented for a part of the year at all events. I can say for myself that the eyes of this poor bird haunted me at night so that I could not sleep, and I endeavoured to divert my thoughts by writing this letter to the *Times* in my head as I lay awake." It was in this same letter that he combated the commonly received idea that if you allow birds to increase without check we should soon be eaten up by them. What he said to those holding this mistaken notion was this :—"There are many kinds of our best-known birds against which war has never been especially waged. But has any one of these birds unduly increased in the way suggested—such, for instance, as the wren, the dunnock or hedge-sparrow, the marsh tit-mouse, cole tit-mouse, the robin too, and scores of others ? Will any one pretend that either of these has increased to any appreciable, or still less to any injurious, extent ? Nay, it would rather seem as if they were gradually becoming fewer in number, though I would fain hope not. If

I am asked to account for the fact I cannot do it. I have often said to myself that it would almost seem, at least that the effect is, as if there were some mysterious law of nature to forbid the undue increase of any one kind of creature, with some 'Hitherto shalt thou come and no farther'—almost as if the air of the globe were only sufficient for the support of life of a fixed and limited number of each and every kind."

It was not sport (and this cannot be too strongly emphasised), but cruel and senseless sport, against which he declared war, and carried it on vigorously for so many years. To him the battue itself was the height of paltriness, and the means used for its support much worse than contemptible, abounding as it did in cruelty, and seriously interfering with the balance of nature, without which many interesting species of birds must be exterminated. To show in how ruthless a way hawks, for instance, are destroyed by keepers, a friend once wrote to say what was done in this way on the estate of a neighbouring nobleman. The truthfulness of the story could be entirely depended on, and good use was afterwards made of it. It was this :—

"The keeper here found a hawk's nest this year with five young ones in it. He took four and killed them, but left one with its wings clipped as a decoy to destroy the old ones by. They were both shot the next day in the act of feeding the young one, and the keeper thought it was done with. The next day he came again, and found two other charitable hawks who had come with an adoptive feeling to succour the orphan. These two he killed, and then left the nest. On returning afterwards he found two more charitable individuals on the same errand of mercy. One of these he killed; the other he also shot but could not find. No more came on the like fruitless errand." Facts such as this had only to be made public in order to enlist the sympathy of every humane person; many were the expressions of hearty approval which he received from those who thought with him whenever he put pen to paper in dealing with the question of "sport and slaughter."

Frequently he exposed, and that in no measured terms, the whole system of modern battue shooting. More than once did he describe how, in one of his country walks in the year 1877, he overtook a cart loaded up as high or higher than any cart he had ever seen in his life before; three men went with it, and, according to his wont, he fell into conversation with them. The burden under which the horses laboured proved to be a load of coops which were being taken away for the winter, after having served their purpose for hatching tame pheasants under barn-door hens. How many more cartloads there were to follow did not appear, but some idea may be found when it is known that on this particular preserve a twenty-acre field had been covered over with these hen-coops.

This incident was the peg on which to hang a long letter to the *Times*. In this letter, after describing what took place on this occasion, as well as the way in which the young pheasants were reared and what was the nature of their food, he proceeded to relate what took place when and before the day of slaughter arrived. This he does so characteristically that it will not be unfitting if I quote his own words :—

"For some two or three months or more before the grand scene that is to follow, boys are stationed at the corners of the woods all day long to mount guard, and keep the birds from straying or straggling out. There were three who ought to have been at school thus ignobly employed at one of these grand preserves, to my knowledge—say ten in all. I could but pity one of the poor lads whom I spoke to one day, his only shelter in the sadly wet season we had being a few turves supported just over his head on four short sticks stuck in the damp ground. Well might he ask me what time of day it was! When it becomes dark they may go home, no doubt; but then relays come on the scene in the shape of the keepers, who patrol the woods all night long to keep the foxes from their foster-broods, and make night hideous with their shouts and all kinds of noises, disturbing the rest of farmers and all or any within hearing of them.

"The long-expected day arrives—the day for the grand *battue*, a French name and a French practice, and due preparation, you may be sure, has been made for such an important event. A full hundred 'beaters' or more (I am stating a matter

of fact) have been engaged to drive the frightened
game before the shooters, paid each of them—the
beaters, I mean, not the shooters—3s. a day, besides
a lunch of bread and cheese and beer ; and another
hundred or more cast in their lot with them to pick
up their crumbs in the best way they can, in a share
of the provender, or any lost or wounded birds, or
other matters they can purvey for themselves.

"Now we shall come to see what it has all been
for. Each one of these shooters has several guns
ready loaded for him by attendants as fast as he
can fire, and hit or miss being the order of the
day, a fusillade is carried on as long as daylight
lasts, as if they were defending their lives behind
some hastily thrown up redoubt against an over-
whelming force of enemies in the deadly breach.
Tens of thousands of shots are fired in these few
hours. It reminds me of More of More Hall and
the Dragon of Wantley :—

> ' So to it they went with hand and with foot,
> And the word it was hey, boys, hey ! '

But not without a result ! No ! Here are a few of
the ' chronicles of the Canongate.' The said chronicles are duly sent to the newspapers by some
friend or other of the shooters, who knows what
admiration they will think their prowess will excite,
and so become public property. Here, I say, are
a few of them ; they have all been placed on
record :—

"The Duke of ——, Colonel ——, Lord ——,

General ——, Colonel ——, Lord ——, and Lord —— shot last week over Lord ——'s estate at ——. The distinguished party bagged 1495 pheasants, 727 hares, 1231 rabbits, 23 partridges, and 17 woodcocks—making a total of 3493 head ; . . . in all (after calculation), 7 tons 12 cwt. 66 lbs.

" Lastly, a distinguished party in eight days this last year shot 10,500 head, . . . a grand total of, say, some 17 tons. I would suggest that in future some newspaper space would be saved if, instead of enumerating the number of heads of game thus destroyed, the sum total were to be put down by weight. Thus let it be chronicled that on such and such a day Mr. ——, Lord ——, Mr. ——, and a distinguished party of congenial companions shot so many tons, or so many hundredweight, as the case may be, of game—hares, say two tons ; partridges, ten hundredweight ; rabbits, one ton ; pheasants, fourteen hundredweight ; and so on— total, so much. And this is sport !

" By all means let country gentlemen have their shooting to their hearts' content, as in days of yore, when they loaded their own guns, and enjoyed a good day's sport with, at the most, a brace of dogs ; but let this trumpery un-English practice no more expose those who are guilty of it to the jeers, behind their backs, of the very peasantry."

It was not against the battue only that his lance was aimed ; with no less vehemence did he attack fox-hunting. For this pursuit he had nothing to urge in its favour ; in his eyes it was full of cruelty, a gross waste of time and money, and bred a vast amount of selfishness to boot.

For those who would not be convinced by the ordinary form of sober argument, he clothed the expression of his views on the question in a livelier garb, and published them in a pamphlet which had a wide circulation at the time, his remarks having previously appeared in the columns in the *Animal World*. The title-page of the publication at once bespoke its character. It represented a bit of retributive justice in a picture of a huntsman on foot flying for his life pursued by a pack of foxes, who were close upon his heels and ready to tear him to pieces. The author gave his name in full, adding as one of his honours this, namely, that he was "Knight of the most noble Order of St. Francis," a title which, by the way, one of his correspondents afterwards took quite seriously, firmly believing that he had been solemnly dubbed by some unknown sovereign a knight of that particular order, and, therefore, it may be presumed that he wore the ribbon of the said order—a little episode which the "Knight of the Order of St. Francis" himself greatly enjoyed. The pamphlet was written in dialogue form, the principal characters being a squire, a nobleman, a farmer, and a country parson ; the scene was laid on a village green ; the occasion, a meet of the hounds. There were present on horseback Lord Redgauntlet, Lord Newman, Squire Holdhard, Mr. Goahead, Mr. Smash, Mr. Leapwell, and a large and somewhat motley gathering of others; while on foot appeared Farmers Hardy, Turnbull, and Cowfold, Mr. Lookout, and Mr. Stopgap; also huntsmen and hounds, and a number of children who ought to be at school, but are playing truant to "see the hounds." A lively conversation follows, and the arguments for and against are fairly heard. The views of the parson, Mr. De Bracy, are clearly the views of the writer himself. A quotation or two will suffice to show what the nature of those views was. Mr. Smash interposes with the question for the parson, "Then you have not a very high opinion of hunting?"

"*Mr. De Bracy*. If my own opinion stood alone, it would not matter what I thought about it, but a very large and increasing number of educated persons of all ranks think in the same way on the subject.

"*Mr. Smash*. They think it a paltry pursuit, do they?

"*Mr. De Bracy*. No doubt; very many persons do.

"*Mr. Smash*. As how?

"*Mr. De Bracy*. As how! Why, that fifty men, with fifty horses and fifty dogs, should go scouring over the country, breaking fences, injuring growing crops and what not, and all in pursuit of a frightened little animal of less than three feet long which runs off for the bare life as soon as it hears the cry of the hounds, and is not only of no use when dead, but has been artificially preserved at an enormous waste of good money, and still more valuable time, to do much mischief for this so-called sport! It would be just as consistent for you to import wolves

R

and preserve them for the like purpose. They, too, would do harm enough. There would at all events be some show of manliness in hunting them as dangerous animals, and they would be quite as useless as the fox when killed."

The "Knight of the most noble Order of St. Francis" had been in his younger days a keen fly-fisher, and therefore he is made to give an account of his opinion on that head. Mr. De Bracy has to admit his former devotion to the gentle art. "'But,' asks Sir Plantagenet, 'you think differently now?'

"*Mr. De Bracy.* I do; that is to say, I find much more pleasure in other things.

"*Sir Plantagenet.* Then you do not blame those who do follow those pursuits?

"*Mr. De Bracy.* Far from it; as I said before, I have not a word to say against them when practised in moderation and in the old-fashioned and sports-man-like manner.

"*Sir Plantagenet.* Then what difference do you draw between fox-hunting, shooting, and fly-fishing?

"*Mr. De Bracy.* All the difference in the world. Shooting and fishing are useful for procuring good food for the use of man. The fox is of no use. There is also the cruelty in his case, which there is not in the others.

"*Sir Plantagenet.* But there is cruelty in the case of wounded birds sometimes?

"*Mr. De Bracy.* There is suffering—I do not call it cruelty—to some, and every one is sorry for it. It is a drawback from the pleasure of every sportsman.

But these are exceptional cases; the other is the universal rule. There is no more merciful way of killing any animal than by shooting, and it is also the quickest. Besides, there is no suffering caused by the pursuit of birds, or in throwing the artificial fly for fish till they are caught, and even then the mouth is a sort of bone, which can have no feeling."

After dealing with several of the commonly received arguments in favour of fox-hunting, the parson replied thus to one of the party who argued that at all events hunting was a source of pleasure to those who engaged in it:—"That is the turning-point of the whole thing; the very main objection to it is, that pleasure is derived from the pain of the hunted animal. It therefore is, and must be, intrinsically wrong, and no argument can make it right." Much more might be quoted from this lively pamphlet, as well as from various letters which he wrote subsequently, on the subject of hunting. I will, however, only add what he once said when writing to a small country newspaper in 1879, for his remarks are characteristic, and well express what he thought:—

"Some three thousand a year is well known to be the ordinary amount that is considered necessary to keep up a pack of fox-hounds in what is considered a proper style; and as there are some one hundred and seventy packs in the kingdom, besides harriers, stag-hounds, otter-hounds, &c., any one can soon tell what the total loss of money in one way or another comes to, even in one year. Could not the very large sum that is thus yearly required for each establishment for this purpose be better employed? Would not the horses be more usefully engaged in ploughing the land for some small farmers, rather than in injuring the crops, as they now so often do? Could not the rugs that cover them be put to a better use on some poor persons' beds? Could or could not the number of men whose sole occupation is to tend on them be better at work in some one or other of a thousand useful ways? Could or could not the food that the animals are so highly fed up with be more creditably used to feed the poor? . . . The whole thing is nothing but selfishness from beginning to end, and cruelty from first to last. For, whatever pleasure these wasters of time may take in the chase itself, the height of it is allowed on all hands to be in being ' in at the death.' Then the poor little hunted animal which has run for its life in terror of a whole pack of its enemies, hounded on after it, till its breath can hold out no longer, must at last come to a standstill, to be torn in pieces by the dogs. I only ask others to give, themselves, the answer to the question, Is this a sight for *gentle*men and *gentle*women to take pleasure in ?"

XIII

STRAY NATURE-NOTES

For many years Mr. Morris was a frequent contributor to the pages of the *Naturalist*. His name appears as early as 1837 in connection with a paper he wrote on the nomenclature of British Ornithology, a subject which, from his frequent reference to it, seems to have had for him a more than ordinary interest. Among others whose articles or notes find place in the same volume may be mentioned that of his old friend Mr. J. C. Dale, whose knowledge of all matters bearing on entomology was so remarkable, of whom a word presently, together with that of Mr. William Macgillivray, the well-known and reliable authority on British birds. Among other topics on which Mr. Morris wrote in this year were "Migratory Birds," "Arrivals of Birds," "Scarcity of the House Sparrow near Doncaster," "A Chapter on the Varieties of Animals," "On the Value of Faunas," "An Explanation of the Latin Names of British Birds," "Sense of Smell in Carrion Birds," "Notice on the Discovery of a New Insect," "The Note of the Corn-Crake." On the last-named of these he remarked :—" Mr. Bree says that he likes the harsh scream of the Swift almost as well as the melody of the Nightingale. I entertain a similar sentiment with respect to the Corn-Crake, whose creaking voice I love to hear even better than the Thrush's—to my mind the finest songster of the grove. The Corn-Crake is associated with my earliest recollections. Where I once lived it was abundant—I can now hear its note. I used always to consider it a bird of mystery, and I never hear it without the most delightful pleasure."

For five years (1851-1855) the *Naturalist* was under the editorship of Mr. Morris's brother, Dr. Beverley R. Morris, the author of "British Game Birds and Wild Fowl;" this gave my father an additional interest in the magazine, and scarcely a month passed without his adding something to his former contributions to its pages. Occasionally, in giving an account of an interesting fact in natural history, he would characteristically add some little personal experience or other reminiscence which seemed to be inseparably connected with it in his mind. Let the following, which gave an account of a rabbit taking the water, serve as an illustration. The incident took place in Ireland, when my father was a boy. He was standing under a steep cliff, to the base of which the tide nearly came up at high water, when, as he described it, "a rabbit, seemingly disturbed by some persons walking at the top of the cliff, dashed down it, and, whether from choice or impelled by the necessity of its downward impetus I know not, entered the sea and swam out a little way, when it was captured by the servant who was with us—one of the best swimmers, by the way, I ever knew, and my successful instructor in that art. His method was a very simple one; he took me out into deep water, out of my depth, and then let me go—sink or swim—keeping near for fear of accidents. I struck out at once, and was a swimmer ever after." Geoffrey Connell (such was the servant's name) came to an untimely and extraordinary end. He afterwards went to sea, and was believed to have been one of the crew of a merchant-ship, the captain of which turned out to be insane. The poor fellows, as if their own senses had taken leave of them, allowed themselves to be tied down one by one by this madman, who then deliberately cut their throats.

When Dr. Morris left England for America in 1856, my father succeeded him as editor of the *Naturalist*, and continued to act in that capacity for several years; this of course added considerably to his literary work, for he frequently wrote himself for the magazine, and the entire direction of it fell upon him for some time, though for a year or so he was associated with Mr. C. R. Bree, who conducted the entomological department. Many interesting and widely varied articles and nature-notes filled the pages of the magazine, and few were more readable than those of Mr. Thomas Edward, who for several years was a constant contributor to the periodical.

In 1856 Mr. Morris began what he called a " *Systema Naturæ* " in the pages of the *Naturalist;*

that is to say, a systematic catalogue of Nature.
He was quite aware of the vastness of the undertaking, and of his own incapacity to supply in his
lifetime the deficiency which he felt to exist. Still,
he was anxious to make a beginning, which he did,
and carried on the work as long as the *Naturalist*
existed. As he said at the outset of the task, " I
am so deeply convinced of the greatness of the
want, that I have determined to endeavour to carry
into effect the idea which I have long wished and
intended to make an attempt to work out. . . . The
following is only meant to be, as it were, a first and
rough 'proof-sheet' of an 'Annual,' which, whenever brought to its temporary end, may then be
yearly 'revised,' with 'corrections and additions ;'
until at last, long, probably, after I myself shall
have left the scene, it may, '*teres atque rotundus*,'
show in one wide but comprehensive view the vast
extent of the works of the Great Creator." Portions
of this catalogue of Nature were given month by
month till September 1860, when the *Naturalist*
came to an end, Mr. Morris having been connected
with it as editor for more than four years and a half.

It may be thought a matter of surprise as well as
regret that he never undertook to write a " Natural
History of Nunburnholme." Such a History, syste-
matically carried out, would doubtless have proved
an interesting volume, for he might have had endless opportunities of observation ; and having lived
here for so many years, he would have had much
to record, especially of bird-life. That he contem-

plated such an undertaking at one time is certain ; indeed, he went so far as to make a beginning of it in the pages of the *Naturalist*. He did not, however, proceed far with his History, if indeed he can be said seriously to have taken it in hand at all, probably for lack of time. He only noticed in his papers, and that very briefly and disjointedly, about ten different species of birds, although from twenty to five-and-twenty kinds had been known to build in his garden from time to time ; and, besides these, there were many others, of greater or lesser rarity, that had been at different times seen in the neighbourhood.

He frequently expressed the wish that a rookery might be formed in the trees around the Rectory, and in the spring of 1880 there seemed every prospect of the permanent establishment of one.

This event was a matter of the greatest interest to him, and for many weeks he carefully watched and noted down the movements of the birds, and the progress they made in the work of colonisation. The habits of the Rook are so curious and mysterious that the faithful record of any lengthened observation of their ways, especially, perhaps, in such a work as the formation of a new rookery, is worth noticing. The following are some of the notes, rough and incomplete though they be, which were made in this case :—

" 1880, February 3rd—Rooks making a great cawing overhead. March 1st—The first rooks' nest began to be built here ; about finished on the 14th.

March 28th—A second rooks' nest begun. April 5th—The first rooks' nest seemed forsaken, as if the old bird had been shot; but a rook was seen on the edge of the nest, and then flying off with something in its bill, seemingly an egg, so that it may have been robbed by strange rooks, as I had two or three times before seen the old ones driving off others, as if interlopers. May 6th—The young rooks out of the nest. May 18th—Three rooks about the first nest; one of them broke off a small twig and flew away with it in its bill. August 25th—The families of the two rooks' nests in the trees this morning making much cawing; and so on, backwards and forwards, to the 20th of October.

"1881, January 27th—The rooks came back to the nests. 30th—One rook roosting at night in the shrubbery not far from one of the nests, as if keeping guard. February 6th—A pair of rooks about the first old nest in the afternoon. March 14th— Eleven rooks about the nests this morning for a short time. March 16th—A few rooks about the nests for a short time. 18th—Three or four rooks. 19th—Three or four again. 28th—Two in the forenoon about the nests. 29th—Seven before breakfast at the nests. 30th—Three before breakfast about the nests. 31st—Three in the middle of the day, two at one nest, and one near the other. April 1st—Three in the morning, and three or four in the middle of the day. 2nd—Two or three about the nests (and so on more or less till May 27th).

October 16th—One at noon. 18th—Two in the morning.

"1882, April 1st—Four rooks a good deal about the old nests. 2nd—Three about them, one of them keeping guard over one of the old nests. 3rd—Three or four about them. 4th—One of the old nests built on. 5th—The last remains of the other of the old nests blown away to nothing by a high wind." This was the *finale*. From these notes it will be seen that nothing came of all the coming and going in the second year beyond the partial repairing of one of the nests.

The East Riding wold country must in former years have been a "happy hunting-ground" for the ornithologist. Its wide, open tracts, well-wooded valleys here and there, and its comparative nearness to the sea, afforded natural characteristics favourable for the occurrence within its boundaries of a widely varied congeries of species.

In the first half of the present century few birds were more interesting to those dwelling on the wolds of Yorkshire than the Bustard. During part of that time these birds used to breed in the parish of Nunburnholme, and there are those still living who remember to have seen them in the neighbourhood. It interested my father greatly to learn from one of his parishioners in 1876 that he remembered a nest of the Bustard having been found in the parish, and described the egg, which he had seen accurately. Many, no doubt, claimed to possess as a specimen the last bird known to have been shot or taken in the country, and it may be difficult, if not impossible, to verify any particular specimen as absolutely the "last of the Mohicans." My father's brother, Dr. B. R. Morris, had in his possession a splendid specimen of this bird, which he had apparently good reason to believe was one of the last "drove" of British-bred ones which was exterminated in the year 1838. He was only just in time to rescue it from being sold to a man for making fishing-flies of its feathers. It is certain, however, that specimens here and there were taken in England long after this date ; indeed, the one from which the figure was drawn for Mr. Morris's " History of British Birds" was killed so recently as 1851. The drawing of this bird was made by Mr. John Gatcombe of Plymouth, who wrote to the author, under date February 14, 1853, saying, " I feel much pleasure in sending you a drawing of the Great Bustard obtained in this neighbourhood about a twelvemonth ago, thinking you would like to figure from an undoubted British specimen, and the last recorded to have been killed in England." An account of this specimen Mr. Gatcombe had given in the *Naturalist* for February 1852. He had himself examined the bird at the house of Mr. Drew, of Stonehouse, a bird-stuffer there, to whom it had been sent for preservation by J. G. Newton, Esq., Millaton Bridestow, Devon, the bird having been shot on December 31, 1851, and was perfectly fresh when Mr. Gatcombe saw it. It proved to be a female, and the stomach contained a large quantity of turnip-leaves mixed with several flat flinty stones about the size of a sixpence. The base of the feathers on the breast and back were, according to the description, of a beautiful rose-colour. Mr. Gatcombe was an excellent authority on birds, and a frequent and valued correspondent of Mr. Morris's.

It was impossible for my father to live for any length of time in a place without noticing something of the bird-life of the district. This is abundantly exemplified with regard to every parish where his lot, as a clergyman, was cast. Indeed, the foregoing pages will have given some proof of this. It nearly always happened that any unusual occurrence he observed in this way was carefully noted down.

The spring of 1868 was remarkable at Nunburnholme for the scarcity of birds. In the previous year some score pairs of Martins built under the eaves of the church. This year not a single nest was seen, and only a bird at rare intervals. A pair or two of Swallows, which used to build about the place, did not appear on this occasion. Even the Sparrows, generally so numerous, were only represented by two or three pairs. " In short," wrote the Rector, " out of the twenty-five species of birds which have been in the habit of building in the gardens and grounds immediately adjoining this Rectory house—about twenty of them regularly—I cannot make out more than four or five, if so many, that have done so this year—namely, the Black-Cap, the Mistletoe Thrush, the Starling, and the Sparrow.

These are all that I can speak positively about. On the other hand, Nightingales have turned up within sound of our windows, as also in numbers between Scalby and Scarborough, and others at Kilnwick Percy and Everingham, near here." He said it was a popular error to suppose that Nightingales did not come so far north as Yorkshire; for, as he observed, they abound in Edlington Wood, near Doncaster, where he used formerly to see and hear them in numbers, and he had no doubt they would abound in all that neighbourhood, if only they were unmolested. Many evidences are at hand to show how full of interest he was while a curate at Doncaster in all that pertained to the natural history of the neighbourhood.

Always having an eye for a bird, and especially a rare one, it was with no little delight that he used to watch the Crossbills, which at that time frequented the neighbourhood of Doncaster in considerable numbers. Their tameness, for birds in a wild state, was quite remarkable; indeed, a friend once informed him that, when first he used to visit the wood where they abounded, they would allow him to fire his gun at them repeatedly without leaving the tree on which they were perched. Later they became more wary; but still, at the time when Mr. Morris saw them, he said they were the tamest wild birds he had ever seen. They attracted his attention especially by the extraordinary strength' they possessed in their feet, grasping the branches of the trees with wondrous tenacity, swaying their bodies in various directions, and putting themselves into all kinds of curious attitudes in order to get at their food.

Some of the geological peculiarities of the district had for him a special interest. Among the places near Doncaster which he, as a naturalist, found well worth visiting was the curious level district known as Hatfield Chase. What the history of this striking formation was afforded food for inquiry and speculation. From observations which he made on the occasions of his visits to the Chase, he came to the conclusion that it had been at one time a tangled forest; at another, covered by fresh water; and at another period, inundated by the sea. On one of these visits he came across workmen engaged in clearing out a deep dyke. When at about eight feet below the surface, and two and a half below low-water sea-level, they found parts of the trunks and roots of trees in an upright position; others of a similar kind were seen nearer the present surface; so that he came to the conclusion that the ground at the time when these trees were growing was more undulating than it is at present. In other places he discovered that many curious land-shells had been dug up, together with nuts and acorns. The bones of animals, probably deer, were also from time to time unearthed. In a paper which he contributed to the *Naturalist* he gave the following as the most probable theory as to the history of this curious region, namely, that at some remote period "a vast stream must have flowed through these tracts; that its course on some occasion must have been impeded by an accumulation of fallen trees. . . . Its outlet being thus obstructed, the natural consequence was the overflowing of the low land in its vicinity, and the water was in all probability prevented from running off into the sea again by such low eminences as still exist, and are now useful to keep out the tide in the Trent from forcing its way, in its turn, over the land inside. The deluge of this river probably remained for some considerable time, until at length some obstruction was removed from staying its onward course; and when it retired it left an accumulation of soil, such as a river will always bring down upon the previously levelled surface which the action of the sea (*i.e.*, on the supposition that the sea was the first invader) had already prepared for its reception."

From his Oxford days onwards my father's intense devotion to the study of entomology never waned. One of his most valued and interesting correspondents was his friend of boyhood, Mr. J. C. Dale, already mentioned.

Mr. Dale's collections of British insects and stuffed birds was very extensive, one of the rooms of his house being entirely occupied by them, and he was said to have possessed the most complete private entomological library in the country. He was a perfect enthusiast in regard to entomology, and thought nothing, even in those days of coaches, of a journey to Scotland or the Lakes in search of some rare butterfly or other. He for many years corresponded with my father, and his letters were curiosities in their way, being as full as they could hold of entomological lore, varied by animated arguments and discussions on various points connected with insects and his collections, together with not a few eccentricities of diction. He usually wrote at great length, and his epistles contained so many Latin names of moths and butterflies that, at the first glance, it seemed as though he might be writing some unintelligible Latin exercise. Here are one or two extracts from a letter under date Glanvilles Wootton, near Sherborne, 3rd October 1842 :—

"I have just heard from your doctor, and he has given a hint which I take at once for fear of exciting your wrath against me for not giving you a specimen of my handwriting since your last *non-entl:* epistle. If you want to hear what I have done lately in collecting only, that will be very short—almost amounting to just nothing at all— one *Perænea cristana, Sarrothripus Afzelianus* one, *Leptogramma Squamana* one, *Tortrix piceana* one, one Death's Head sent from Sherborne wh. yr. 'Counsellor' took to London to a friend. I believe this is nearly all I have taken, but not all I have added. I have a box here now of Scotch insects from Weaver; . . . a new Crambus allied somewhat between *Baccæstria, Sylvallus,* and *Dumetorium.* . . . A new Oporobia (*Polata Duponchell*) has been taken in Scotland and near Manchester in plenty; it bears the same affinity to *O. Dilutata* as *P. Artaxerxes* to *Agestis,* and *Davus* to *Typhon,* &c. Mr. Haworth

S

talked of *sub-species ;* the late Mr. Burney said it was 'highly unphilosophical' and species or no species for him. Now I do not think *Polata* is a distinct species, neither can you call it a 'permanent variety,' because it varies quite as much as the genuine *Dilutata. O. camlinca* bears, again, the same relation, and whether you call it a 'local variety' or a 'sub-species' matters little to me. *Charissa obscuraria, C. pullaria, C. serotinaria,* and *C. dilucidaria* are called by some people distinct species because, in their respective haunts, they have a peculiar character, affected no doubt by the soil or herbage where they are found; but if these four are distinct, how many more might there be ?—at least double, if not *ad inf."* Much more did he write in this letter, which is a short one compared with many. In concluding his letters, he signed himself "Yours entiy," which probably was an abbreviation for "yours *entomologically"* (!). Mr. Dale was quite capable of such a piece of originality !

Of all branches of natural history, there was none, as before stated, that my father pursued with greater zest than this, and none to which he gave more time and attention. Of this proofs are not wanting. Let the following, which dates from the year 1865, suffice. He had long felt it to be an entomological want to have, as far as possible, a complete catalogue of our British insects in all the orders. Nothing of the kind had been attempted since those published by Curtis and Stephens many years previously. These were now out of date, much progress having been made since those days. While his "History of British Moths" was in course of publication he undertook to prepare such a catalogue, and the work was completed and published early in 1865. With a view to making the catalogue as useful as possible, one feature of it was, that it could be made available for the mutual exchange of specimens. The names, too, being printed on one side of the paper only, could easily be utilised for fixing in cabinets. The work was one of some difficulty; indeed, it could not have been carried out without assistance, and on its completion he gratefully acknowledged the help he had received from Mr. W. F. Kirby, and from others who were engaged at the British Museum. The catalogue extended to 125 pages, and the looking through of the proofs only must have needed the greatest care. It is certainly remarkable that such a by-work should have been carried out at a time when the "History of British Moths" was in course of publication—an undertaking which involved such untold trouble and difficulty. This is, indeed, one of the many standing proofs of the extraordinary patience and perseverance of the author, and his unbendable determination to overcome all difficulties that stood in the way of anything on which he had set his mind to accomplish.

Not least among the large collection of Nature-notes that he had in course of years brought together was the extraordinary mass of anecdotes of animal sagacity and character that had come before his notice, or that of his correspondents and others. Most of these he from time to time published in some way or other. To some of them allusion has already been made. To the *Fireside Magazine*, for instance, he contributed a "Thousand and One Stories from Nature," his "Anecdotes in Natural History" contained one hundred and seventy-five, and his "Records of Animal Sagacity and Character" three hundred and eighteen—in all, nearly fifteen hundred. The year 1882 found him still with a considerable number of such animal stories on hand. Accordingly he contributed in that year to the pages of the *County Gentleman* a hundred of these, which he headed "A Century of Anecdotes of Animals and Birds," characteristically adding at the end of his few introductory words, " I most sincerely hope that the stories may tend to the promotion of a good and kind feeling towards all God's creatures." This, indeed, might have been prefixed to all he wrote about them either in this or any other way, for it truly expressed what he himself felt.

Indications of this kind might be almost indefinitely multiplied showing what a store of facts connected with various branches of natural history came before his notice from time to time, either from his own observations or those who corresponded with him.

XIV

DECLINING YEARS (1873–1893)

ALTHOUGH living such a quiet and, in one sense, uneventful life at Nunburnholme, Mr. Morris's time was nevertheless as fully occupied as it was possible to be ; he was never idle. As nature abhors a vacuum, so his energies seemed as if they must perforce be continually finding exercise in something. It appeared impossible for him to pass any portion of his time without occupation of some kind. We are told of Thomas Bewick that odd moments at meal-times were seized by him to perform a few touches of his truly marvellous art ; in a somewhat similar way, as regards the economising of time, my father would daily snatch such moments for providing for his feathered flock and other creatures their morning meal of crumbs and other fragments. People used sometimes to wonder how it was he did not wear himself out by this perpetual motion of mind and body. But nature was kind to him, and he was always able to sleep off any wear-and-tear of the previous day. This recuperative power was invaluable to him ; without it he must have utterly broken down. He was never what would be called an early riser, but "took it out" in sleep; though when awake he was wide awake, and that instantly.

If at night he was by chance sleepless at intervals, or if he awoke betimes, he used sometimes to jot down on a writing-tablet, kept by his bedside for the purpose, any thoughts that occurred to him that he wished afterwards to recall, for fear of forgetting them. This he could do in the dark in characters that he himself, but probably no other, could decipher.

To this gift of easily sleeping the fact is no doubt due that advancing years—that irresistible power which with so many writers causes a slackening in the speed of the pen, or perhaps even periods of stoppage altogether—had in Mr. Morris's case no such result. It is probable that for the last twenty years of his life he was fully as actively employed in this way as he was in the twenty which preceded them.

While it is true that all his more voluminous works may be assigned to the earlier period, the last published of them being the "County Seats," still, what with the publication of numerous pamphlets, small treatises, innumerable letters to newspapers as well as to private individuals, to say nothing of corrections of proofs and emendations of volumes already published, the years from 1873 onwards were years of ceaseless literary work and activity in many directions. A leading feature in all this mass of writing and work was the large and increasing share given up to the cause of humanity, for the longer he lived the more strongly did he seem to feel on all that pertained to the kindly treatment of dumb animals; while, needless to say, his crusade against vivisection was to the very last unabated, and for some years during the last decade of his life he would send out by post almost daily large numbers of circulars, letters, and leaflets bearing on that question.

Thus the months and years rolled on, each day bringing with it opportunities for work of various kinds, not only in his own parish, but, as far as in him lay, wherever he felt he could speak or act for the great cause he had so much at heart. Never was he so happy as when he felt himself permitted to be instrumental in doing his own small share in mitigating the world's evils, increasing its store of happiness, and in promoting anything that made for righteousness, justice, and truth. All this with him was a religious duty, and literally a *business*.

Sunday was to him a welcome day. Its duties refreshed rather than overtaxed his powers. The church itself in which he officiated for so many years was very small, and needed no strain of voice to fill. To say nothing of other considerations, the very fact of his Sunday work being a change was to him almost as good as a rest.

Although considerable improvement had been effected in the general appearance and fittings of the little church at Nunburnholme shortly after Mr. Morris came to the parish, yet anything like a complete restoration of the dilapidated building had never been taken in hand. For many years he shrank from the work, thinking it would not be possible in so small a place to raise sufficient money for the purpose. However, after many delays, and the exercise of a certain amount of persuasion from some members of his family, he finally determined to attempt the task; and after having engaged the services of Mr. George Gilbert Scott, junior, to make a survey, he issued a circular to the public appealing for funds. This appeal met with an encouraging response. Lord Muncaster, one of the principal landowners, generously contributed £400, and Lord Londesborough £150, the total outlay being close upon £1000; the rest of the sum was made up by Mr. Morris's parishioners, relatives, and friends. The only portion of the church that was not included in the restoration was the tower, which still, for lack of funds, remains *in statu quo*. The work was completed by the spring of 1873. It was a happy day for the parish when the church was reopened, which it was on April 18th in that year. The Archbishop (Dr. Thomson) kindly came to preach on the occasion, and he prefaced his sermon with a brief but fitting allusion to the rector and his tastes. He remarked :—" Time was when the learning of the world was concentrated in the clergy. That is not so now; but I hope the time is very far distant when the clergy shall lag behind in the knowledge of science and in general cultivation. Whatever may be said on this subject, in this place knowledge and culture reign, and I am

sure that your pastor has never abridged one hour
of his labour amongst you for the subjects which
he has studied so well and so devotedly.   I am sure
that nothing which he says in this place will be
weakened because he takes a great interest in the
works of God's creation, and I am sure that his interest in the souls of those to whom he ministers is
none the less that he has spared a thought for the
migratory birds which sometimes pass over this
part of the country.   I am reminded of the words
of one of our poets, who says—

> ' He prayeth well who loveth well
> Both bird and man and beast.' "

The general effect of the work of restoration was
highly approved of, all the old and interesting
features of the fabric being carefully preserved
where possible, thus connecting in itself the present with the centuries long past, and preaching a
silent but still forcible sermon in stone.

The restoration of the church renewed in him a
desire for a rearrangement of a portion of the parish.
The little hamlet and chapelry of Thorpe-en-le-Street,
situated some three miles distant, had from time im-
memorial been served by the rectors of Nunburnholme.   The chapel itself had fallen into decay
generations ago, and no services had been held
there since ; the population, too, was exceedingly
small, the whole township consisting of a couple
of farms with their dependencies.   For years Mr.
Morris had wished for a new parish to be formed

out of this isolated ancient chapelry and part of the parish of Market-Weighton called Shipton. Accordingly, in conjunction with the vicar of Market-Weighton, he set to work to accomplish his object, and was glad to be enabled to see this carried into effect a few years later; thus the new ecclesiastical parish of Shipton-Thorpe was formed. This, indeed, severed a connection which had been in existence certainly for over six hundred years, which, from one point of view, was regrettable, though this connection is so far maintained in that a portion of the tithes of Thorpe is still payable to the rectors of Nunburnholme. My father always felt great satisfaction when this work was accomplished, and that he had been in a measure instrumental in having this new .ecclesiastical parish formed and a residence for a clergyman built. He was strongly in favour of the multiplication of even smaller parishes than were, perhaps, by most people thought desirable.

It was very seldom that he went far from home, especially in the latter years of his life. He was always happiest in doing his work quietly in his own parish, and in the constant exercise of his pen. Only on urgent business or from a strong sense of duty would he ever consent to travel so far as London. One such call of duty occurred in June 1873, when he felt he ought, in compliance with an invitation, to make a journey there in order to be examined before a Committee of the House of Commons on the subject of bird protection. His exami-

nation would have been a protracted one, but, at
the Chairman's suggestion, he preferred to hand in
a written statement embodying his views on the
details of the question. His oral evidence, while it
lasted, was given very strongly in favour of the rook,
which bird he always stoutly defended against indiscriminate slaughter, maintaining that it did more
good than harm to the farmer. "Do you think,"
asked one of the members of the Committee, "that
the farmers and occupiers of land are the best
judges whether or not the rooks are doing harm,
and that they should be allowed to destroy them
if they pleased?" "No; I fear they are often very
bad judges indeed." "Then what would you do in
that case? Have you been a farmer?" "No, I
never was a farmer." "If you yourself had a field
of corn and you saw a number of rooks settling
down in your corn-field, what course would you
follow in order to prevent the destruction of your
crops?" "I would frighten them off by firing a
gun or I would shoot them." "Then you do not
desire to prevent the farmers or others shooting
them in such cases as that?" "Certainly not, nor
any bird that does harm at other times of the year."
"The same remarks would apply, I suppose, to any
other bird that will destroy produce or crops in
gardens?" "Yes, certainly." The replies that he
made on this occasion were in accordance with all
he had said and written upon the subject years
before that time as well as afterwards; in fact, he
seldom saw reason to modify the opinions he had

originally formed after careful observation and reflection.

Before the beginning of 1876 the value of the "Humanity Series of Schoolbooks," which had been published a year or two previously, was acknowledged on all hands, and their usefulness received a stimulus in course of time owing to a lady, well known for her benevolence, having contributed a considerable sum for giving away the books to poor schools. A large number of applications were received for these gifts, and it was a revelation to find what heavy sacrifices many of the clergy in some of the very poorest parishes had made, and were making at that time, on behalf of their schools. Thus, for instance, one clergyman wrote to say that he did not know whether his case would come under the definition of " Poor Schools," for others might be poorer ; but he did know that the previous year's account left him with a heavy balance to meet, which a living of but £95 a year could ill afford to make good, the adverse balance being nearly £28. Another wrote that his parish contained a thousand very poor people, among whom he had worked for sixteen years, building church, rectory-house, and schools ; he added: "I cannot imagine a parish where the 'Humanity Series of Schoolbooks' would be of greater service. I would gladly purchase this series of books for the children were it in my power." Dozens of similar cases might here be quoted showing clearly enough how well bestowed the good lady's gift was, and that there was a loud call throughout the land for the teaching of humanity. In a certain district from which an application was received this was made plain by the following testimony of a schoolmaster :—" Since my appointment here I have noticed such determined and wanton cruelty towards birds that I have thought over and over again what could I do to remove such unkindness. I was told not long since that a boy had caught twenty-five birds under a sieve, and then wrung their necks only for sport ! Bird-killing—chasing with stones—is an everyday amusement."

The horrors of the growing practice of experimentalising on living animals were never long out of his mind during this period of his life.

In March 1877 he issued one of his feeling appeals to the public in support of an address to be presented to Mr. Secretary Cross, then at the head of the Home Office, in favour of the total suppression of vivisection, or, as he worded it, " The purport of the address will be to urge the Government to support a Bill for the entire prevention of the unhallowed, degrading, and unmanly practice referred to." It had been found that the Act passed in the previous session was insufficient for the purpose for which it was designed, although no doubt it was generally looked upon as a step in the right direction by those opposed to vivisection. Accordingly, continues the circular, " I ask you in the name of God's dumb creatures, they being unable to ask you themselves, to sign and return to me the address in the behalf of Mr. Secretary Cross, a copy of which I send with this.

.   .   .   .   .   .

"I have had before me the authority of Lord Shaftesbury for stating that never since the agitation on the factory question has the feeling of the country been so deeply moved as it has been by the martyrdoms of our 'dumb companions.'" At the end of his appeal for signatures he added in a footnote the expression of many eminent men on this question, most of which were couched in the strongest language, though it may, I venture to think, be said with safety that not one of those whose words were cited felt more strongly upon the subject than the writer of the circular himself. It was a matter of deep regret to him, therefore, that the Government did not see its way to amend the law in the way desired, and to the last he never ceased to deplore the laxity of the application of adequate measures of repression.

With the early spring of this same year (1877), when the aconites in the Rectory garden were still a blaze of gold and the birds were beginning to make their voices heard, came a heavy blow to the rector and his family, and one that cast a gloom over the household and parish. In the early part of March my mother met with a grievous accident. She was incautiously standing behind a cart while speaking to its occupant, when the horse suddenly backed, and she was thrown violently to the ground, the wheels of the cart passing over her; she was severely injured, and in spite of all that skilled medical aid and devoted nursing could do, she never recovered from the terrible shock to the system.   For several weeks she lay in a critical state, her life, as it were, hanging in the balance, and it was not till April 18th that she was released from her patiently endured sufferings, when she quietly and peacefully passed away. She was laid to rest in the little churchyard hard by the home where she had spent so many happy years, beloved by all who knew her.   It may truly be recorded of her that she left "her kind deeds and happy, gracious ways shining like a track on the waters behind her."   Acutely as my father felt his loss, he bore up against the blow bravely, his naturally hopeful, sanguine, and cheerful spirit standing him in good stead in the heavy trial he then passed through.

Nothing could be greater than the kindness of friends and neighbours at this sad time ; to none was he more beholden for kind sympathy than to his valued friend, Canon Wilton of Londesborough, who, in preaching at Nunburnholme on the Sunday following the funeral, made touching allusion to the sad circumstances attending Mrs. Morris's death, taking for his text the words of David in 1 Sam. xx. 3, "There is but a step between me and death." Never did my father feel the help of his devoted daughter Laura of greater value than now, and he always spoke of it in terms of the deepest affection, satisfaction, and thankfulness.   He did not lay aside his work in any respect, but seemed to find comfort after his bereavement in renewing his many-sided labours with something at least of his old force and vigour. Whether suggested by the circumstances connected with this time of sorrow or not I cannot say, but before the close of April 1877 he had compiled a small "Hand-Book of Hymns for the Sick Bedside," which in after-years he found most valuable in visiting the sick in his parish. It included many of those hymns which were his own favourites, among which may be named, "Art thou weary, art thou languid;" "O let him whose sorrow;" "Lead, kindly light;" "Abide with me; fast falls the eventide;" "Rock of Ages, cleft for me;" "O Lord, how happy should we be;" "O God, our help in ages past;" "My life's a shade, my days apace to death decline," the last-named being one which he specially valued. As with nearly all his works, both great and small, he inscribed a motto on the title-page, so in this little compilation also he did the same; in this case he chose the appropriate words from the 89th Psalm—"Misericordias Domini in æternum cantabo." He always in after-years kept a small stock of this "Hand-Book of Hymns" by him, and frequently gave them away in his own parish, and to many outside it also; they were always much appreciated by the sick.

At no period did he carry on his crusade against the heartless practices of the vivisectionists more persistently than in the last decade of his life. His greater literary works being then accomplished, he no doubt felt himself freer to agitate for a more organised attack against this particular form of cruelty, which he always looked upon as a disgrace to our age and country, as indeed, in his eyes, it would be to every age and every country, when men were found to put their hand to such abominations under any pretence whatever. For several years he was in the habit of sending off almost daily by post countless packets of papers bearing upon the question, in the hope of enlightening the minds of people to what was really going on around them, and exposing the horrors of the whole system, the very first principles of which he looked upon as an outrage on civilisation. Of his views on the subject generally I have spoken elsewhere, and therefore need not here dwell further upon them. It is only here again alluded to in order to show that he never allowed the subject to drop, but that to the very end of his life he was found vigorously preaching the gospel of kindness and mercy, in the most practical and forcible way that lay in his power, to thousands and tens of thousands beyond the boundaries of his own parish.

He kept his eye on passing events during these latter years with quite as much interest and keenness as ever. It was remarkable how sometimes things seemingly unimportant had for him an interest that astonished his friends. Those who attain the allotted threescore years and ten may well claim a certain indulgence for not displaying an active concern in the events of the day or the hour; no such indulgence was ever claimed by my father. The fact was, he was never an old man except in years, for he had none of the ways of old men about him ; his mind and memory were fully as fresh and active at eighty as they were at fifty, and he was as thoroughly alive to the questions of the day and the events that were passing around him at the latter period as he was at the former. His sight and hearing were practically as good in 1892 as in 1872 ; if his step was not quite as elastic a year or two before his death as of yore, he could at least walk several miles without fatigue.

No trouble was too great for him to take in order to rectify any statement which seemed to him to need correction, but which the ordinary reader would have let pass without comment. His action on these occasions can best be described, perhaps, by saying that he appeared ever on the look-out, and was ready to fall upon the unwary scribe like a hawk that had been hovering over its prey.

I need not mention names, but, as an instance of this, will only say that one Mr. X. had been contributing his opinions to a certain Church paper on a point connected with the headings to the chapters in the Bible. This correspondent had, in the course of his observations, made some extraordinary statements which need not here be entered into ; they were such, however, as to carry absurdity on the face of them, and most of those who read them would assuredly have at once seen the palpable errors, and not have considered the writer worth the powder and shot necessary to demolish him. Not so Mr. Morris. He took the trouble to give a whole series of quotations to show the wrongness of the assertions, and filled nearly a column of the paper with his exposure of him.   Had he been asked why he expended his energies on so trivial a matter, he would no doubt have replied, that somebody might have accepted the statement as correct without inquiry, and so harm would have been done, and, at all events, that Mr. X. himself needed a little instruction.

He was specially quick to animadvert upon anything that might appear in print in disparagement of the Church, of which he was so devoted a son. Points which most men would either not notice, or, if they noticed them, would not think it worth while to take any trouble to rectify, these my father would never let pass, but would take any amount of trouble to expose and put straight.   Many illustrations of this might here be given, but let a single one suffice. The frequent use he made of tracts has been elsewhere spoken of.   He circulated many of those of the Society for the Promotion of Christian Knowledge, though more frequently those published by the Religious Tract Society.   One of these latter he had been reading, and in one particular at least had occasion to communicate his views to the editor. It was this.   The tract told, as my father read it, how a poor man got no good by going to church, but at once became converted by going to the "little chapel" close by.   This, as he observed, was not keeping true to the principle the Society professed, of holding an even balance between Church and Dissent.   On bringing this before the editor's notice, it was pointed out in defence that the person spoken of as having failed to receive spiritual good at the church was not the same as the one spoken of as having become converted at the "little chapel." This was true enough, and should not have escape his notice ; still, as Mr. Morris observed, the fact remained that the one first spoken of did not receive benefit from attending church, while the second spoken of did receive benefit from attending the "little chapel," and thus the main point referred to was left untouched. The editor further suggested, though he did not lay stress upon it, that the word "chapel" might have been meant for a Church of England one ; this, however, as Mr. Morris pointed out, could hardly have been intended by the writer, but the contrary ; and on this he proceeded to explain what the exact meaning of the word "chapel" is, and quoted John Wesley's own words in which he warned his people not to call the houses where they assembled anything else but preaching-houses. He further added that he disliked the term "place of worship," which might apply equally well to a heathen temple or a Mohammedan mosque, and although the expression "House of God" did not meet the case altogether, he preferred it to the other. This incident, insignificant though it may seem, is sufficient to show the way in which he dealt with points of this kind that casually came across his notice. Had he felt it necessary, he would have taken ten times the trouble he did to correct what appeared to him erroneous.

The chief part of what he wrote against the Evolution theory, as adopted by followers of Darwin, was published during the last twelve or fifteen years of his life.   His general line of argument has been indicated in another section of this memoir, and therefore need not be dwelt upon here.   To enter into the details of his combative methods would be an endless task ; they are, moreover, generally well known.   It need here only be repeated that nothing short of a positive duty would have led him to have expended so much time and labour in a cause which, from his point of view, he deemed to be sacred, and this the more when he saw how many there were who were carried away by extravagant ideas founded upon theories which could not be, or at least had not been, proved.   One word only need here be added in this connection.

When so many of those eminent in the scientific world gave their adhesion to the doctrines of Darwin, it was something of the nature of a consolation to Mr. Morris to find men of such sound judgment and sober sense as the late Lord Hatherley and Lord Selborne (both of whom had filled the office of Lord Chancellor) expressing themselves as altogether on the opposite side.   The former, in a letter he wrote to Mr. Morris, uttered no halting opinion as to what seemed to him the unphilosophical conclusions arrived at by some of the Darwinian school.   He shall speak for himself :—

"THE RED HOUSE PARK, IPSWICH,
December 2, 1876.

" REV. SIR,—I owe you an apology for not sooner
acknowledging your courtesy in sending me a copy
of your valuable exposure of Darwinism, but I
usually, when I hope to read a book, wait till I have
so done before thanking the author.

" I have only this day perused the pamphlet, and
most heartily thank you for it.   I believe that your
mode of treating the preposterous fictions of Darwin
is the only way to shake the self-confident tone of
would-be philosophers.   Newton's grandest saying
(after ' *Deus non est Æternitas sed Æternus* ') was
' *Hypotheses non fingo.* '   I have more than once
quoted this, and once at a Royal Society dinner.

"Newton kept back his Principia for years because a mistake had been made in the measurement
of an arc of the meridian, so closely did he keep to
experimental truth.   Now the crudest fancy, nothing
like so ingenious as the Ptolemaic cycles, because
really the Darwin fancy stumbles at every step, is
exalted into a rank exceeding that of the discovery
of gravitation.

" I remember —— excommunicating from the
scientific fold any one who believed that man could
come from a single pair, regard being had to the
negro, Chinese, &c., &c., and then saying, at the
meeting of the British Association, he had wholly
forsaken his former view, and Darwin is the new
Mahomet, and all are to be excommunicated who

do not believe that man comes from a proto-plasm, in company with sea-anemones, crocodiles, monkeys, &c.

"In a very clever sermon by Pritchard (now Savilian Professor at Oxford, and formerly President of the Astronomical Society), preached before the British Association when Grove presided, he exposes the folly of this stuff, and in his appendix to a print of it, proves that the chances against the eye being formed by development are more in number than those of Darwin's book being taken by the printer to pieces and tumbled into a bag, and then thrown back on the table in the same order as they went in.

"But I am not going to write a treatise, and only add that I am, yours respectfully,

"HATHERLEY.

"The Rev. F. O. MORRIS."

So, too, Lord Selborne, writing to him on June 4, 1877, although he had not then had time to read through the pamphlet which my father had lately published, knew enough of its contents to be able to say, "Your opinion of 'Darwinism' is evidently the same as my own."

To this same period may be assigned many of his letters to the *Times*, to some of which allusion has already been made elsewhere. Most of these letters had reference to birds, though by no means all. Among these communications may be found letters on "Thrift," "Gleaning," "Humanity Teaching in Schools," "The Rat," &c.

It is remarkable—-might we not say touching ?—to see with what persistence Mr. Morris devoted himself at all times to the cause of his feathered friends. Advancing years were no barrier to him, nor in anywise cooled his ardour in his ceaseless activities and earnest labours on their behalf.

In the autumn of 1885 the fashion was at its height of decking ladies' hats, bonnets, and dresses with stuffed birds or portions of them. It was impossible for such a fashion to escape the censure of him who had attempted and accomplished so much in defence of the birds. It was not to his thinking enough simply to decry the fashion. He therefore threw himself heart and soul into an organised crusade against it. Accordingly, towards the close of the same year, at the suggestion of Lady Mount-Temple, he took the lead in establishing what was called "The Plumage League." The membership was restricted to ladies. Its main object was to discourage by every means in their power—by their example, their practice, their influence, their words, and their writings—the use of small and other birds stuffed for the supposed adornment of dresses, hats, and bonnets. It was urged in the circular announcing the formation of the League that, if ladies wished to adorn themselves in this way, they should use artificial birds ; a new industry would thus be developed for this purpose, after the manner of the industry for the manufacture of artificial flowers.

On December 19th in this year a letter signed

F. O. Morris appeared in the *Times* drawing attention to the movement, and enlisting sympathy and help for the poor birds. He quoted a letter from Lady Mount-Temple to him, in which she said :—"You have probably, with your usual zeal for our dear friends the birds, written on the subject of this shameful destruction to meet the tasteless fashion of covering ladies' bonnets, hats, and ball-gowns with lovely specimens of them, and in some cases with our special favourites and home pets. They parade the massacre, showing the heads and throats sometimes stretched, as if in dying agonies, on the hat. A milliner told me she had put twelve birds on one. Another told us of a ball-dress covered with canaries. I am glad to say the wearer of it, though handsome, had no partners." Even the kingfishers on the Thames were destroyed for this same contemptible and cruel purpose. The letter concluded with an earnest appeal to the ladies of England to put a stop to this hateful and cruel fashion.

The following day a leading article appeared in the *Times* backing up the plea urged by their "old and welcome correspondent, the Rev. F. O. Morris," as they were pleased to describe him, concluding with a forcible expression of their opinion on the subject by saying:—"Surely Lady Mount-Temple and her ally, Mr. Morris, will not be left to plead in vain for those who have so much to say for themselves, could they but say it. As a mere matter of taste there can be no doubt about the matter. A live bird is a beautiful thing. A dead bird is a very ugly thing. Even when stuffed and in a glass case, it is a barely tolerable curiosity."

Inserted in the circular were several of his friend the Rev. Richard Wilton's tasteful and telling sonnets, and the principles of the League were set forth at the end. Lady Mount-Temple and the Hon. Mrs. R. C. Boyle acted as secretaries. It was argued that every one would acknowledge that "the enjoyment of Nature is immensely enhanced by the lovely forms and movements of the birds of our woods and shrubberies, filling the air as they do with song, and answering in the most endearing way by their familiarity and friendliness to any kindness shown to them on our part. The display of the dead and distorted bodies of these lovely creatures is obnoxious also to good taste, and the plumage, which is doubtless ornamental, can easily be obtained by fair means."

It may be interesting here to state the relationship between the Plumage League and the early history of the Selborne Society, an organisation which has since widely extended itself. This I gather from a short circular issued in May 1888 by George A. Musgrave, Esq., who with Mrs. Musgrave were the originators of the Selborne Society, or, as it was then called, the Selborne League. Cards of membership were issued on December 17, 1885. The circular states :—"The Plumage League was a happy suggestion made by the Rev. F. O. Morris, the veteran champion of the birds, on the 18th December 1885, in the *Times*." Lord and Lady Mount-Temple kindly defrayed the printing expenses connected with the formation of the Plumage League, and on January 28, 1886, Mr. Morris, who was one of the earliest members of the Selborne League, at the suggestion of the Hon. Mrs. R. Boyle, at once consented to merge his Plumage League in Mr. Musgrave's Selborne League.

In all this work which Mr. Morris undertook for those that could not speak for themselves he never gave a thought to himself or his own interests, and this remark applies to all he did and wrote through life. He was the last man to tone down his words or trim his sails to catch any favouring gale, from whatever quarter it might blow ; still, it was a cause of satisfaction whenever he knew that his efforts had been appreciated by any whose opinions he valued. It was, therefore, an agreeable announcement to him when he learnt in 1888 that the Government, through Mr. W. H. Smith, then First Lord of the Treasury, had so far recognised his work as a naturalist as to recommend him for a Civil List pension of £100 a year. This recognition of his lifelong labours by the Government of the day was a source of gratification to him, and the addition to his income that it brought him in his declining days was much valued.

In 1886 he was seized with an acute and painful attack of eczema. At one time it was thought the illness might take a serious turn ; in time, however, it yielded to the skill of his medical attendant, and he eventually threw it off, but it left him weakened considerably for some time, though not otherwise injured as regards his general health.

It certainly speaks well for his activity and patience when, in his eightieth year, merely for some literary purpose, he read, or rather looked, Shakespeare through, and not only so, but as he went on, proceeded to put down any short passages which, one knows not how or why, have become "familiar in our ears as household words." These, which make quite an interesting array of quotations, he contributed to the pages of the *Stonyhurst Magazine*, having previously sent some lengthy articles to that publication on ornithological subjects, notably one on the Sparrow, a bird for whom he was always prepared to do battle.

Another small by-work that he undertook in these latter years was to compile from the larger work of Bishop Wordsworth an epitomised commentary of the Book of Revelation; he never did more than write it, beyond contributing portions of it to one of the Church papers. It was evident at least that he must have expended no little time and care upon this task.

From his earliest years everything pertaining to the sea had a great fascination for him; even the sight of a ship always attracted his attention, and he would minutely observe and comment upon the "cut of the jib," the style of her rigging, and general appearance of her lines. He was fond of making models of yachts in his younger days, and the same taste broke out when he was past seventy, for he then began, though never completed, the model of a schooner which took his fancy. It was a

pleasant reminiscence of his Oxford days in connection with this taste when, in his eighty-first year,
he unexpectedly received the following letter from
an old college friend :—

"WISHFORD RECTORY, SALISBURY,
June 13, 1890.

"MY DEAR MR. MORRIS,—'Tis sixty years since
I contracted a debt of gratitude to you, and I have
been all these years longing for an opportunity of
at least acknowledging it to you ; but seeing lately
your honoured name in some newspaper, writing
as usual in the cause of truth and humanity, I am
compelled to make an opportunity. I believe it
was in 1830 that you spared time to come day after
day from Worcester College to the bottom of High
Street to rig up a model of a schooner for me and
my brother, to our wonderful enjoyment for some
years, and again, in the next generation of boys, to
my son and his numerous cousins.

"That venerable vessel still stands in my study,
at the top of book-shelves, with the remains of your
rigging still existing. It is of more interest to me
than Nelson's *Victory*.

"But I have also, in common with thousands, to
thank you for all you have said, written, and done
in behalf of our inferior fellow-creatures, for which
I know many of their superiors love you.

"May you have many happy years even yet added
to your life.—I am very gratefully yours,

"EDWARD HILL."

One of the last papers written by my father.was one on " Mimicry," which appeared in the pages of the *Field Club*, a magazine afterwards merged with *Nature Notes*. Though admitting that there was just a substratum of truth in the idea, he did not, as it may well be supposed, hold with the general conclusions of the theory. " No doubt," he said, " very many insects closely resemble the objects on which they are wont to repose ; but if it is by this likeness that they have been preserved, how has it come to pass that a vastly greater number of others, which are as unlike their *loca standi* as the former are like them, have survived, and far more numerously, both specifically and individually, as we can see for ourselves every day ? How was it that the unfavoured ones have not been long since exterminated, as Darwin says it was their fate to have been, on his theory ?" As to the idea that birds generally will not attack and devour butter-flies owing to a scent which is distasteful to them, Mr. Morris suggested what seemed to him a more probable and common-sense explanation, namely, that the birds are not tempted to feed on butterflies owing to the large and tasteless wings of the insects surrounding, as he expressed it, " such very small morsels as their bodies to reward their capture—a halfpenny worth of bread to such an intolerable amount of parchment."

XV

LAST DAYS

HE is something more than a strong man who, after passing the extended limit of fourscore years, does not feel that life's fires are cooling down and its former energies growing weaker. And yet it scarcely seemed, until my father had reached this age, that his natural force was to any great extent abated; certainly his mental faculties at that time were as clear and active as ever they were. It is true his bodily frame was less vigorous than of yore, but, as he often thankfully acknowledged, he felt as well in health as ever he did. This gradual weakening of physical power made itself felt in various ways. He could not, for instance, walk the long distances he had been accustomed to do, and his pace, though never what would be called slow, even to the end, lost not a little of its wonted quickness and elasticity. Frequently would he allude to this gradual failure, though never but to look upon and own it as a kind warning of his Heavenly Father. This confession was with him no form of speech, though few, surely, needed such a warning less than he, whose whole life was spent in a practical realisation of the fact that he was daily drawing nearer the stream that cannot be avoided.

Though thus slowly losing strength, nothing would have induced him to give up his duty as long as he could possibly do it with any degree of satisfaction.

Even after one or two alarming seizures of faintness, he would not consent to forsake his usual work. His recuperative power after these attacks was remarkable ; nothing robbed him of his happiness in doing work connected with his calling in life, and his cheerfulness and contentedness never failed him, and he used to say he never *felt* old.

It was not until the autumn of 1892 that he obtained permanent help in his clerical duties ; and even then he did not abstain from doing his share of work to the utmost of his strength, but would still visit constantly among his parishioners, and give general instructions as to what should be done. His birds were as punctually fed, morning by morning, as ever, upon the table he had provided for them in front of his study window ; his letters continued to be answered as promptly as in former years ; his interest in all that went on around him was as keen as of old.

One of the last publications that came from his pen was a series of small papers entitled " Politics for the People ; " these were completed towards the end of this year, and were written in his old trenchant, half-serious, half-humorous style, which those who had read other similar productions of his knew so well. Dealing in these papers with political and ecclesiastical questions, he was plain and outspoken, as he always was, going straight, as it were, into the enemy's camp, and striking with good effect. If his opponents were not convinced by his arguments, they could hardly fail to give him credit for honesty of purpose in his endeavours to expose the fallacies of those who seek to injure the usefulness of the Church, and destroy her influence in the land. Into these questions it would be unfitting here to enter; they are only mentioned as affording proof of his interest in such questions at this period of his life, and of his activity in dealing with the points raised in these lively and entertaining papers.

The early winter of 1892 was in the East Riding, as elsewhere, one of great severity; keen winds and storms swept over the wolds, and penetrated with cruel effect even to the sheltered valley of Nunburnholme. Still, they were not sufficient to keep my father indoors, unless the day happened to be exceptionally stormy. Most days he made his regular walk into the village, or beyond it, to call upon his parishioners and others. Christmas came and went, with all its peaceful joys, and the New Year dawned upon the venerable rector, enfeebled, indeed, as compared with what he was the previous New Year, but still by no means laid by. At this time, and for some months previously, he was engaged in what proved to be his last piece of literary work. This was the revision of the proof-sheets of the

U *

seventh edition of his favourite treatise, the "Natural History of British Butterflies," which Mr. John C. Nimmo had undertaken to publish along with other of my father's works. This task was duly performed, and the proofs sent, with additions and corrections, to Mr. Fawcett's office in Driffield, where this edition was printed, as the first had been about forty years before. The last pages were completed, as previously mentioned, by the author only a very few days before he died. It is worthy of remark that his old associate, Mr. Fawcett, died at the beginning of 1893, being a year or so his senior.

Up to this time he continued with more or less frequency to keep up his correspondence in the newspapers; the last letter that he penned of this kind was one he wrote to the editor of the *Yorkshire Herald*, headed "Winter and Winter," being dated January 16, 1893, and contained, as so many previous ones had done, kindly thoughts for others. It spoke, as it were, forebodingly of the severity of the season, as may be seen from the following quotation. He wrote :—

"My words have come only too true as to the continuance and increase of the cold weather we have had, are having, and may have before we have done with it, or it with us. It has been a most unusually trying time for all, young and old, rich and poor. I was thankful to you for making room for my letter the other week advocating some better provision for the poor shoeblack boys, as

well as the cabmen and their horses, and as I have
no doubt but that every member of the North-
Eastern Railway Company sees the *Yorkshire Herald*,
I can only hope that something may be done ; and
surely the sooner the better, in face of the winter
we are having and may have."

Subsequently to this he corresponded with private
individuals, and every letter he wrote and received
was scrupulously entered in his diary—a practice
he had adopted for many years.

The severest part of the winter seemed now over,
and it was hoped, as he had escaped thus far without
any serious attack, that a further length of days and
usefulness was in store for him ; but, to the great
sorrow of his many friends and relations, these hopes
failed of their fulfilment.

Towards the end of January he caught a chill,
which took an unfavourable turn and developed
into an acute form of bronchitis. The stubborn-
ness of the malady completely prostrated him, and
he was compelled to take to the bed from which he
rose no more, though it seemed at one time as if
his natural powers might still prove superior to the
forces of the ailment. His medical attendant, Dr.
Jefferson of Market-Weighton, who had treated him
so successfully when, a few years previously, he was
well-nigh mastered by the attack of eczema, was at
this trying time unremitting in his attention ; while
his beloved daughter Laura continued, as she had
ever done, to watch over him with the tenderest
care and devotion. But though everything was

done that could be done by loving relatives and friends, the years of my father's active and devoted life were rapidly drawing to an end. At times he suffered much from his breathing, but no word of complaint passed his lips. As he had lived so he met his end ; he had nothing to fear, and he feared nothing ; his whole life had been spent in his Master's service, and it is not too much to say of him that each day was lived as if it were to be his last. He was absolutely resigned ; "in God's hands" he owned himself to be. By daily intercourse through life he knew Him in whom he had believed, nor did he find Him to fail. During the afternoon of February 10th he peacefully passed away. There was something of pathos in the fact that shortly before he breathed his last a favourite collie-dog who was in the room came up to his master's bedside as if to bid him farewell, an approach which was responded to by the gentlest of touches.

His body was laid to rest near the south wall of the little church in which his well-known voice had been so often heard. The words of faith and hope were feelingly read at the grave-side, as they had been sixteen years before at the grave-side of his beloved wife, by his good friend and neighbour, Canon Wilton. Though but mid-February the day was bright and warm, with signs of spring in the early budding flowers and the voices of the birds in the Rectory garden close at hand—no unfitting accompaniments for the occasion. Of him truly it may be said, " He being dead yet speaketh."

APPENDIX I

From a Sermon preached by Canon Wilton in Londesborough Church on Sunday Morning, February 19, 1893.

" I protest by your rejoicing which I have in Christ Jesus our Lord, I die daily."—I COR. xv. 31.

THESE words were read on Wednesday morning in Nunburnholme Church at the funeral of my friend and neighbour for twenty-seven years, the Rev. F. O. Morris. The removal of one who for so long a period has lived in the next parish, and whom through his writings I have known for a still longer time, must needs be an impressive fact for me. I cannot but recall the many hours I have spent with him in intercourse at once friendly, literary, and religious, for we often met to discuss Scriptural subjects. You all know what a lover and friend he was of birds and beasts—how he pleaded in the papers and the pulpit and in his books for dumb animals. They have lost a fearless advocate in him. But the lover of God's creatures was a lover of God—a lover of His House, of His Holy Word, of His glorious Gospel. He was eminently a godly man, a man who lived in the fear of God all the day long ; conscientious, nay scrupulous in the discharge of duty, always placing his work as a minister of the Church before his work as a naturalist; seeking first the kingdom of God and His righteousness, and finding that all other things were added unto him. Though he had lived beyond the allotted fourscore years, he continued until very lately to perform his own clerical duty, and I remember his saying to me that although he found it difficult of late to write altogether new sermons, he tried to put more of Christ into the old ones. And throughout his numerous volumes there is at once " such a hearty enjoyment of Nature and such a devout recognition of the God of Nature, that, while the mind is elevated, the heart is warmed in the contemplation of the wonderful works of the Almighty."

No wonder, then, that Mr. Morris was a cheerful man, always looking at the bright side of things, hoping the best, and trying to bring it about by word and example.

But life, though very real and interesting to him and full of activities, was always passed under the shadow of eternity ; the feeling of our text was ever present to him—" I die daily." He realised the certainty of death, and that gave seriousness to life and tranquillity to his closing days. He had no fear. He left himself, as he explained it, in God's hands. " I am in God's hands," he said, and so his end was peace.

APPENDIX II

LIST OF PUBLICATIONS BY THE
REV. F. O. MORRIS.

1834. "A Guide to an Arrangement of British Birds; being a Catalogue of all the Species hitherto discovered in Great Britain and Ireland." 20 pp. Longmans.

1840. "Extracts from the Works of Rev. John Wesley." 51 pp. Simpkin & Marshall.

1840. "Penny Postage: A Plan for Ensuring the Safe Delivery of every Letter under the New System."

1849. "A Bible Natural History." Groombridge.

1850. "An Essay on the Eternal Duration of the Earth." 15 pp. Groombridge.

1850. "An Essay on Baptismal Regeneration." 31 pp. Groombridge.

1850. "An Essay on Scientific Nomenclature." 10 pp. Groombridge.

1850–57. A Natural History of British Birds." 6 vols. royal 8vo. Groombridge. 3rd Edition; Revised, Corrected, and Enlarged. John C. Nimmo, 1891. 4th Edition (in course of issue); vol. i., 1895; vols. ii. and iii., 1896.

1851–53. "A Natural History of the Nests and Eggs of British Birds." 3 vols. royal 8vo. Groombridge. 3rd Edition; Revised, Corrected, and Enlarged. John C. Nimmo, 1892. 4th Edition (Edited by W. B. Tegetmeier), 1896.

1852. "A Natural History of British Butterflies." Royal 8vo. Groombridge. 6th Edition, 1889. John C. Nimmo. 7th Edition, 1893. 8th Edition, 1895.

1853. "National Adult Education." 23 pp. Groombridge.

1854. "An Account of the Battle of the Monongahela." 10 pp. Groombridge.

1854. "An Account of the Siege of Killowen." 8 pp. Groombridge.

1854. "The Present System of Hiring Farm Servants in the East Riding of Yorkshire." 10 pp. Groombridge.

1854. "A Letter to Archdeacon Wilberforce on Supremacy." 32 pp. Groombridge.

1855. "The Precepts of the Bible." Groombridge.

1855. "The Maxims of the Bible." Groombridge.

1856. "A Book of Natural History." Groombridge.

1858. "A Practical Solution of the Church-Rate Difficulty."

1859–70. "A Natural History of British Moths." 4 vols. royal 8vo. Longmans. 5th Edition, 1896. John C. Nimmo.

1860. "Anecdotes of Natural History." Longmans.

1860. "The Yorkshire Hymn-Book." 122 pp. Longmans.

1861. "Records of Animal Sagacity and Character." Longmans.

1864. "The Gamekeeper's Museum. A Series of Letters to the *Times*, with Additions."

1864. "A Catechism of the Catechism." 34 pp. Macintosh.

1864. "The County Seats of the Noblemen and Gentlemen of Great Britain and Ireland." 4 vols. 4to.

1865. "A Catalogue of British Insects in all the Orders." 125 pp. Longmans.

1869. "Words of Wesley on Constant Communion." 48 pp. Macintosh.

1869. "None but Christ." 63 pp. Macintosh.

1869. "Difficulties of Darwinism." Read before the British Association, 1868. 68 pp. Longmans.

1870. "Dogs and their Doings." Partridge.

1870. "A Double Dilemma in Darwinism." Read before the British Association, 1870. 15 pp. Poole.

1872. "The Humanity Series of School Books." 6 vols. Partridge.

1876. "A Dialogue about Fox-Hunting between a Squire, a Nobleman, a Farmer, and a Country Parson." 23 pp. Poole.

1877. Handbook of Hymns for the Sick Bedside." 28 pp. S.P.C.K.

1877. "All the Articles of the Darwin Faith." 45 pp. Poole.

1879. "The Paradise of the Soul." Poole.

1880. "The Darwin Craze. A Paper on the Plumage of Birds and Butterflies." 14 pp. Poole.

1880. "Letters to the *Times* about Birds." Poole.

1882. "A Handbook of Church and Dissent." 104 pp. Poole.

1885. "A Hundred Reasons against the Land Craze." 10 pp. Elliot Stock.

1886. "The Curse of Cruelty." A Sermon preached in York Minster. Elliot Stock.

1886. "The Seagull Shooter." 79 pp. Partridge.

1886. "The Sparrow Shooter." 72 pp. Partridge.

1892. "Politics for the People." A Series of Six Small Tractates.

Dates uncertain.

"A Letter about the Land, the Church, and the Factory." 46 pp. Poole.

"A Letter to J. Chamberlain on the Unearned Increment."

"The Ghost of Wesley." 24 pp.

INDEX

INDEX

ACHILL ISLAND, west of Ireland, its bird-life, 193

Albert, Prince, gets the Queen to accept the dedication of Mr. Morris's " History of British Birds," 90 ; on its production, 91

Alington, Richard, ornithologist and lifelong friend of Mr. Morris, 14, 76, 79 ; his original drawings for the " History of British Birds," 73 ; his sketch of the Kestrel, 73 ; a valuable assistant to Mr. Morris, 74

Amherst, Lord, godfather to Amherst Morris, 6

Angevine, sexton at Yonkers, U.S.A., cited for an incident of the marriage of Roger Morris and Mary Philipse, 4 *note*

Animal World, The, object of its production, 137

Astley, A. F., on the bird-life of Achill Island, west of Ireland, 193

BAILLIE, Hon. and Rev. John, vacates the Rectory of Nunburnholme, 39

Barnes, Rev. H. F. (now Canon Barnes-Lawrence), advocates the protection of bird-life, 143

Battue-shooting, Mr. Morris's description of modern, 253

Berkeley, Hon. Grantley, cited, 198

Bewick, Thomas, his excellence as an engraver, 72 ; his industry, 277

Bibliography of Mr. Morris, 311

Bird, W. F. W., a correspondent of Mr. Morris, 87

Birds, Mr. Morris's campaign in favour of their protection, 135 *et seq.*

Boyle, Hon. Mrs. R. C., joint-secretary of the Plumage League, 298

Braddock, General, killed at the battle of the Monongahela, 1

Branson, Rev. Henry John, Vicar of Armthorpe and Christ Church, 24

Bree, C. R., 261, 263

Bridlington, destruction of sea-birds at, 142, 149

Bright, John, Mr. Morris's aversion to his opinions, 233

Brightwen, Mrs., cited for the effects of kindness to animals, 200

Bromsgrove School, 11, 12

Brown, E., engraver of the illustrations for the " History of British Moths," 108

Buckland, Frank, advocates the preservation of bird-life, 137, 144

Bulwer, Sir E. Lytton, cited for the future existence of the animal creation, 157

Burdett-Coutts, Baroness, her interest in elementary education, 242

Burke, Sir Bernard, his interest in the " County Seats of the Noblemen and Gentlemen of Great Britain and Ireland," 164

Burney, Mr., cited, 274

Bustard, the, once frequent at Nunburnholme, 267

Butler, Bishop, cited for the future existence of the animal creation, 156

317

X

Printed by Ballantyne, Hanson & Co.
Edinburgh and London

9 781331 351450